S0-BAF-149

January 1, 1997.

Dear Paul,

I fondly remember watching episodes of Miss Marple, Poirot, and Tommy and Tuppence in #2204 with you and my Mom. I hope that this book is of interest to you. Thank you for the days of peace that we three had in Vermont and for being with the Pearmain & Thomson clans in Boston and Lincoln during Christmas.

P.S. Thank you also for your generous Christmas present.

Love,
David

AGATHA CHRISTIE

Murder in Four Acts

AGATHA CHRISTIE

Murder in Four Acts

A Centenary Celebration
of 'The Queen of Crime'
on Stage, Film, Radio & TV

Peter Haining

VIRGIN

This book is for my family
PHILIPPA, RICHARD, SEAN & GEMMA,
with love

First published in Great Britain in 1990 by
Virgin Books
A division of W.H. Allen & Co Plc
26 Grand Union Centre
338 Ladbroke Grove
London W10 5AH

Copyright © 1990 Peter Haining

This book is sold subject to the condition that
it shall not, by way of trade or otherwise,
be lent, re-sold, hired out or otherwise circulated
without the publisher's prior written consent in any
form of binding or cover other than that in which
it is published and without a similar condition
including this condition being imposed upon the
subsequent purchaser.

British Library Cataloguing in Publication Data
Haining, Peter, *1940–*
    Agatha Christie: murder in four acts: a centenary
    celebration of 'The Queen of Crime' on stage, films,
    radio & TV.
    1. Fiction in English. Christie, Agatha, 1890–1976
    I. Title
    823.912

    ISBN 1–85227–273–2

Designed by Cecil Smith

Set in Concorde and Bodoni by
Phoenix Photosetting, Chatham, Kent

Printed and bound in Great Britain by
Butler & Tanner Ltd, Frome & London

'There is nothing immoral
in my books, only murder.'

Agatha Christie

AGATHA CHRISTIE · 1890~1990

Queen of Crime

MURDER
=IN=
FOUR ACTS

CONTENTS

FOREWORD by Sir John Gielgud   9

'THE QUEEN OF CRIME': An Introduction   11

CURTAIN UP ON MYSTERY   21

MAYHEM IN THE CINEMA   39

RADIO SERIAL MURDERS   55

DEATH ON THE SMALL SCREEN   68

THE LITTLE GREY CELLS OF M POIROT:
Ten actors who have starred as the great Belgian detective   88

A LADY WITH MURDER TO REPORT:
Six actresses who have portrayed the famous sleuth of St Mary Mead   122

PARTNERS IN CRIME-FIGHTING:
Four couples who have played the resourceful Tommy and Tuppence Beresford   148

ACKNOWLEDGEMENTS   160

FOREWORD

By Sir John Gielgud

q am greatly admiring of Agatha Christie's wonderful skill and ingenuity – although I have to admit that I have read only a handful of her books. But I have enjoyed working in the adaptations of several of her murder mysteries for films and television, as well as watching others on television at various times.

I never actually met Dama Agatha, although I did see her at the preview of *Murder on the Orient Express.* She sat in the corner of the foyer and was soon surrounded, so I did not think I should add to the throng.

I have never travelled on the Orient Express either, but acting in the film directed by Sidney Lumet was a very pleasant experience, working with so many stars. The film *Appointment with Death* was also great fun, though I was really just a feed for Peter Ustinov – a Doctor Watson to his Sherlock Holmes. I was actually the only character who was *not* a suspect so there was only a line here and there for me to speak! But I like Peter Ustinov so much that I did not mind at all.

Shortly after Dame Agatha's death I was very touched when her husband wrote to me asking me to speak at her memorial service, and said that she had been a great admirer of my acting. I was very sad to have to refuse on account of a previous commitment.

I send all good wishes for the success of this book!

John Gielgud

Wotton-Underwood, Buckinghamshire
October 1989

SIR JOHN GIELGUD has a unique association with Agatha Christie. Early in her career as a playwright she wanted him to appear in one of her productions, and actually sent him the script of Akhnaton, *a drama set in Ancient Egypt, which she wrote at the same time as* Death on the Nile. *In a letter which Agatha treasured, he politely declined her offer, saying the play had interesting points but would be too expensive to produce. Subsequently, Agatha actually wrote him into* Sleeping Murder, *the last Miss Marple novel, when the lady detective attends a performance of* The Duchess of Malfi *at Her Majesty's Theatre in 1945 with Gielgud playing Ferdinand and speaking the famous line, 'Cover her face', which causes the heroine to run screaming from the auditorium. He also starred in two of the most successful Poirot films: firstly, as the butler, Beddoes, in* Murder on the Orient Express *(1974); and secondly, as the Head of the British Forces in Palestine in* Appointment with Death *(1987). And, most recently, he has given memorable performances in the London Weekend Television productions of* Why Didn't They Ask Evans? *(1980) and* The Seven Dials Mystery *(1981), which have heralded a whole new era of Agatha Christie on television.*

Novelist's Life With Arabs

CLUES TO A LOST CIVILISATION

Miss Agatha Christie, the novelist, has just arrived back in England, after an adventure as romantic as anything in her own novels.

For six months she has been living in an Arab's house in the Mesopotamian desert, with her husband, Mr. M. E. Mallowan, and other members of the British Museum expedition to Tal Arpachiyah, near Nineveh. Here she has been helping to unearth clues to a lost prehistoric civilisation.

Miss Agatha Christie

The discoveries made by Miss Christie and her husband throw light on the mode of life, customs, and religious rites of a people who lived at least 7,000 years ago—centuries before the rise of Ur.

Finds made in the excavations, Miss Christie said yesterday, include :

Mud and brick houses clustered round a central court.

Pottery of egg-shell thinness, decorated in bright black and red paints in geometric designs and shapes, which compare with the finest work of classical Greece.

Marble pendant of an ox's head, of exquisite workmanship.

Tiny terra-cotta figures of goddesses, whose painted clothing is suspended by braces !

Jewellery, including amulets and beads.

A circular granary, containing wheat thousands of years old.

"It was exciting work," Miss Christie told a "News-Chronicle" reporter yesterday. "My job was to clean the finds, and you can imagine the thrill of rubbing away dust and dirt to find, say, an amulet worn 7,000 years ago.

"I was also in charge of the photographic work, and in addition acted as chief cook and washer-up

Shortly the finds will be on view in the British Museum.

Newspaper report from the News Chronicle *of 7 June 1933, and (above) a rare book cover actually depicting Hercule Poirot*

The first detective story Agatha Christie read – 'a particularly baffling mystery', she later called it

'THE QUEEN OF CRIME'

An Introduction

The statistics of the Agatha Christie phenomenon – for such it undeniably is – are awesome. Since the publication in 1920 of her first book, *The Mysterious Affair at Styles*, featuring a curious little detective named Hercule Poirot, her works have sold more than a billion copies in English and at least the same number again in approximately 44 other languages. Only the Bible and the plays of Shakespeare have sold more editions than her murder mysteries.

In a career that spanned over half a century, she published in all 78 crime novels, nineteen plays (of which seven are adaptations of her books), six romantic novels under the pen-name Mary Westmacott, and four non-fiction titles. And in the year which marks her centenary, it is true to say that Agatha Christie is the most widely published writer of any time and in any language, and the royalties deriving from her books alone now run in excess of £2 million every year! (A short while ago, an American detective story writer, Emma Latham, wrote, with perhaps the slightest tinge of envy, that to keep just one of Miss Christie's most popular titles, *4.50 from Paddington*, in print in the USA required the chopping down of 5,000 acres of woods in the state of Maine every year!)

Yet it is also true that the books represent only a proportion of her impact on the general public. For few other writers can match Agatha's achievements in the world of entertainment or have given such pleasure to audiences of uncountable millions: on the stage, in films, and on radio and television. For ever since the first theatrical and cinema adaptations of her work (both in the same year of 1928), she has provided a constant source of material for the four media. Indeed, a decade after her death her stories of murder and mystery are, if anything, proving to be even more popular with viewers and listeners around the world. During her lifetime, Agatha annually produced without fail a new 'Christie for Christmas', and now no festive season would be complete without the reshowing of one of her old films plus a new adaptation of one of her stories on radio or television.

It is this unique and extraordinary achievement which I have set out to record for the first time in *Murder in Four Acts*.

The story of Agatha Christie's energetic and productive life – she was born in Torquay, Devon, in 1890 and died peacefully at Wallingford, Oxfordshire, in 1976 – has, of course, been recounted in several biographies, not the least of these being her own fascinating *Autobiography*, written over a number of years and finally published posthumously in 1977. Surprisingly, in none of the books has any substantial attempt been made to draw together all the strands of her contribution to the world of entertainment. This contribution amounts to at least twenty major theatrical productions on both sides of the Atlantic (not to mention a vast number of touring productions and repertory performances); two dozen films for the cinema; in excess of fifty radio programmes; and an even larger number of individual stories and series for both British and American television.

Although it has to be admitted that the records for all these media are not totally complete, the resulting picture of Agatha Christie's characters transposed from the printed page into the public imagination is nonetheless very impressive. For someone who was never over-keen on the adaptation of her work, and indeed vetoed the plans of dozens of producers and impresarios, the achievement is even more striking. What is sad from the author's own point of view is that so few really outstanding adaptations were made while she was alive: their general quality has improved substantially only in the last ten years or so.

Interestingly, while Sir Arthur Conan Doyle, a writer whose work greatly influenced Agatha Christie, has become overshadowed by his creation, Sherlock Holmes, her own name is still writ as large as those of her two best-known characters, Hercule Poirot and Miss Marple. Neither is mentioned without reference to their creator and her reputation is as well founded and enduring as theirs.

Poirot is perhaps the more celebrated of the two, having featured in 33 novels and ten volumes of short stories. His constant reference to his 'little grey cells' is just as famous as Holmes's 'Elementary, my dear Watson' (although the famous detective *never* actually said that in direct conversation). The detective-story writer C. H. B. Kitchen accorded the little Belgian detective, with his twirled moustache and egg-shaped head, this resounding compliment in the *Times Literary Supplement* of February 1955: 'He is always real, as Sherlock Holmes is real, not to mention Malvolio, Pickwick and Peter Pan – a figure without which the human kaleidoscope would be poorer.'

Jane Marple, the tall, thin inquisitive sleuth of St Mary Mead, with her china-blue eyes and profound insight into human nature, has her legions of admirers, too – though she appeared in far fewer cases: twelve books and twenty short stories. According to Gordon Ramsey in his *Agatha Christie: Mistress of Mystery* (1968) she 'remains the English gentlewoman, and may well be the twentieth century's most famous example of the breed'.

Agatha has given some indication of the origins of both Poirot and Miss Marple. She was, she says, a reader of detective fiction from her childhood, spurred on by her elder sister, Madge.

The first detective story she recalls reading was *The Mystery of the Yellow Room* (1907) by the French writer Gaston Leroux (1868–1927) who has recently enjoyed a renaissance as a result of Andrew Lloyd Webber's adaptation of his novel, *The Phantom of the Opera* (1911), as a spectacular musical. Leroux's crime mystery, of the seemingly impossible attempted murder of a beautiful young woman in a sealed room, was solved by a precocious young amateur detective named Joseph Rouletabille, and the young Agatha declared it to be 'a particularly baffling mystery, well worked out and planned'.

She also read the stories of Eugene Valmont, the first humorous detective in English litera-ture, written by the Scotsman, Robert Barr (1850–1912) and published as *The Triumphs of Eugene Valmont* (1906). Not surprisingly, this sleuth's enormous ego, elegant clothes and ever-present wit as well as certain other physical characteristics have led one or two his-torians of the genre to see Valmont as the inspiration for Poirot. A better case, though, can be advanced for Hercules Popeau, the creation of Marie Belloc Lowndes (1868–1947), sister of Hilaire Belloc, and the author of the most famous Jack the Ripper novel, *The Lodger* (1913).

Popeau, who appeared in a number of short stories and three novels including *The Lonely House* (1920), is a retired French detective from the Paris Sûreté now living in England. He is short and stout, incredibly vain and conscious of his dignity, while being inquisitive and a shrewd student of human nature. He also has a 'brave and loyal' friend in Captain Angus Stuart.

Agatha Christie was certainly aware of these stories – indeed both Poirot and Popeau were

"Miss Marple thinks the butler did it with the pate!"

BRIDGE

Miss Marple plays a thriller

The old-fashioned suit was more appropriate for the English countryside than Deauville. She was not tall, but carried herself well. Her blue eyes were alert; her grey hair, with the exception of one thin strand, perfectly in place. Despite her friendly greeting I should have known that here was Miss Marple.

Pairs. Deauville. Love All. Dealer North

```
            ♠ J 5
            ♡ K Q J 9
            ◇ 10 9 7
            ♣ K Q 6 2
♠ 9 6 2        N        ♠ A 3
♡ A 10 5 4   W   E      ♡ 8 2
◇ 8 6          S        ◇ K Q J 5 4 2
♣ 10 9 4 3             ♣ A 8 7
            ♠ K Q 10 8 7 4
            ♡ 7 6 3
            ◇ A 3
            ♣ J 5
```

W	N	E	S
		Flint	Marple
—	1♣(1)	1◇	1♠
No	1NT(2)	No (3)	3♣
No	No	No	
			Opening lead ◇8

(1) Not exactly an obligatory opening bid.
(2) Horrible, but what else?
(3) Vainly hoping for more no trumps

Miss Marple won my ◇J with the Ace, and craftily played the ♣5 to the ♣Q and my Ace. I cashed the ◇K and persisted with the ◇Q. Miss Marple ruffed with the ♠10, and without any perceptible pause, made the remarkable play of successfully running the ♠7. I ducked that trick, won the trump continuation and tried for a trump promotion by playing another diamond. Unhappily for us Miss Marple's far-sighted trump finesse permitted her to ruff with the ♠Q, and draw West's remaining trump. She then graciously conceded a heart, making exactly nine tricks for an excellent score.

"Well played," I said, when I had recovered from my astonishment.

"Oh, good heavens, I didn't do anything: I just thought that if you had long diamonds, well, I mean it was natural to play your partner for long spades." Her voice trailed away. It came almost as a surprise that there was no reference to life at St Mary Mead.

Jeremy Flint

The 'Miss Marple' phenomenon: as cartoon hero (in the Evening Standard, *29 August 1989); the inspiration for a bridge game (in* The Times, *20 November 1988); and even setting a new fashion! (*Mail on Sunday, *25 September 1988)*

anthologised together in collections – and she chose a virtually identical title for her 1947 Poirot book, *The Labours of Hercules*, to Mrs Belloc Lowndes's Popeau short story, 'A Labour of Hercules'. (To enable the reader to make a comparison, I have reprinted an extract from the Popeau story *The Lonely House*, on the facing page.)

It seems much less likely that she was aware of Monsieur Poiret, a portly, retired Parisian police officer, known as 'Old Pawrey', who settled in London and helped to solve mysteries in a series of short stories written by Frank Howel Evans in the *New Magazine* in 1909–10. Although it has recently been suggested that these stories by Evans, a former actor and contributor to the *Boy's Own Paper*, could have been influential on Agatha, she *was* only nineteen at the time, and the *New Magazine* had a smaller circulation than most of the other popular magazines of the time like the *Strand*, the *Windsor*, etc. For interest, though, one of H. M. Brock's illustrations of M Poiret from 'The Disappearance of the Duchess' (November 1909) is reproduced below.

Whatever the influence of Leroux, Barr or Mrs Lowndes, Agatha decided on making her detective a Belgian, having been deeply moved by the plight of First World War refugees from that country living near her home in Torquay. She also wanted him to be meticulous, tidy and very clever. And for his name? 'He would be a small man – Hercules: a good name,' she later wrote in her autobiography. 'His last name was more difficult. I don't know why I settled on the name Poirot, whether it just came into my head or whether I saw it in some newspaper or written on something – anyway it came.'

Above: *One of the earliest illustrations of Poirot, by Norman Keene, for Agatha's short story, 'The Second Gong' (1926).* Left: *'Old Pawrey' in a scene from 'The Disappearance of the Duchess' by Frank Howel Evans*

A Case for Hercules Popeau

'I am here,' said M Popeau quietly, 'because a sad thing befell this lady, Miss Fairfield, today on her way to the English church service. She is staying in a villa called La Solitude, some way above Monte Carlo, and, wandering a little way off the path, she suddenly came across a dead body! Of course, it gave her a terrible shock.'

To Lily's astonishment, M Bouton did not look surprised.

'Very sad,' the Commissioner of Police murmured. 'The matter will have my very earnest attention. If Mademoiselle will give me a few particulars as to the locality where she made this painful discovery I will see to the matter at once. Would you kindly come this way?'

He opened the door, and passed on, in front of them, into a room built out at the back of the house. It was obviously his own study.

'Here is the plan of our principality,' he observed, and Lily, glancing up, saw that a huge map covered one entire side of the room.

'Will you point out the exact spot where you made your sad discovery?' went on M Bouton, handing her a long, light stick.

Lily stared anxiously up at the map, but she had no bump of locality on her pretty head.

M Popeau took the thin stick from her hand. He laid the point lightly on the map, and pushed it up and up and up!

'Here is La Solitude,' he said at last, 'so now we shall be able to find the exact place.'

'Ah, yes,' said M Bouton. 'La Solitude belongs to Count Antonio Polda. He and the Countess are nice, quiet people, almost the only people in Monaco with whom I have never had any trouble! It is my impression that somewhere about the fourteenth century a Grimaldi married a Polda – so the count is distantly related to our sovereign.'

'Mademoiselle is a niece of the Countess Polda,' said M Popeau quietly. 'She is staying at La Solitude for the winter.'

M Bouton looked at Lily with enhanced respect.

'Now take La Solitude as the point of departure, and try to concentrate your mind on where you found the body,' said M Popeau, handing Lily back the cane.

She moved the point slowly, hesitatingly, down the map.

'Surely you are going too far!' cried M Popeau.

'Perhaps I am –'

She knitted her brow in some distress. 'Do you remember the place where our taxicab stopped?' she asked.

M Popeau took the wand from her hand. 'Here it is – this little white spot.'

'It was just below there,' said Lily.

'Was it? How very strange!' exclaimed M Popeau. And then he looked at the other man. 'Do you remember what happened just there, six years ago, the last time I was at Monte Carlo, Bouton?'

The other shook his head.

'The Affair of the Mexican Millionaire!' exclaimed M Popeau.

The Commissioner of Police turned round quickly. 'I remember all about it now! Why, you're right – it was just at that spot that he was found dead, too. What a strange coincidence! They mostly do it, as you know, within a very short distance of the casino. You'd be astonished to know the number of poor devils who go and destroy themselves in that rather lonely place just beyond the station. They rush out of the casino full of

Hercules Popeau on the trail of a murderer – an illustration from The Lonely House *by Mrs Belloc Lowndes*

anguish and despair, and wander down the road. I always have a man stationed on point duty there – he has stopped more than one poor fellow from destroying himself. Ah, our beautiful, brilliant Monte Carlo has a very melancholy reverse side, has it not?' and he sighed.

But M Popeau was still staring at the map. 'It is indeed an amazing coincidence!' he muttered. 'The more one thinks of it, the more amazing it is.'

THE LONELY HOUSE
by Mrs Belloc Lowndes
(Hutchinson & Co, 1920)

Miss Butterworth Investigates

Without waiting for any further confirmation of my discovery, I jumped into the buggy and made my way to the detective's side.

'Ah, fresh news!' exclaimed Gryce. 'I see it in your eye. What have you chanced upon, madam, in your drive into town?'

'I have something to add to the investigation,' said I. 'Mr Gryce, I have just come from the other end of the lane, where I found a clue which may shorten the suspense of this weary day, and possibly save Lucretta from the painful task that she has undertaken in our interests. Mr Chittenden's ring –'

I paused for the exclamation of encouragement he is accustomed to give on such occasions. He did not fail me in the exclamation.

'– was not found by Mother Jane, or even brought to her in any ordinary way or by any ordinary messenger. It came to her on a *pigeon's neck*! The pigeon you will find lying dead among the bushes in the Knolly yard!'

He was amazed. He controlled himself, but he was very visibly amazed. His exclamations proved it.

'Madam! Miss Butterworth! This ring – Mr Chittenden's ring – whose presence in her hut we thought an evidence of guilt, was brought to her by one of her *pigeons*?'

'So she told me. I aroused her fury by showing her the empty husk in which it had been concealed. In her rage at its loss, she revealed the fact I have just mentioned. It is a curious one, sir, and one I am a little proud to have discovered.'

'Curious? It is more than curious; it is bizarre, and will rank, I am safe in prophesying, as one of the most remarkable facts that have ever adorned the annals of the police. Madam, when I say I envy you the honour of its discovery, you will appreciate my estimate of it – and you. But when did you find this out, and what explanation are you able to give of the presence of this ring on a pigeon's neck?'

'Inspector, to your first question I need only reply that it was two hours ago, and to the second that everything points to the fact that the ring was attached to the bird by the victim himself – as an appeal for succour to whoever might be fortunate enough to find it. Unhappily it fell into the wrong hands. That is the ill-luck which often befalls prisoners.'

'Prisoners?'

'Yes. Cannot you imagine a person shut up in an inaccessible place making some such attempt to communicate with his fellow creatures?'

'But what inaccessible place have we in –'

'Wait,' said I. 'You have been in Deacon Spear's barn?'

'Certainly, many times.' But the answer, glib as it was, showed shock.

'Well,' said I, 'there is a hiding place in that barn which I dare declare you have not penetrated.'

'Do you think so, madam?'

'A little loft way up under the eaves, which can only be reached by clambering over the rafters. Didn't Deacon Spear tell you there was such a place?'

'No, but –'

'William, then?' I inexorably pursued. 'He says he pointed out such a spot to you, and

Miss Butterworth spots a clue

that you pooh-poohed it as inaccessible and not worth the searching.'

'William is a – Madam, I beg your pardon, but William has just wit enough to make trouble.'

'But there is such a place there,' I urged, 'and, what is more, there is someone hidden in it now. I saw him *myself*!'

LOST MAN'S LANE
by Anna Katharine Green
(G. P. Putnam's Sons, 1898)

Just as Holmes has his Watson, Agatha provided Poirot with Captain Arthur Hastings, albeit for only a number of the early cases. The first of these was, of course, *The Mysterious Affair at Styles*. At a stroke, Sherlock Holmes had a rival who, in time, would seriously challenge his popularity with the public.

Agatha Christie then achieved something that had proved beyond the powers of her predecessor, Sir Arthur Conan Doyle: she created another character the equal of Poirot, and a woman to boot, Miss Jane Marple, first introduced in *The Murder at the Vicarage* in 1930. Miss Marple's origins are much more definite – she is a composite of the author's grandmother and some of her old cronies. 'Grannie' had a considerable insight into human nature, and though cheerful by nature always expected the worst of people, according to her granddaughter.

Though Miss Marple does not have an associate like Poirot, she does have an entourage of helpers, the most frequently employed being her nephew Raymond, who eventually becomes a best-selling novelist. There are also several policemen of varying ranks and capabilities.

But just as Hercule Popeau lurks in the wings of Poirot's life, so the diligent researcher comes across Miss Amelia Butterworth, a spinster lady of formidable detective powers in six novels by Anna Katharine Green (1846–1935). This American authoress was the first woman to write detective fiction, and her classic novel, *The Leavenworth Case* (1878), was another of the crime novels that Agatha was encouraged to read by her sister.

Miss Butterworth is a well-bred amateur sleuth with a penchant for poking her nose into other people's business whenever wrongdoing is suspected. She is also 'methodical in her methods even under the greatest excitement', to quote from her second case, *Lost Man's Lane* (1894). She usually resides in an apartment overlooking Gramercy Park in New York, though her cases sometimes take her into the countryside. More often than not she is summoned to aid a bewildered police officer called Detective Gryce. I have also selected an extract from one of the Miss Butterworth cases to illustrate the parallels.

Agatha Christie's literary creativity did not, however, end with Poirot and Miss Marple. There are plenty of admirers of her mysterious investigator, Mr Harley Quin; of Mr Parker Pyne, the detective who deals in matters of the heart; and also of those resourceful 'partners in crime', Tommy and Tuppence Beresford. Like the Belgian and the spinster of St Mary Mead, all of these have been adapted for the world of entertainment and will be found featured in this study. In particular, I have given especial attention to the Beresfords who were created in Agatha's second book and who appeared in the very last work to come from her pen. Her lifelong devotion to this charming pair deserves, I think, more detailed study than it usually receives.

Agatha Christie ended her days the object of world-wide fame and admiration; her achievements in Britain were honoured by a CBE in 1956 and then by being made a Dame in 1971. In 1972, a likeness of her was placed in Madame Tussaud's, wearing clothes and shoes she had actually worn, and in the company of world leaders and royalty – many of whose real-life counterparts she could number among her readers!

Since the death of 'The Queen of Crime' – as she deservedly became known – interest in her work has grown at a tremendous rate, although its use in any medium is carefully controlled by Agatha Christie Ltd, which is part of the entertainments division of Booker Plc, and which endeavours to see that producers remain faithful to the author's text.

Despite the stewardship of those involved with the estate, there have still been some strange manifestations of the Christie cult over the years. Poirot's 'death' in the novel *Curtain* in August 1975, for example, prompted a front page obituary in the *New York Times* and a whole column in the centre pages of *The Daily Telegraph*. The little detective has also been the subject of satires by writers such as J. I. M. Stewart and C. Day-Lewis, while there is a Hercule Poirot Museum in Belgium and an American company has manufactured a 'Hercule Poirot Moustache Mug'.

Though Miss Marple is perhaps a less obvious figure for such exploitation, she has been featured in several cartoons, a newspaper bridge game, and in the autumn of 1988 was the inspiration for a new style of ladies' fashions.

Agatha Christie's own name also regularly crops up in newspaper headlines when parallels between her plots and real-life events are drawn by resourceful journalists. Doubtless some of the comparisons would not have pleased her, but she would have been quietly pleased at the tributes her work still earns.

Rosalind Hicks, for one, is quite sure of the reason for her mother's success. 'She had a genius for starting books,' Mrs Hicks explains. 'Once you read the opening of *A Body in the Library* you can't put it down. And have you noticed the way her chapters stop, before you're bored?'

Critic Robert Barnard's view in *A Talent to Deceive* (1980) would also have brought a modest smile to her lips because of its comparison to another of her great literary heroes. 'Christie's appeal,' he wrote, 'like Dickens's, is universal, cutting across every possible barrier of race, colour, class and intelligence.'

Fellow detective-story teller, Margery Allingham, has put the Christie success even more specifically. 'She appeals directly to the honest human curiosity in all of us. The invitation she gives her readers is to listen to the details surrounding the perfectly horrid screams from the apartment next door.' Miss Allingham has also claimed that 'Agatha Christie has entertained more people for more hours at a time than almost any other writer of her generation.'

As the pages of this book will make plain, she has now done virtually the same thing for cinema and theatregoers, as well as radio and television audiences.

But although we know a great deal about Agatha Christie's work, the lady herself still remains an enigma, as puzzling and elusive as the best of her stories. She disliked personal publicity, gave very few newspaper interviews and refused to appear on television. Yet, just as we must look in her books for the clues to solve the mysteries she sets, so there too can be found the clues to the author herself.

Dr Janet Morgan, her biographer, has explained this facet of her subject in these words:

> As a wife, a mother and a friend she held back, self-protective. As a writer, she gave generously and incessantly, book after book ... The feelings and beliefs Agatha revealed through her writing, if only there, were genuinely and strongly held. That, as well as the fact that her work dealt with familiar, universal themes, accounts for the success of her books and plays.

To the books and plays must be added the recent films, television series and radio programmes which have all ensured the continuing growth of the Christie phenomenon. Just how this has happened will become apparent as the story unfolds.

'I specialise in murders of quiet, domestic interest,' Agatha Christie once wrote rather self-deprecatingly. Yet it is those self-same cases written during a lifetime of dedication to her craft that have made her, in the years leading up to her centenary, so spectacularly and internationally famous! And with each new generation of readers and viewers discovering the special Christie magic, there seems little doubt she will continue so for many more years to come.

So, let the curtain rise!

Peter Haining
April 1990

DAME AGATHA'S FINAL SOLUTION FOR POIROT

By GODFREY BARKER

M. HERCULE POIROT, the well-known Belgian detective, has died at the home of a friend in Styles St Mary, Essex, his physician, Dr John Franklyn, announced yesterday.

A report certifying the cause of death as coronary thrombosis is due on Sept. 29 from his close friend and inspirer, Dame Agatha Christie.

The 'death' of Hercule Poirot made headlines around the world in August 1975. This report is from The Daily Telegraph *of 7 August*

Other close friends of the moustachioed gastronome maintain, however, that his death occurred through far from natural causes.

But the fact remains that Poirot, who has figured in dozens of the 90-plus mysteries, novels and short stories of Dame Agatha, 85, is now dead and gone.

Rot sets in

From the moment that Poirot hobbles on stage in this epilogue to a great career, " Curtain—or Poirot's Last Case," it is clear the rot has set in.

The jet black of his sleek hair now comes out of a hair-dye bottle; his emaciated frame is supported in a wheel-chair, arthritis grips him.

Twenty four hour nursing is now required to keep the famous " grey cells " in tune. The once besplendent pudgy figure in his mauve silk dressing gown now has to be washed, put to bed, doped with sleeping tablets and dressed in the morning.

" His health's rotten, of course," his doctor declares revealingly outside the bedroom door after another touch of the shudders around Poirot's heart.

For once, the famous remedies do not work. All the coats, mufflers and scarves to protect him from draughts, the Perrier waters to calm the liver, the noxious tisanes for the fluxions poitrines (flu to us) are of no avail.

Poirot is but a shadow of the vigorous dandy who used to demolish two tornados, a delicate cream cheese, coffee and liqueurs at lunch-time, pick locks and clamber into coal lifts if need be, and put his large foot in criminals' front doors throughout North London and the Home Counties.

" Sacré !   Sapristi ! "   and " Mille tonnerres ! " he would cry at grease stains on his grey suit, in whose bulging pockets he kept talcum powder, clothes brushes, silk thread for placing across door jambs, a large turnip watch, a whistle, a pocket-book and curling tongs for his moustaches.

He would occasionally " have a go " at the criminal classes, in his younger days.

" Allez! " he cried on one typical occasion as he enveloped the neck of an intruding Italian with a woollen scarf.

Much vaunted brainpower

In his heyday the tri-lingual sleuth who never grasped English, was the greatest international detective of them all, the employee of aristocrats such as Lords Cronshaw, Estair and Yardly and " perfect women " like Miss Esmèe Farquhar though he was not above working for insurance companies if need be.

His much vaunted brainpower was based on close reading of "The Daily Megaphone" and "The Daily Newsmonger." Faded copies of " Society Gossip " littered his coffee table; the " Almanach de Gotha." and Burke's Peerage (which he preferred to Debrett) were in the bedroom.

Signs of decay

Physically fearless, Poirot regarded dead bodies as routine— " it is not pretty " was a typical rejoinder — and was totally unmoved by ghosts, even when they appeared with blood dripping from their fingers in the dark.

An excellent judge of diamonds, a connoisseur of scent, Poirot was " un peu snob " (as the Belgians say) and affected a cane. But his image was occasionally dented when his moustaches fell into the soup.

But the signs of decay were always there. Too much thick, sweet chocolate; too many tiny Russian cigarettes; too many taxis and too little walking; seasickness on his way to Egypt for a cure; disaster on the camels when he arrived.

But lovers of Dame Agatha's novels will be relieved that Miss Marple, her other ace detective, remains in good health, and a mystery will continue to appear every autumn for the future as it has done every year since 1924, according to Collins, her publishers.

Readers can rest assured that the novel, though Poirot's last, is one of Dame Agatha's best. It dates from 1940, in the middle of her vintage period, and has lain in a vault for 35 years.

Editorial comment—P14

AMBASSADORS THEATRE, West St. Cambridge Circus, W.C.2

Sole Proprietors: Ambassadors Theatre Ltd.   Lessees: J. W. Pemberton & Co. Ltd.
Managing Directors: W. G. Curtis & H. J. Malden.
Licenced by the Lord Chamberlain to J. F. H. Jay.

Monday to Friday: 7.30	Saturday: 5.15 and 8.0	Tuesday: 2.30
Stalls: 15/-, 10/6, 8/6;	Dress Circle: 15/-, 10/6, 8/6, 5/6;	Pit (unreserved): 3/6.

BOX OFFICE
Temple Bar 1171

Peter Saunders presents

Richard Attenborough
Sheila Sim in

THE MOUSETRAP
by Agatha Christie

With
Jessica Spencer
Aubrey Dexter
Mignon O'Doherty
Allan McClelland
John Paul
and
Martin Miller

DIRECTED BY PETER COTES   *Décor by Roger Furse*

CURTAIN UP ON MYSTERY

In London there exists one unique and perennial reminder of Agatha Christie's talent as a mystery-maker – her stage drama, *The Mousetrap*, the world's longest-running play, now in its 37th year. No other theatrical work at present comes anywhere near the run of this phenomenal production which opened in 1952, has been performed close to 16,000 times, and is a 'must' for theatregoers from all over the world visiting the capital city. It has truly become as much a part of a London Tour as Buckingham Palace and the Tower of London – and the mecca for all mystery story lovers.

The curtain first rose on *The Mousetrap*, with its assorted cast of characters trapped in a snowbound Berkshire guesthouse knowing there is a murderer in their midst, at the Ambassadors Theatre on 25 November 1952. Though there had been problems in the provincial tour, it was greeted with a standing ovation and enthusiastic press notices, John Barber of the *Daily Express*, for one, declaring that, 'Even more thrilling than the plot is the atmosphere of shuddering suspense.'

In the next twenty years, the play became a show-business legend, breaking all theatrical records. Then on 25 March 1974, it transferred to the slightly larger theatre next door, the St Martin's, where it has continued to play without interruption ever since. And during these years the drama's eight characters have been performed by a total of 200 actors, while the original director, Peter Cotes, has had a dozen successors to re-direct the various cast changes.

Peter Saunders, the London impresario who first read the script, remembers that the show received a lukewarm reception in the provinces before reaching London, and he and Agatha Christie had to carry out extensive re-writing before the opening night at the Ambassadors.

'Agatha realised she had written neither a thriller nor a comedy-thriller,' he explained recently. 'In those days it had a few laughs in it, but the whole thing fell between two stools. So the two of us sat up all night removing quite a few jokes – just the reverse of what a playwright and producer normally do together in those circumstances. We still were not absolutely sure we had got it right when the curtain went up – but neither of us had the faintest idea of the phenomenon we had set in motion.'

The Mousetrap had actually evolved from 'Three Blind Mice', a short radio play which Agatha had written for Queen Mary's 80th birthday in 1947, and though it is only one of the twelve full-scale dramas and three single-act plays she wrote, it has probably done more than anything else from her pen to keep her name alive in the consciousness of the public as a whole. Even those who may never have read any of her novels, nor met Hercule Poirot or Miss Marple on the screen, nor even seen one of her plays, cannot fail nonetheless to be aware of *The Mousetrap*. Its fame is truly international – and what other play can boast of having been performed in over 40 countries, having an annual horse race, 'The Mousetrap Challenge Cup Handicap' named after it, and being celebrated by an annual party on 25

Original poster for the opening of The Mousetrap *in 1952*

Above: *A line-up of 30 of the 35 actresses who have played Mollie Ralston in* The Mousetrap, *with Sir Richard Attenborough, the original Detective Sergeant Trotter, at a gathering to mark the play's 36th anniversary on 25 November 1988*

Agatha with Peter Saunders and Richard Attenborough at The Mousetrap's *tenth anniversary party in 1962*

November when an ever-increasing number of former cast members gather to mark the mystery that, in several cases, was a stepping stone to success in their acting careers?

So large, indeed, have these celebrations become that in the 1988 gathering at the Savoy Hotel, only 30 of the 35 actresses who have played Mollie Ralston, the female lead, could squeeze together for a photocall with the original leading man, Dickie (now Sir Richard) Attenborough, the first Detective Sergeant Trotter. And among these ladies was the first Mollie Ralston, Sheila Sim, who later became Lady Attenborough.

Agatha Christie's own original estimation of her play was that it might 'run for eight months perhaps'. Before it in fact eventually outlived *her*, she wrote in her autobiography in 1977:

> People are always asking me to what I attribute the success of *The Mousetrap*. Apart from replying with the obvious answer, 'Luck!' – because it *is* luck, ninety per cent luck, at least, I should say – the only reason I can give is that there is a bit of something in it for almost everybody: people of different age groups and tastes can enjoy seeing it. Young people enjoy it, elderly people enjoy it . . .
>
> But I think, considering it and trying to be neither conceited nor over-modest, that, of its kind – which is to say a light play with both humour and thriller appeal – it is well constructed. The thing unfolds so that you want to know what happens next, and you can't quite see where the next few minutes will lead you. I think, too, though there is a tendency for all plays that have run a long time to be acted, sooner or later, as if the people in them were caricatures, the people in *The Mousetrap* could all be real people.

Though none of Agatha's other plays have come near matching the singular triumph of *The Mousetrap*, the story of her contribution to the theatre is one of continuing success – a fact that is due in no small measure to the care which she, and later her executors, have exercised over the performance of these plays. The rights are rigorously controlled and only one play may be produced annually, 'no doubt the better to keep the public in suspense', according to a wry comment in *The Times* in February 1982.

In the sixty years since Agatha's first play, *Alibi*, was staged in London, the number of productions of her work plus the adaptations in this country, let alone the rest of the world, has passed into the realms of the uncountable. The performances of touring companies, repertory theatres and amateur dramatic societies are simply legion, and it is only possible here to consider the 21 major London productions. Though, like all playwrights, Agatha Christie had her flops and short runs, her name outside a theatre has long exercised a tremendous attraction for the public, and spelt gold for the management. The theatre historian, J. C. Trewin, has, I think rightly, referred to her work as 'a Midas gift to the theatre'.

The first performance of a work by Agatha occurred at the Prince of Wales Theatre on 15 May 1928, with a version of her 1926 novel, *The Murder of Roger Ackroyd*, retitled *Alibi*. Adapted by Michael Morton and directed by Gerald du Maurier, the play also marked the debut of Hercule Poirot, played by Charles Laughton.

Michael Morton effected several changes in transferring the mystery from the book to the stage, including dropping the character of Caroline Sheppard, a spinster lady deeply involved in village society, and an obvious prototype of Miss Marple. Instead, to Agatha's disapproval, a bright young thing played by Gillian Lind took her place. Among the rest of the cast were Basil Loder, Henry Forbes Robertson, Iris Noel and Henry Daniell, later to become well known playing villains in Hollywood movies.

For a first play, *Alibi* attracted a considerable amount of publicity, including a full-page feature with photographs in *The Graphic* of 9 June 1928, headlined 'Expressions of a Sleuth', which commented that Poirot was being 'admirably impersonated by Mr Charles Laughton'.

EXPRESSIONS OF A SLEUTH

Close-ups of Mr. Charles Laughton as Hercule Poirot in "Alibi" at the Prince of Wales Theatre

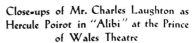

Mr. Charles Laughton, the twenty-six-year-old actor as he is in real life

"Englishmen conceal only one thing—their love." The detective in one of his philosophical moods as a rest from sleuthing

"I appeal to you, Mees Flora—tell me ze truth." The relentless Poirot in plaintive mood

Poirot at work. The effective curtain to Act I, when the detective sits alone in front of the murdered man, turns down the lights, and mentally reconstructs the crime

"Each one of you has something to hide." Poirot grows suspicious of everybody

"Poirot may play the fool, but there is a reason behind his actions," he says to the unsuspecting criminal

"To me it grows clearer." Poirot has a clue which he keeps to himself

"Ze person who killed Sir Ackroyd is in zis room." The detective in one of his "je sais tout" moods

The play enjoyed a successful run of 250 performances before it was transferred to the Booth Theater in New York with Laughton continuing to play the lead. There, unhappily, it failed to repeat the London success and closed after just 24 performances.

Even before *Alibi* was put on in London, however, Agatha had actually written a play herself entitled *Black Coffee*, and, encouraged by the reception of the Poirot mystery, decided to see if this mystery also featuring the detective might be worth putting on. Years later she wrote: 'It was a conventional spy thriller, and although full of cliches, it was not, I think, at all bad. Then, in due course, it came into its own. A friend of mine from Sunningdale days, Mr Burman, who was connected with the Royalty Theatre, suggested to me that it might perhaps be produced.'

The producer who took up *Black Coffee* was Andre van Gyseghem, and after a try-out at the Everyman Theatre in Hampstead, the play opened at the Embassy Theatre on 8 December 1930. There was a new Poirot in the bulky form of Francis L. Sullivan, with supporting roles played by Donald Wolfit, Josephine Middleton, John Boxer, Richard Fisher and Joyce Bland.

Although Agatha had the same reservations about Sullivan playing Poirot as she had about Charles Laughton – his height and weight – she could not fail to be delighted by the *Times* review which said: 'Mrs Christie steers her play with much dexterity.'

FRANCIS L. SULLIVAN

VAUDEVILLE THEATRE
STRAND, W.C.2
Proprietors — J. & R. GATTI
Licensed by the Lord Chamberlain to — R. & J. A. GATTI
EVENINGS at 8.10   MATINEES: TUESDAY, THURSDAY & SATURDAY at 2.30

HERBERT MASON

presents

FRANCIS L. SULLIVAN

AS

AGATHA CHRISTIE'S

GREAT DETECTIVE

"HERCULE POIROT"

IN A NEW PLAY

PERIL AT END HOUSE

Adapted for the Stage by ARNOLD RIDLEY (Author of "The Ghost Train")

CAST INCLUDES

OLGA EDWARDES   IAN FLEMING
BRIAN OULTON   PHOEBE KERSHAW
TULLY COMBER   MAY HALLATT
WILFRED FLETCHER   JOSEPHINE MIDDLETON
ISABEL DEAN   WILLIAM SENIOR
BECKETT BOULD   NANCY POULTENY
         CHARLES MORTIMER

Produced by A. R. WHATMORE

Décor by DANAË GAYLEN

OLGA EDWARDES

Left: *The first Hercule Poirot, Charles Laughton, featured in a page of photographs from* Alibi *in* The Graphic, *9 June 1928*

Above: *A rare poster featuring the second Poirot, Agatha's friend Francis L. Sullivan, in* Peril at End House *in May 1940*

Black Coffee ran for five months before closing, but, strangely, was not transferred to New York. It was, however, revived twenty years later and has since done well in repertory. A recent successful round-Britain tour in 1981 with Patrick Cargill as a dapper and exuberant Poirot has further underlined the durability of Agatha's first effort.

Francis Sullivan made a second appearance as Poirot in 1940 in *Peril at End House*, adapted from Agatha's 1932 novel. With a script by Arnold *(Ghost Train)* Ridley and directed by A. R. Whitmore, the play opened at the Vaudeville Theatre on 1 May 1940, during that inauspicious summer which began with the Battle of Britain and turned into the autumn of the German blitz on London. Despite the undoubted quality of *Peril at End House*, the uncertainty of life in the capital conspired against show business as a whole, and the play closed after three months. There was no transfer to New York.

It was to be five years after *Black Coffee* that the next Christie appeared in London. This was *Love from a Stranger*, which Frank Vosper, a well-known playwright and leading man in the British theatre, had adapted from one of Agatha's short stories, 'Philomel Cottage', in her collection, *The Listerdale Mystery* (1934). Vosper stuck closely to the dramatic story of a young wife who has recently come into a fortune and is living in fear of her former lover, and cast himself and Marie Ney as the husband and wife. The play was directed by Murray Macdonald and the co-stars were Geoffrey King, Charles Hodges and Muriel Aked.

Love from a Stranger opened at the New Theatre on 31 March 1936, and earned outstanding reviews. 'A brilliant terror play,' said the *Daily Herald*, 'our blood was gloriously curdled.' *The Daily Telegraph* also enthused, 'Quite obviously it is going to hit the present taste for cleverly manipulated horror,' and the *Daily Mail* added, 'Thanks to Miss Agatha Christie who wrote the story and Mr Frank Vosper who adapted it, *Love from a Stranger* is first class entertainment.'

In fact, the play ran for 149 performances, and then transferred to New York's Fulton Theater in September 1936. But it shared the same fate as Agatha's previous play, closing after 31 performances. Still, the power of the drama was undeniable, and apart from several revivals in repertory, it has also twice been filmed, in 1937 and 1947.

It was the extraordinary story of *Ten Little Niggers* which Agatha wrote in 1939 that assured her fame as a playwright. At first glance this complex mystery set on Nigger Island off the Devon coast to which ten people are lured in order to be murdered seems an unlikely candidate for adaptation to the stage. And, indeed, those members of the theatrical fraternity to whom the script was first shown shook their heads and felt that audiences would fall about laughing at such a plethora of corpses.

But the authoress had taken great care in writing the original book and fancied the challenge of making it work in the theatre.

'It seemed impossible', she agreed later in her autobiography, 'because no one would be left to tell the tale, so I would have to alter it to a certain extent. It seemed to me that I could make a perfectly good play of it by one modification of the original story. I must make two of the characters innocent, to be reunited at the end and come safe out of the ordeal.'

However, several impresarios turned the play down before finally Bertram Meyer, who had backed *Alibi*, decided to take a chance with it. He signed Irene Hentschel to direct and assembled a cast of experienced actors including Terence de Marney, Allen Jeayes, Henrietta Watson, Linden Travers, Percy Walsh and Gwyn Nichols. After a try-out at the Wimbledon Theatre, *Ten Little Niggers* opened at the St James's Theatre on 17 November 1943 and everyone, Agatha included, held their breath for the critics' verdict.

W. A. Darlington, the doyen of *The Daily Telegraph*, led the chorus of approval. 'You see what a task Mrs Christie sets herself,' he wrote. 'She must play fair because her reputation depends on it. She must stick to her pattern. And she must somehow contrive to keep you and me guessing, even when the choice of suspects has narrowed down. Well, she succeeds!'

The Times was equally enthusiastic, and singled the producer out for especial praise. 'This

Linden Travers and Terence de Marney in Ten Little Niggers, *which opened at the St James's Theatre in November 1943* (John Vickers)

is not a play,' the newspaper wrote, 'it is a kind of theatrical game, with Miss Irene Hentschel pitting all her wits as a producer against our natural tendency to weary of flagrant absurdity prolonging itself throughout three acts. She has some admirable actors at her disposal; the stage action she invents for them is unfailingly ingenious; and she wins her game very comfortably.'

Playgoers loved the mystery, too, and it ran for 260 performances at the St James's until a German bomb forced the theatre to be closed. But Hitler only temporarily interrupted the success story, for *Ten Little Niggers* moved to the Cambridge Theatre where it continued for several months more. In June 1944, the play was put on in New York at the Broadhurst Theater – retitled *Ten Little Indians* so as not to offend audiences – and with Halliwell Hobbes, Michael Whalen, J. Pat O'Malley and Claudia Morgan notched up a very creditable 425 performances.

In 1966 the play was similarly retitled *Ten Little Indians* in the UK, and it has proved a popular revival item with numbers of repertory companies. It has been adapted for British television, too, in 1949, and filmed no less than three times, in 1945, 1965 and 1975, with varying degrees of success.

As the Second World War drew towards its merciful end in the spring of 1945, Agatha prepared another of her pre-war novels, *Appointment with Death* (1938), for the stage. However, in adapting this Hercule Poirot case of the murder of the horrendous Mrs Boynton during a tour in the Holy Land, she took the bold decision to delete the little Belgian and put the enquiry into the hands of another member of the party, one Colonel Carbury! She also made the killer a quite different person from the one in the book.

There has been much discussion as to exactly *why* the authoress should have chosen to remove her most famous character. It has been suggested, on the one hand, that she may have come to the conclusion that he was so overwhelming a personality that he dwarfed all the other characters on stage; on the other, that he was nothing more than a collection of mannerisms and was exposed as such when impersonated. Agatha herself only gave one less-than-satisfactory answer – that she removed the detective because he was too difficult to cast satisfactorily!

The man signed to direct *Appointment with Death* had actually been one of the stars of *Ten Little Niggers*, Terence de Marney, and his first-hand knowledge of Agatha Christie's work obviously helped him in the staging of the production. Among the cast, Mary Clare was outstanding as the sadistic Mrs Boynton; Owen Reynolds made an impressive Colonel Carbury; and Percy Walsh an amusing Alderman Higgs. Also to be found among the supporting roles was an actress who was to reach the climax of her career, forty years on, thanks to Agatha Christie – Joan Hickson, the current television Miss Marple, who then appeared as a diffident little spinster, Miss Pryce.

Appointment with Death opened at the Piccadilly Theatre on 31 March 1945 and ran until the autumn. In 1987, the story was filmed by Michael Winner, with Poirot reinstated as the investigator and played by Peter Ustinov.

Almost exactly a year after *Appointment with Death* opened, Agatha had a second play with an exotic setting on in the West End, *Murder on the Nile*. Again she had adapted this play from an earlier book, *Death on the Nile* (1937), and removed Poirot from the case.

The original novel remained one of Agatha's favourites throughout her life – based as it was on her own experiences in Egypt – and she adapted the story of a murder on a cruise boat with what was now becoming practised skill. Interestingly, among the cast assembled by producer Claude Guerney for the opening at the Ambassadors Theatre on 19 March 1946 was another actress whose later career was to be influenced by the playwright. She was Helen Hayes, then playing Miss ffolliot-ffoulkes, but destined to be another of the screen's Miss Marples.

The chief crime investigator devised by Agatha for the play was a sharp-witted cleric, Father Borrowdale, who was finely played by David Horne. Also in the cast were Hugo Schuster, Ivan Brandt, Joanna Derrill, Walter Lindsay and Vivienne Bennett. On the whole, though, the newspapers were not impressed by *Murder on the Nile, The Times* calling it a 'Who did it?' piece 'in almost its crudest form'.

Despite the press reaction, though, the play was transferred across the Atlantic – where it was rather curiously retitled *Hidden Horizon*, opening at the Plymouth Theater, New York on 19 September 1946. The cleric had also risen in the Church during the interim, for he was now Archdeacon Pennyfeather. This part was taken by Halliwell Hobbes, and among his co-stars were the beautiful Diana Barrymore, David Manners, Peter von Zerneck, Blair Davies and Barbara Joyce.

Unhappily, the American critics disliked the play even more than their British counterparts – the *New York Times* calling it 'dull in theme, dull in story, dull in the acting' – and it closed after just twelve performances. Yet despite this failure in both Britain and America, a much rosier future awaited *Murder on the Nile* when EMI filmed it in 1974 with Peter Ustinov as the reinstated Hercule Poirot . . .

Considering how determined – not to mention skilled – Agatha Christie had become at

A sketch by Ronald Searle of the first Miss Marple, Barbara Mullen, in The Murder at the Vicarage *at the Playhouse in December 1949, with Stanley van Beers as Detective Inspector Slack and Jack Lambert as the Reverend Leonard Clement*

adapting her work for the theatre, it comes as something of a surprise to discover that it was not she who was responsible for bringing her other famous sleuth, Miss Marple, to the stage in 1949. The play in which the remarkable amateur detective of St Mary Mead made her debut was *The Murder at the Vicarage* (1930), the intriguing tale of the murder of the 'pompous old brute' Colonel Protheroe, whose wife is having an affair with a handsome young artist.

The idea for dramatising this particular book had been put to Agatha by Barbara Toy and Moie Charles, two playwright friends of Bertie Meyer, the producer who had gambled on *Ten Little Niggers*. By all accounts she readily agreed to this suggestion, though quite how she took Barbara Toy's reason for believing the story would succeed with the public is debatable. 'Sex and religion', Miss Toy said, 'always goes down well!'

However, though Agatha did not write the script of *The Murder at the Vicarage*, she took a very keen interest in its adaptation, making numerous suggestions. She even sanctioned a major change to the ending and an up-dating in the time period from the Thirties to the year 1949. And when the play was finally put into production, she went to watch director Irene Hentschel at work and found the lady who had made such a good job of *Ten Little Niggers* was repeating the process once more. In particular, she was getting spirited performances from the stars: Barbara Mullen as Miss Marple; Reginald Tate as the artist, Laurence Redding; Alvys Mabon as Anne Protheroe; and Stanley van Beers as the bemused Inspector Slack.

Barbara Mullen proved an inspired choice as the first Miss Marple – though she was, in fact, a good thirty years younger than her character – and received glowing notices for the play which opened in London at the Playhouse on 14 December 1949, and ran for 1,776 performances.

When, two years on, Agatha was approached for an adaptation of her own, her choice fell on another of her Poirot stories, the ingenious but complex story of *The Hollow*, written in 1946. This baffling case of a woman who is found standing over a dying man with a smoking revolver in her hand was dedicated to Francis L. Sullivan, the second actor to play Poirot on the stage, and was also partly based on his country home. Yet once again Agatha excised all signs of the Belgian from her play.

This time, though, she was quite unequivocal about why Poirot had to go. 'He was all wrong there,' she said. 'He did his stuff all right, but how much better, I kept thinking, would the book have been without him? So when I came to sketch out the play, out went Poirot.'

Two of the first people to see the script of *The Hollow* expressed grave reservations. Agatha's daughter, Rosalind, one of her firmest and fairest critics, declared, 'It's a good book, and I like it, but you can't *possibly* make it into a play.'

Bertie Meyer simply did not like the script and thought it would be impossible to cast.

At this point Peter Saunders made his first appearance on the stage of Agatha Christie's life. A relatively new impresario, he admired her work and wondered if she might have something he could produce. Thus began one of the most fruitful partnerships in recent English theatre history.

To direct this new play, Saunders engaged the light comedy actor, Hubert Gregg, who made up for his lack of knowledge about directing with boundless enthusiasm. Several of his rehearsals were attended by Agatha, anxious to see whether she or Rosalind was right.

Initially, Gregg gave himself a small part in the play, but other commitments prevented him continuing this once the play had opened at the Fortune Theatre on 7 June 1951. Also in the cast were Jeanne de Casalis, Colin Douglas, Beryl Baxter and George Thorpe. Martin Wyldeck played Inspector Colquhoun, the Poirot 'replacement'.

The theatre critics were quick to express their approval of Agatha's gamble, *The Times*'s man declaring: 'Once the fatal shot has been fired and the police arrive to ask questions, there can be nothing but admiration for the impudent skill with which she directs suspense first this way, then that, and yet contrives to let certainty arrive in due course with an effect of genuine surprise.'

The public flocked to the production and it ran for eleven months, with a total of 376 performances. Since then, *The Hollow* has become one of the most popular of Agatha's plays with both touring and repertory companies. One production in South Africa even made news because of a real mystery associated with it in 1984.

Under the headline, 'A Real Life Whodunnit', the *Sunday Express* reported on 11 March 1984: 'A stage hand has been charged with attempted murder in a real life "whodunnit" backstage at a Johannesburg theatre where an Agatha Christie play was showing. The man was charged after poison was found in the cast's kettle only fifteen minutes before the villain in *The Hollow* "died" on stage . . . of poisoning.'

The success of *The Hollow* and, the following year, the opening of *The Mousetrap* began Agatha Christie's 'golden period' in the theatre. Her reputation as a playwright had grown with each new production, and with the triumphs that followed in the Fifties she earned a place in stage history which few can equal.

Consolidation of her fame – if such she needed – came with her very next play, *Witness for the Prosecution*, which Peter Saunders produced in 1953. Curiously, it was Agatha herself who had doubts about this project when Saunders suggested that she should adapt the short story of the same title which he had read in her collection, *The Hound of Death* (1933). She felt she would not be able to write a convincing courtroom drama.

But pressed by Saunders to try (the impresario even went so far as to write a first draft himself to convince her it could be done), Agatha started by reading up on trial transcripts and discussing details of procedure with several barristers and solicitors. When, finally, she sat down to write the play, she also decided to change the ending of the short story for something more visually dramatic and violent.

Agatha wrote the play in a single creative burst, taking less than three weeks. Once she had delivered the typescript to Peter Saunders, he too was caught up with the excitement of the courtroom play and rushed it into production, casting David Horne as Sir Wilfred Roberts, the QC briefed to defend Leonard Vole (Derek Bloomfield) against a charge of murder.

Patricia Jessel co-starred as Vole's wife, Romaine. *Witness for the Prosecution*, directed by Wallace Douglas, opened at the Winter Garden Theatre on 28 October 1953.

Agatha was a bundle of nerves before the curtain went up – but she remained in her seat for what she afterwards described as 'the one night at the theatre which will always stand out in my memory'.

The production was a triumph – the press, the public and even Agatha herself said so. 'I was as nearly satisfied with that play as I have been with any,' she remarked later.

'Agatha Christie must be happy this morning,' the *Daily Mirror* critic wrote without fear of contradiction the next day. 'While one thriller, *The Mousetrap*, is packing them in at the Ambassadors Theatre, another play opened with great success last night at the Winter Garden Theatre.' And of the play itself, *The Times* added, 'Mrs Christie has got the audience

Agatha attending a rehearsal of Witness for the Prosecution *in October 1953. The judge was played by Percy Marmont, and the two QCs by David Horne and D. A. Clarke-Smith*

in her pocket . . . the evidence brings the trial to a triumphantly satisfying conclusion. It is only then that the accomplished thriller writer shows her real hand.'

Agatha admitted she got just as much pleasure from the jostling crowds outside the theatre that first night who were anxious to shake her hand, get her autograph or tell her of their enjoyment at her play. In London, *Witness for the Prosecution* ran for 468 performances, then crossed to America where it enjoyed even greater success at the Henry Miller Theater following its opening on 16 December 1954.

Heading the American cast as Sir Wilfred Roberts was Agatha's actor friend, Francis L. Sullivan, with Gene Lyons playing Vole, and Patricia Jessel reprising her part as Romaine. The Broadway production ran for 645 performances and won the New York Drama Critics' Circle award for the best foreign play. Agatha had now triumphed on both sides of the Atlantic.

Three years later, in 1957, *Witness for the Prosecution* became more than just a classic of the stage: it became a classic of the cinema, too, when Billy Wilder filmed the play for United Artists with another former stage Poirot, Charles Laughton, as Sir Wilfred. Co-starring as the Voles were Tyrone Power and Marlene Dietrich.

In 1954, though, with this successful transition to the screen still to come, Agatha had written another page of theatre history when a third play from her pen opened in London,

SAVOY THEATRE, STRAND, W.C.2
Licensed by the Lord Chamberlain to HUGH WONTNER, M.V.O.
Proprietors SAVOY THEATRE LTD. General Manager: FREDERIC LLOYD
Box Office Phone TEMple Bar 8888

PETER SAUNDERS presents

Margaret Lockwood

in

Agatha Christie's

SPIDER'S WEB

Directed by WALLACE DOUGLAS   Decor by MICHAEL WEIGHT

Original poster for Spider's Web, *which Agatha wrote especially for Margaret Lockwood in 1954*

Spider's Web. Now, with a trio of productions packing audiences in during the Christmas season, she was not only the 'Queen of Crime' but the 'Queen of Theatreland' as well!

This new play about a diplomat's wife who discovers a body in her drawing room and then tries to dispose of it was specially written for its star, the vivacious English actress, Margaret Lockwood. Earlier in the year, Agatha had been invited to lunch by the actress who told her she was growing tired of playing 'wicked ladies' and wanted to try her hand at something new, perhaps a thriller with some elements of comedy?

The two women took an immediate liking to one another, and within a month Agatha had answered the request with *Spider's Web*. In choosing the name for her somewhat impulsive central character, Agatha had used her mother's name, Clarissa, for she had been a lady prone to similar if less extreme experiences. But in Clarissa's love of daydreaming, there was something of herself as well.

Margaret Lockwood had hoped that the other major role of Sir Rowland Delahaye might be played by the master of stage comedy, Wilfred Hyde-White, but he declined, and instead the part was taken with great relish by Felix Aylmer. Playing the two policemen investigating the crime were Campbell Singer (Inspector Lord) who had appeared in the first Agatha Christie play to be televised (*Ten Little Niggers*, in 1949), and Desmond Llewellyn (Constable Jones), later to become famous as 'Q', the gadget master, in the James Bond films.

Directing *Spider's Web* was Wallace Douglas who had so capably put *Witness for the*

Prosecution on the road to success, and he again extracted superb performances from his leading players. The press and public at once hailed a third triumph for Agatha when the play opened on 13 December 1954 at the Savoy Theatre. Alan Dent in the *News Chronicle* spoke for everyone when he declared, 'It is always a pleasure to be baffled by Agatha Christie!'

Agatha enjoyed writing *Spider's Web* as much as she did seeing it on the stage. 'It ran for two years and I was very pleased with it,' she said. 'When Margaret Lockwood proceeded to lead the police inspector up the garden path she was enchanting . . . She is a very good actress, and has that perfect timing which enables her to give lines their true weight.'

The play did not transfer to New York, but it was later adapted for filming in 1960 by the Danziger brothers, although surprisingly the actress Glynis Johns was preferred to Margaret for the lead role. Agatha was initially optimistic that the picture might enjoy the same success as it had done on the stage, but somehow the web had become tangled and lost its power to grip.

And, although no one could have known it at the time with the euphoria of three shows running in London, *Spider's Web* was to be one of Agatha's last major theatrical successes . . .

One thing that Agatha Christie insisted upon in the studies that were written about her plays or books was that the killer – or killers – in her stories should never be revealed. For obvious reasons, the restriction has continued since her death.

When a London reviewer indiscreetly gave the game away in the last paragraph of his review of *Towards Zero*, Agatha's 1956 production at the St James's Theatre, the effect could well have been disastrous – for what attraction is there in a murder mystery when the audience knows in advance 'whodunnit'? It says a great deal for Agatha's skill at being able to spin out the interest, that this intricately plotted adaptation of her 1944 book still managed to run for six months. The revelation did not prevent one of her keenest fans, the Queen, from arriving unannounced one evening to watch the play from a seat in the front row.

The story of Superintendent Battle's investigation into the sinister events at a seaside house which is to become the focal point for a psychopathic killer was jointly adapted for the stage by Agatha Christie and Gerald Verner. Directed by Murray Macdonald, it starred William Kendall as the superintendent, with the other leading parts taken by Cyril Raymond, Mary Law, George Baker, Gwen Cherrell and Michael Scott.

Agatha attended the rehearsals and was her usual forceful self when any untoward suggestions of changes were made. The reviews after the first night, on 4 September 1956, fell somewhat short of the notices she had received for her previous trio of plays, and the majority took the line of *The Times*: 'A not too strenuously diverting evening in which we do not smell a rat until it is too late.'

Agatha's next play, *Verdict*, directed by Charles Hickman, was also marred by an unfortunate incident on the opening night at the Strand Theatre on 22 May 1956. Because of a misunderstanding, the final curtain dropped sooner that it should have done, completely blacking out the sudden re-entrance of an important character, and thereby entirely changing the ending of the play. For perhaps the only time in her theatre career, Agatha Christie was booed: *Verdict* appeared to be a complete damp squib. True, the piece was not a detective story or thriller in her usual vein, but without the surprise finale it stood no chance of acceptance with audiences. W. A. Darlington, the *Telegraph*'s theatre critic, who was present at that first night, said the last scene, 'rang false and fell flat'. A day later, however, he was explaining to his readers what had *really* happened:

> *Verdict*, the play by Agatha Christie, was more enthusiastically received last night, when the company took six curtain calls. On Thursday, the first night, there was

booing from the gallery. It was revealed yesterday that the curtain had been rung down 40 seconds too soon, before the vital two lines between Gerard Heinz and Patricia Jessel. These lines complete a happy and more satisfactory ending to the play. The mistake in lowering the curtain was due to an error by a member of the stage manager's staff.

Verdict tells the story of some middle-European refugees, Professor Karl Hendryk, his crippled wife and his secretary, now living in London, and of how a female student, besotted with the professor, kills his wife. It was a play of which Agatha thought very highly – placing it second only to *Witness for the Prosecution* – and the fact that it survived for only a month deeply disappointed her. Yet, as she wrote in her autobiography, she believed she understood the reasons for this:

> It failed, I think, because it was not a detective story or a thriller. It was a play that concerned murder, but its real background and point was that an idealist is always dangerous, a possible destroyer of those who love him – and poses the question of how far you can sacrifice, not yourself, but those you love, to what you believe in, even though they do not.

Aside from the central performances by Gerard Heinz and Patricia Jessel as the professor and his secretary (the latter fresh from her triumphs in both London and New York in *Witness for the Prosecution*), Viola Keats was notable as the wife, Moira Redmond obsessive as the student, and Michael Golden dogged as Detective Inspector Ogden. Nonetheless, the show closed on 21 June.

Peter Saunders, however, was quick to cheer Agatha with the news that while *Verdict* may not have been the success she had envisaged, *The Mousetrap* had by then played for more than 2,239 performances and thus become the longest-running production in history. He also urged her to put her disappointment behind her and write something new, which she promptly did, delivering *The Unexpected Guest* to him just four weeks later.

Hubert Gregg was rehired to direct this tense and gripping story of a stranger who arrives one night at the door of a fog-shrouded house in South Wales to discover a woman who has just murdered her crippled, sadistic husband. In conjunction with Peter Saunders, Gregg lined up a strong cast including Nigel Stock (as the stranger), Renée Asherson (the wife), Violet Farebrother, Michael Golden and Tenniel Evans.

The play opened on 12 August 1958, and soon proved that Agatha had not lost her touch, by running for a total of 604 performances. *The Times* and *The Daily Telegraph* were both happy to comment on the playwright's instant return to form, with the *Guardian* underlining the point in purple prose:

> Only seven weeks after her last play was booed off the stage, Agatha Christie stumped defiantly back into a London theatre last night. She had a new whodunnit ready and watched from the back of the circle, white-faced and apprehensive. But no boos came this time. No rude interruptions. At the end she heard the kind of applause that has given her *Mousetrap* a record six-year run.

Even allowing for a little artistic licence, the *Guardian* fairly set the seal of success on *The Unexpected Guest*, which has since joined the roster of other Christie plays which are continually popular with amateur groups and touring companies.

For her next play, in 1960, Agatha decided to adapt another of the Poirot novels, *Five Little Pigs* (1943), and once more removed the detective from events. Inspired by the children's nursery rhyme, the story is concerned with the poisoning of a famous painter, Amyas Crale, for which his wife, Caroline, is found guilty, subsequently dying while serving her sen-

Margaret Lockwood in Spider's Web *with (l. to r.) Harold Scott,
Judith Furse and Sidney Monckton, and Felix Aylmer beside her on the sofa*

tence. In the book, Poirot is asked some years later by the couple's daughter to clear her mother's name by interviewing the five other people who were present at the time of the murder.

For the stage version, called *Go Back for Murder*, Agatha chose to put the enquiry into the hands of a young solicitor called Justin Fogg, and Hubert Gregg, who was again directing, chose Robert Urquhart for the role. Ann Firbank played both the mother and daughter, and there were strong supporting roles for Mark Eden, Laurence Hardy, Lisa Daniely and Nigel Green. The play opened at the Duchess Theatre on 23 March 1960, but it disappointed both the press and the public.

The Times was openly hostile: 'It must be said that Miss Christie has often got more excitement from the routine police investigation than she manages to get from this variation on the routine.' And the *Daily Mail*'s critic added, 'I felt cheated by this play.'

Go Back for Murder played for 31 performances and was then closed by a dismayed Peter Saunders. Though Agatha Christie was to produce two more plays for the stage, her reign as the undisputed ruler of London theatreland came to an end at that moment – even if her mark on theatre history was indelibly fixed for all to see.

In 1962 she tried the experiment of writing three one-act plays which were put on in London in the run-up to Christmas under the collective title, *Rule of Three*. The plays, 'The Rats', 'Afternoon at the Seaside' and 'The Patient', were again directed by Hubert Gregg,

A rather glum-looking Miss Marple played by Dulcie Gray in the 1977 version of A Murder Is Announced *at the Vaudeville. The cast are (l. to r.) James Grout, Dinah Sheridan, Elenor Summerfield, and (seated) Dulcie Gray, Barbara Flynn and Patricia Blake*

A Daily Mail cartoon of Glynis Barber as the femme fatale in And Then There Were None *at the Duke of York's in October 1987*

with a cast which included Betty McDowall, David Langton, Mercy Haystead and Raymond Bowers.

'The Rats' was a melodrama about four rather unpleasant Hampstead characters; 'Afternoon at the Seaside' concerned a stolen necklace and was seemingly derived from Agatha's short story 'The Rajah's Emerald'; and 'The Patient' dealt with a totally paralysed patient in a nursing home trying to make known the identity of the person who had pushed her from a balcony window.

After a not uneventful pre-London tour in Scotland, *Rule of Three* opened at the Duchess Theatre on 20 December 1962. Although the trio of plays was to run through the holiday season and for ten weeks into the spring of 1963, the press's lack of enthusiasm was matched by the returns at the box office.

'A harmless, naive evening,' was *The Times*'s verdict. 'The plays will probably appeal to amateurs and the less demanding reps, but are hardly, one would have thought, a probable addition to West End entertainments.'

Agatha's final play, a comedy-thriller called *Fiddlers Three*, written when she was 80, was to prove a sad finale for such a successful playwright. Even though it was toured in the provinces by the actor-manager James Grant Anderson (where it was first called *Fiddlers Five*), Peter Saunders decided not to bring this story of four conspirators, trying to conceal a body in order to get their hands on a £100,000 inheritance, into the West End. He would have done so had Agatha pressed him, he later admitted, but felt it would have harmed her reputation.

However, the impresario Cameron Mackintosh, who today dominates the West End with shows like *Les Miserables*, *Phantom of the Opera* and *Miss Saigon*, did urge a director friend, Alan Davis, to see if he could restructure the play in order to make it work. This he did, and *Fiddlers Three* was actually performed at the Yvonne Arnaud Theatre in Guildford, Surrey, on 1 August 1972 with a cast including Doris Hare, Raymond Francis, Gabor Baraker and Arthur Howard. However, despite the efforts of all those involved, this last Christie drama has never made it to the London stage.

Since Agatha Christie's death in 1976, her plays have continued to be performed in countless numbers by amateur and rep companies all over the world. In London, however, only three further major productions have been mounted in the intervening years.

The first of these was an adaptation of the Miss Marple case, *A Murder Is Announced*, which Peter Saunders staged at the Vaudeville Theatre, opening on 21 September 1977. Agatha had actually given her blessing to this project in 1975, but did not live to see Leslie Darbon's faithful adaptation which starred the demure Dulcie Gray as the lady sleuth, with James Grout (Inspector Craddock), Dinah Sheridan (Letitia Blacklock) and Eleanor Summerfield (Dora Bunner).

The story of a game of Murder played in Chipping Cleghorn which results in a real killing was the first new Christie in London for fifteen years, and *The Financial Times*, for one, was prepared to welcome the return, even if perhaps a little over-enthusiastically: 'There is no reason, intellectual or dramatic, why it shouldn't run as long as *The Mousetrap*,' the paper said. It didn't, of course – but it still lasted for 429 performances.

Dulcie Gray, as Miss Marple, was given a mixed reception, with Sheridan Morley writing in *Punch*, 'Dulcie Gray's Miss Marple is a long way from Margaret Rutherford and I suspect in the wrong direction – though Christie purists may prove me wrong.'

On the other hand, Ned Chaillet commented in *The Times*:

> Here Dulcie Gray is given a very animated Miss Marple to play, constantly poking her head in to comment on the crime – or rather, crimes, for there is another murder – and being taken surprisingly seriously by the investigator in charge of the investigation. Her fabled dottiness is hardly in evidence, and in this play her deductions and questions are unfailingly reasonable.

When, in 1981, Peter Saunders decided the time was ripe for another Christie, he chose a Poirot novel, *Cards on the Table* (1936), and followed Agatha's tradition by asking Leslie Darbon to remove the sleuth from the story. The playwright also dropped Colonel Race from this mystery of the death of the millionaire card-player, Mr Shaitana, and put the onus for the enquiries on to Superintendent Battle and Agatha's alter ego, Mrs Ariadne Oliver. Director Peter Davis cast Gordon Jackson as the policeman, and Margaret Courtenay as Mrs Oliver, with Derek Waring as Dr Roberts, Gary Raymond as Major Despard, and Belinda Carroll and Mary Tamm as two very different young ladies.

Once again the production opened in time for the Christmas season, on 9 December, at the Vaudeville Theatre, and both *The Observer* and *The Times* agreed that there were still good reasons for welcoming a play by Agatha Christie.

'The acting style is in the spirit of the play,' said *The Observer*, 'and is the closest approximation to a prewar "quota-quickie" movie likely to be found in the West End. We're in french-window and lily-pond territory. Gordon Jackson binds the play together superbly.'

And *The Times*'s view: 'Leslie Darbon's new Christie adaptation, *Cards on the Table*, is a puzzle with as many wrong turnings as a Rubik cube with a merry line in deception. Some may hate this breed altogether, but, of its kind, *Cards on the Table* is a champion.'

Cheered by such notices, the play ran for over six months.

The most recent production of all has been a revival of that classic Christie whodunnit, *And Then There Were None*, which Bill Kenwright put on at the Duke of York's Theatre on 7 October 1987. Using basically the same script as Agatha herself had written back in 1943, director Kenneth Alan Taylor marshalled an impressive cast of victims on his Devon island setting including Miriam Karlin, John Fraser, Jack Hedley, Rodney Bewes and Glynis Barber.

For two of London's best-known critics, opening night brought a nostalgic trip back to childhood. Jack Tinker of the *Daily Mail* and Jeremy Kingston of *The Times* had seen the play as boys and it had had a considerable impact on both of them.

Jeremy Kingston recalled seeing an amateur dramatic society performance at Thames Ditton. 'My late Aunt Margaret played the spinster,' he wrote, 'and when the needle was found in her I was child enough to be thrilled.'

However, of the 1987 London production, he said: 'Agatha Christie's elimination comedy, formerly known as *Ten Little Niggers* and frequently regarded as a thriller, shows what a master of laughs the old "Queen of Crime" could be, even without trying.'

For Jack Tinker his youthful experience had an even more profound effect:

> This is the play which changed my life. It is, in fact, the first play I ever saw and I came home in such a thrall of terror and hypertension I could not wait to return to the Oldham Repertory Company as soon as pocket money permitted. As I was only eight at the time and the effect of video nasties and violence on formative minds was totally unknown, it was perhaps more than fortunate that my taste was tempered by the following week's offering, which was *Peg O' My Heart*.
>
> Suffice it to say I was hooked on the theatre for evermore. And seeing this early Agatha Christie vintage thriller now, after all these lifetimes, I can only say it is the most collectable tosh. What director Kenneth Alan Taylor has realised is that the play's only remaining strength is its rattling narrative and that he must make virtues of all its remaining defects.

And Jack concluded his notice, 'It is amazing to find there is a whole new generation which genuinely does not know who-dunnit.'

Long may it continue so, for therein, I believe, lies the key to the appeal of Agatha Christie in the theatre. For each generation has kept the secret to enable the next to have the chance to be puzzled, excited and, in all probability, outwitted by a lady who is unquestionably one of the masters of stage mystery.

MAYHEM IN THE
CINEMA

For sixty years – a period which spans the coming of the talkies and the present-day big-budget extravaganzas – Agatha Christie's murder stories have proved a continuing attraction for film-makers in Britain, America and Europe. Yet despite the fact that over two dozen feature-length productions for the cinema have been made from her work, few of those created during her lifetime pleased the authoress. And, in truth, in only a handful of cases on the big screen has anything approaching justice been done to her memorable characters and complex, baffling plots.

Because of the liberties which producers have consistently taken with her work it is no surprise to learn that Agatha remained sceptical throughout her life about the wisdom of granting film rights. She believed she had good reason, too, as she explained to Francis Wyndham in an interview for *The Sunday Times* in February 1966:

'I kept off films for years because I thought they'd give me too many heart-aches,' she said. 'Then I sold the rights to MGM, hoping they'd use them for television. But they chose films. It was too awful! They did things like taking a Poirot book and putting Miss Marple in it! And all the climaxes were so poor, you could see them coming! I get an unregenerate pleasure when I think they're not being a success.'

Yet despite her dissatisfaction with what was done to her stories by the film industry, an examination of the varied range of productions since the very first in the late 1920s provides some fascinating insights – as well as revealing a very substantial contribution to cinema entertainment by 'The First Lady of Crime'.

There are two major surprises which the researcher into Agatha Christie on film comes across when looking at the first picture, made in 1928. Firstly, it does not feature Hercule Poirot, who was by then already a household name (Miss Marple, of course, was not created until the following year); and secondly, it was based not on a novel but on a magazine short story, 'The Coming of Mr Quin'.

The central figure of the story is Mr Harley Quin, a rather strange, illusionary man seemingly possessed of supernatural powers. Agatha Christie had for years been interested in spiritualism (as can be seen in collections such as the fantasy tales in *The Hound of Death* and the novel *The Pale Horse*) and created Quin as a kind of mysterious figure who appears whenever crime threatens the happiness of lovers: a fact which earns him the soubriquet 'The Love Detective'. His name (a play on 'harlequin') reflects the authoress's interest in the commedia dell'arte.

'The Coming of Mr Quin' was spotted on its original publication in *Pearson's Magazine* by the enterprising producer-director, Julius Hagen of Strand Films, who promptly made an offer for the film rights. If the authoress was at all surprised that the first film-maker to approach her should want Mr Quin, this was no doubt offset by the affection in which she already held this unusual character. Years later in her autobiography she confessed he was one of her favourites:

> Mr Quin was a figure who just entered into a story – a catalyst, no more – his mere presence affected human beings. There would be some little fact, some apparently irrelevant phrase, to point him out for what he was: a man shown in a harlequin-coloured light that fell on him through a glass window, suddenly appearing or disappearing . . .
>
> I wrote the Mr Quin stories not very often, at intervals of perhaps three or four months, sometimes longer still. Magazines appeared to like them, and I liked them myself, but I refused all offers to do a series for any periodical.

Agatha did, though, accept Julius Hagen's film offer, and the story was adapted for the screen by Leslie Hiscott. Unhappily, though, not only was the title inexplicably changed to *The Passing of Mr Quinn* (with a second 'n' added to the hero's name), but the introductory tale was changed out of all recognition. Instead of an intriguing story about Mr Quin's special ability at solving mysteries, it became an investigation to save an ill-treated wife, Mrs Appleby, whose sinister professor husband has been found poisoned while having an affair with the couple's maid.

Playing Mr Quin was a popular matinee idol of the day, Stewart Rome, who had begun his career on the music halls in 1906, and then become a pioneer star of British silent films in 1913, making over 200 pictures. His name had become revered in the acting profession after he won a law suit in 1919 against the Hepworth Company, establishing that an actor's professional name belonged to *him* and not to the company that had given it to him. (Rome's real name was Septimus William Ryott.)

With his Ivor Novello-like profile, Rome was one of the first actors to receive star billing on the screen, though his salary was usually little more than £6 per week. Also appearing with him in *The Passing of Mr Quinn* were Trilby Clark as Mrs Appleby and Ursula Jeans as the maid.

During a radio talk Stewart Rome gave about his career in August 1953 entitled, 'Merely Players', he mentioned the film: 'I played a villain in my very first picture, *Justice*, for which I received a fee of twelve shillings and sixpence per day. After that I became a detective in *The Great Poison Mystery* in 1914 and earned a little more! But in those early days there was such an atmosphere of goodwill and comradeship in the studios that the question of salary was unimportant . . .

'I also played a detective in *The Passing of Mr Quinn* which was the first film to be made from an Agatha Christie story. I believe there was going to be a series about Mr Quin if it was successful. My last picture, made in 1950, was called *Let's Have a Murder* – so you might almost say I had a career in crime!'

Strand Films obviously had high expectations for *The Passing of Mr Quinn*, for not only was it extensively advertised in the newspapers (with Agatha Christie's name given prominence, an indication of her popularity even in 1928), but also a full-length 'book of the film' was written by G. Roy McRae and published by The Novel Library at sixpence. Agatha Christie had no hand whatsoever in the writing of this book, as one glance at the pulp fiction prose will immediately reveal.

Despite some enthusiastic write-ups about the movie in film magazines such as *The Picturegoer*, the film was only moderately successful at the box office and any plans for another Mr Quin film were not pursued. Julius Hagen, though, was already casting his eyes over Mrs Christie's other books, in particular one featuring Hercule Poirot.

Scarcely had *The Passing of Mr Quinn* reached the British cinema than another Christie adaptation, this time from Germany, was released early in 1929. This was entitled *Die Abenteuer GmbH* (Adventurers Ltd) and was based on Agatha's 1922 novel about her two young

55.

*Mr Quinn at the gateway to the future... A
rare still from the first film of an Agatha
Christie story,* The Passing of Mr Quinn, *made
in 1928 and starring Stewart Rome*

The unlikely-looking first screen Poirot, played by Austin Trevor in Lord Edgware Dies *(1934)*

sleuths, Tommy and Tuppence, which she had originally planned to call *The Young Adventurers Ltd* before settling for *The Secret Adversary*. (When the German movie was shown in Britain it was billed as *The Secret Adversary* as well.)

Again it seems curious that the film-maker, Fred Sauer, had ignored Poirot in favour of the pair of young detectives – especially as at that time Germany was in the middle of a craze for pictures about English detectives, such as Sherlock Holmes, and Edgar Wallace's master criminals such as The Ringer.

In 1931, Julius Hagen decided to film a second Agatha Christie story. He had become intrigued by the character of Hercule Poirot, especially in the story of *The Murder of Roger Ackroyd*, which had been successfully adapted for the stage in 1928 as *Alibi* with Charles Laughton in the lead. Hagen believed this success could be repeated in the cinema. He secured the rights and handed the directing of the picture to his former scriptwriter, Leslie Hiscott.

Neither Hagen nor Hiscott had any intention of following Agatha Christie's idea of Hercule Poirot in this film – instead they chose another tall, dark, matinée star, Austin Trevor, to be the first man to play the little Belgian detective on the screen. (The story of the making of this film – and Austin Trevor's two further interpretations in *Black Coffee* (1931) and *Lord Edgware Dies* (1934) – is told in its star's biography in a later chapter.)

While this trio of films was being shot, Agatha Christie was approached by a group of film-makers who wanted her to dramatise another of her novels, *The Secret of Chimneys*. This light-hearted thriller about two young adventurers, Anthony Cade and Jimmy McGrath, who unwittingly become involved in a plot to gain control of a troubled middle European nation, certainly had the ingredients to make a successful Thirties movie, and according to Janet Morgan the film people intimated to Agatha Christie that she 'might make £200,000 out of it'.

Although she did actually complete a dramatisation of *The Secret of Chimneys*, nothing further was heard of these ambitious plans, and the project can be written off as the first of the 'Christie Films That Never Were'.

The year 1937 saw the next of Agatha's stories filmed – again with a popular leading man and also based on a short story. The actor was the South African-born Basil Rathbone, and the story was 'Philomel Cottage' from the collection *The Listerdale Mystery*.

This 1934 anthology is also notable for two other of its short stories. One is the tale entitled 'The Rajah's Emerald', about a young man who discovers a missing precious stone. Nothing unusual in that – except that the young man's name was appropriated twenty years later by another writer for a character who became the most famous secret agent in the world: James Bond! And the second is 'Witness for the Prosecution', a tale from another book (*The Hound of Death*) which was added for the American edition of these stories. This story was, of course, the basis for the classic play and for the films to which I shall refer later.

'Philomel Cottage', the account of a young wife's recurring nightmare that her mysterious ex-fiancé is going to murder her husband, had first been turned into the stage play, *Love from a Stranger*, in March 1936. It had been adapted by Frank Vosper, the former actor and playwright, and also the villain in a number of Alfred Hitchcock's films, who planned to play the leading male role himself. This he did with some success – his final scene with Marie Ney was so brilliantly played on the opening night in London that a number of people in the audience actually fainted. Later in the year the play transferred to New York. Frank Vosper, however, did not long enjoy his success, for the following year, in an incident that might have come straight from the pages of a Christie novel, he mysteriously disappeared overboard from an ocean liner and was never found.

Film producer Max Schach was among the first-night audience at *Love from a Stranger* and decided to film the story at Trafalgar Studios. Another screenwriter, Frances Marion, was brought in to work on the late Frank Vosper's play, and the leading Hollywood director Roland V. Lee came over to England to direct. He recommended Basil Rathbone and Ann Harding for the lead roles, and there was also a small part for a developing young English character actress named Joan Hickson as the maid, Emmy.

Although much of the film was restricted to the studios, Lee produced a stylish and gripping film which has the distinction of being the first Agatha Christie movie to have been released in America (by United Artists). Basil Rathbone was sleekly sinister as the fortune-hunter intent on murdering rich women, and the *New York Times* shared the view of the British press that the whole picture was 'a tense and moving melodrama'.

Many years later in 1963 – four years before his death – Basil Rathbone recalled the picture for a very different reason. 'Although I played a pretty unsavoury murderer in *Love from a Stranger*, it was the picture that Darryl Zanuck saw before he cast me in the first of the Sherlock Holmes films, *The Hound of the Baskervilles* . . . So you can say it was actually Agatha Christie who got me typecast as Holmes for all those years!'

Basil Rathbone as the mystery-man of the title in Love from a Stranger *(1937), with co-star Ann Harding*

Love from a Stranger was also remade again ten years later – in Hollywood this time – by producer James J. Geller for Eagle-Lion Films. It was retitled *A Stranger Walked In* and a new script was written by the American crime novelist, Philip MacDonald, in which a sweepstake winner (Sylvia Sidney) gradually discovers that her charming new husband (John Hodiak) is concealing a very sinister past. The director was Richard Whorf.

There was little for Agatha Christie to smile at when she saw this picture, save, perhaps the naming of one character Auntie Loo-Loo, and the inept performances of two supporting actors with the extraordinary names of Anita Sharp-Bolster (playing Ethel) and Fred Worlock (as Inspector Hobday).

If such a picture reinforced her general dissatisfaction with the way in which the film industry treated her work, at least there was the comfort of *And Then There Were None*, an adaptation of *Ten Little Niggers*, which the French director René Clair made for Twentieth Century-Fox in 1945. It was the first classic film to be made from a Christie mystery, and with three later versions – including one for television – is one of the most filmed of her books.

It was soon after the outbreak of the Second World War that Agatha turned her fiendishly ingenious novel into a play, and after its transfer to New York in June 1944, with its new title of *Ten Little Indians*, two American film companies, RKO and Warner Brothers, expressed interest in the rights. It was, however, Twentieth Century-Fox that finally secured these and put writer Dudley Nichols to work on a screenplay with yet another title, *And Then There Were None*.

Much of the quality of the resulting picture must be attributed to René Clair's innovative direction and the fine acting of a cast which included Barry Fitzgerald, Walter Huston, Louis Hayward, Roland Young, C. Aubrey Smith and Mischa Auer. Aubrey Smith, an exiled British actor and one of the leading lights of the English colony in Hollywood at that time, remembered the film well.

'It was one of those rare pictures where no corners were cut,' he said. 'Everything from the design to the costuming and the casting was first class, and with a really good script to work with all the actors gave splendid performances. The director René Clair's ingenuity with the camera and lighting was the icing on the cake.'

Such was the impact of this picture that it is hardly surprising that it should have been filmed again. Before then, however, BBC Television, though still hampered by its limited post-war resources, produced a 'live' adaptation in August 1949 using the original title, *Ten Little Niggers*.

The man who tried to follow René Clair's achievement in the cinema was the energetic former English radio producer Harry Alan Towers, who got Seven Arts Films to back a remake in 1965. To direct the picture, he chose George Pollock, who, though he had been responsible for four Miss Marple films in the Sixties, was no match for the French director, turning the drama of the string of murders into something approaching a farce.

Nor could the scriptwriters, Peter Welbeck and Peter Yeldham, resist tampering with the classic story: changing the location from an island to the Austrian Alps and substantially altering the characters of several of the ten victims. Among those who starred in the film were Hugh O'Brian, Shirley Eaton, Stanley Holloway, Wilfred Hyde-White, Dennis Price, Daliah Lavi and an American pop singer, Fabian.

The 1965 *Ten Little Indians* is perhaps best remembered for containing the first love scene in a Christie movie (Hugh O'Brian and Shirley Eaton) as well as a 'who-dun-it' break just before the finale, when the audience are given a recap in order to try and spot the killer before all is revealed!

Less than ten years later – following hard on the heels of the success of *Murder on the Orient Express*, of which more shortly – Harry Alan Towers, seemingly unable to leave the story alone, instigated another remake for Avco-Embassy. This time the crimes perpetrated on Agatha Christie's original story were even more horrific.

The scriptwriter, Peter Welbeck (working on his own this time), now updated the murder

Above: *The classic René Clair version of* And Then There Were None, *filmed in Hollywood in 1945. C. Aubrey Smith is at the top right, clutching his head!*

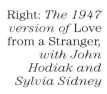

Right: *The 1947 version of* Love from a Stranger, *with John Hodiak and Sylvia Sidney*

The 1965 version of Ten Little Indians, *with* (l. to r.)
Wilfred Hyde-White, Stanley Holloway, Daliah Lavi,
Shirley Eaton and Hugh O'Brian

mystery to the present day and changed the setting to a hotel in Iran. Once more the victims underwent character changes, presumably to suit the international cast of Oliver Reed, Charles Aznavour, Gert Fröbe, Adolfo Celi, Elke Sommer, Richard Attenborough and Herbert Lom. The voice of Orson Welles was also heard on a tape-recorder as the host of the victims. The director was Peter Collinson who had recently finished the hugely successful *The Italian Job* – but the job he did on this film was far less satisfactory, even though Oliver Reed gave a typically robust performance as the master amateur detective, Hugh Lombard.

When the *New York Times* reviewed the picture its comment was typical of many others:

Left: *Charles Laughton and Elsa Lanchester discussing their roles in* Witness for the Prosecution *(1957) with Billy Wilder. Opposite: Laughton gave one of the great performances of his life as Sir Wilfred Roberts*

'*Ten Little Indians* is an international movie mess of the sort that damages the reputations of everyone concerned with it.'

In 1956, however, long before this butchery, not only did the singer Gracie Fields play Miss Marple on television in America, but in Britain, Agatha Christie, having grown tired of what others had been doing to her plots, agreed to prepare a screenplay of *Spider's Web*, the successful 1954 stage comedy-thriller which she had written for Margaret Lockwood.

The Danziger brothers, who were to produce the film, were optimistic about the success of *Spider's Web*. It was to be the first Christie mystery filmed in colour, and two popular actors, Glynis Johns and John Justin, were to star as the diplomat and his wife. Director Godfrey Grayson was noted for his skill at blending comedy and thrills, and had recruited two stalwart character actors, Ferdy Mayne and Jack Hulbert, to bolster the entertainment.

Agatha Christie accepted an invitation from Godfrey Grayson to visit the set and was happily photographed with the stars and inspecting the priest-hole where the corpse was to be discovered. But once shooting was completed, all was silence for some time.

Perhaps the fact that the picture was not released until 1960 indicates that optimism had turned to scepticism – for certainly the film was neither a critical nor a popular success, and it was not even released in America, where Agatha Christie was now selling hundreds of thousands of copies of her books every year.

The year 1957, however, brought another undoubted classic with the first cinema version of the play *Witness for the Prosecution*, which United Artists had secured for the princely sum of £116,000. Although the play had already been broadcast three times on three different American television drama series – in 1949, 1950 and 1953 – here was a riveting drama that in the right hands could surely also enthral cinema audiences.

That year had, in fact, begun auspiciously for Agatha when she learned from her agent that Alfred Hitchcock was interested in filming 'Accident', another of the stories from *The Listerdale Mystery*. This tale of a retired police inspector who suspects a woman he meets of being a husband-killer would have been ideal material for Hitchcock, and it is unfortunate that his plans never materialised.

Witness for the Prosecution proved quite a different matter, however. United Artists and

Left: *Agatha inspecting the 'priest's hole' on the set of* Spider's Web *in 1956 with the film's director, Godfrey Grayson*

Right: *The first cinema Miss Marple, Margaret Rutherford, and her husband, Stringer Davis, filming a scene for* Murder Most Foul *in 1964*

producer Arthur Hornblow Jr decided to put their vast resources behind the making of the courtroom drama, and assigned the vastly experienced Billy Wilder as director. The script was written by Wilder himself in conjunction with Harry Kurnitz, and it stuck faithfully to the stage play.

The decision to shoot the picture in black-and-white was a brave one, as colour movies were all the rage, and almost £100,000 was spent on recreating a replica of the courtroom and passages of the Old Bailey in the Hollywood studios.

In order to ensure secrecy during the making of the picture, Billy Wilder insisted on a closed set and made all visitors sign an agreement not to reveal any of the secrets they might see 'relating to its electrifying climax'. The casting of the picture was also inspired: Charles Laughton, the first man to have played Hercule Poirot on the stage, as Sir Wilfred Roberts; Tyrone Power as Leonard Vole, the man on trial for his life; Marlene Dietrich as his wife, Christine; Henry Daniell as Mayhew; and Laughton's wife, Elsa Lanchester, as Sir Wilfred's fussy nurse, Miss Plimsoll.

Billy Wilder never forgot Laughton's tour de force in this film. 'He took on the dimensions of a barrister,' the director said afterwards. 'We had heated arguments but they always led to something positive. We would have fifteen or more readings and each time the interpretation of lines was different. He was like a musician looking for variations in a theme. You can tell how good an actor is by looking at his script. If he's no good, it will be neat as a pin. Charles's was filthy, it looked like a herring had been wrapped in it. He had obviously digested it and regurgitated it – whole!'

Interestingly, Agatha was visiting America with her husband while filming was taking place, and she took the opportunity to drop in on the Hollywood studios. If she went along with her usual sense of trepidation, for once she left feeling that, *this* time, all was going well with her story.

Considerable excitement greeted the opening of the movie which promptly received six Academy Award nominations. Though it surprisingly failed to capture a single Oscar,

Witness for the Prosecution was ecstatically reviewed and took a staggering $3.75 million at the box office in the first year of its release. It was a popular success and a classic into the bargain – and underlined again Agatha Christie's assertion that if only her work was not so carelessly tampered with, more adaptations for the screen might be successful.

That the lesson was not learned can be judged by the chequered results of the next four stories to be brought to the screen – a quartet of Miss Marple cases made by MGM and starring Margaret Rutherford: *Murder She Said* (1962), *Murder at the Gallop* (1963), *Murder Most Foul* (1964) and *Murder Ahoy* (1964). The second and third of these were actually based on novels in which Hercule Poirot had been the detective, which not surprisingly provoked Agatha's outburst to Francis Wyndham in 1966, quoted earlier.

While these pictures were being made, another MGM producer asked Agatha if she would write a screenplay of her favourite Charles Dickens novel, *Bleak House*. She tackled this with relish, setting the action against the background of the Jarndyce *v.* Jarndyce case which she believed to be the essence of the story. Understandably she wanted to highlight the detective streak that she said she was almost always to be found in Dickens – but despite completing a 270-page draft (which MGM asked her to cut) the project eventually died.

Hercule Poirot made another appearance on the screen in the shape of Tony Randall in

The Alphabet Murders in 1966 which the authoress again found unsatisfactory. She was not best pleased, either, when just over five years later United Artists made a lack-lustre version of another of her favourite novels, *Endless Night*, which she had written in 1967.

This story concerns the London youth of the swinging Sixties, and in particular a working-class boy who marries a 'poor little rich girl' and finds himself the owner of a dream house where strange accidents and deaths occur. Early work on the picture encouraged the authoress: Sidney Gilliat who wrote and directed the movie was an acknowledged master of his craft, and his screenplay remained faithful to the novel. Two talented young actors, Hywel Bennett and Hayley Mills, were cast to play the central couple, with supporting roles given to Britt Ekland, Per Oscarsson and George Sanders.

Excellent locations were found and atmospherically filmed in the West Country, but somehow the film never quite fulfilled its promise, containing – as the reviewers agreed – too many red herrings and an overly intrusive musical score. An erotic scene near the end, showing an uninhibited Hayley Mills dancing in the open air, offended Agatha Christie and clouded her judgement of the film. Though *Endless Night* failed to be released in America after its poor run in Britain, it has subsequently been shown on television on both sides of the Atlantic and has gained a number of admirers.

A new era of Christie on film was to begin dramatically in 1974 with EMI's bold decision to splash millions of pounds on an all-star version of the classic Poirot case, *Murder on the Orient Express*, with Albert Finney as the little Belgian detective. Because of Agatha Christie's disenchantment with the film world, co-producer John Brabourne asked his father-in-law, Lord Mountbatten, to help convince the authoress that EMI was determined to make a faithful version of the mystery, and to that end had signed the top director, Sidney Lumet, to direct, with Richard Rodney Bennett providing the musical score. Albert Finney, for his part, planned to play Poirot with painstaking attention to make-up and character.

When Agatha Christie saw the finished version of *Murder on the Orient Express* she found much to admire in the picture – though she thought Finney's moustache too small for her hero! The critics, too, applauded the picture, and the public flocked to the cinemas in droves, making it the most popular British film of all time.

Hywel Bennett and Hayley Mills, a swinging Sixties couple in Endless Night, *made in 1972*

Left: *Sidney Lumet directing Albert Finney and Sir John Gielgud in* Murder on the Orient Express *(1974).* Below: *The Orient Express locomotive itself, which almost stole the honours*

Above: *The river
steamer which was
the setting for
murder in* Death on
the Nile *(1978).*
Right: *Peter Ustinov
as Poirot cross-
examines one of the
boat's passengers,
played by Bette
Davis*

The producers John Brabourne and Richard Goodwin followed *Murder on the Orient Express* with *Death on the Nile* in 1978. Albert Finney, however, did not wish to play Poirot again, and the role was taken over by that man of many parts, Peter Ustinov. He achieved success in the role, as well as in another picture for EMI, *Evil Under The Sun* in 1981, and in *Appointment with Death* (1987), plus three made-for-TV movies, *Thirteen at Dinner* (1985), *Dead Man's Folly* (1986) and *Murder in Three Acts* (1987).

In 1980, EMI also decided to bring Agatha Christie's other famous detective, Miss Marple, to the screen, and filmed *The Mirror Crack'd*, starring Angela Lansbury, with an impressive list of co-stars including Elizabeth Taylor, Tony Curtis, Rock Hudson, Geraldine Chaplin, Edward Fox and Kim Novak.

If, with hindsight, the Seventies was the decade of superior Christie movies, then the Eighties have become the same for the author's work on television. No longer at the mercy of confined studios and the unpredictability of 'live' broadcasts, the small-screen producers have now been able to bring colour, authenticity and the highest production values to bear on the authoress's books and characters. Apart from the three Peter Ustinov Poirot features, there have been Thames TV's *Agatha Christie Hour*, LWT's Tommy and Tuppence stories, *Partners in Crime*, the BBC's Miss Marple series with Joan Hickson and LWT's *Poirot* with David Suchet.

Only one further movie for the cinema has been made: *Ordeal by Innocence*, which Menahem Golan and Yoram Globus's Cannon Group produced in 1974, and which opened at a Royal Charity Premiere before the Queen and the Duke of Edinburgh on 14 February 1985. Both the Sovereign and her husband are Christie fans and the Queen had met the

Pointing the way to still greater screen triumphs for Agatha Christie? Angela Lansbury as Miss Marple, with Edward Fox as Inspector Craddock in the lavish 1980 production of The Mirror Crack'd

authoress on several occasions, including the premiere of *Murder on the Orient Express.*

Ordeal by Innocence, written in 1958, is the story of Dr Arthur Calgary, a physician who recovers from a period of amnesia to find that a young man he knew has been wrongly executed for murder. It was another of Agatha Christie's favourite books and is set on her native Devon coast. Cannon director Desmond Davis decided to shoot the whole film on location in and around Dartmouth, and cast Donald Sutherland as Dr Calgary (who in the movie is not suffering from amnesia, but instead has been away in the Antarctic for two years), with Faye Dunaway, Ian McShane, Sarah Miles, Christopher Plummer and Diana Quick.

The making of the picture was not without incident, however: on location in February 1984 a thief stole a number of vital documents from producer Jenny Craven's car, including her notes, a number of contracts and firearm permits for the guns used by the cast. In reporting the theft, Jenny told the press: 'We would like to get out property back – it sounds like a case for Miss Marple!' (Sadly, nothing was returned.)

Donald Sutherland took the robbery very much in his stride, confessing how much he enjoyed a good mystery.

'I've always loved whodunnits,' he said during filming. 'Raymond Chandler, Dashiel Hammett, Ngaio Marsh, I like them all. But for a long time I had never read any Agatha Christie, until one day I found myself stuck in a friend's house in France with nothing to read except a couple of Christie books. So I read one and couldn't put it down. I read the second one and immediately went out to the local store where I found another ten or twelve of her books. I bought them all and for a while I always had one of them in my pocket.'

Donald researched his role carefully, and before flying to England for filming, visited a paleontologist in California for background information on his character.

'I came to like Dr Calgary,' he said. 'I liked his earnestness, his pride, his struggle to deal with his self. His problem is that he has disassociated himself so much from human beings that he has lost his instincts about people.'

Though the resulting picture was an enjoyable mixture of atmospherically filmed scenery with some spirited acting, only Derek Malcom of the *Guardian* really enjoyed it. '*Ordeal by Innocence* is not the most lavish of recent adaptations,' he wrote, 'but it can lay fair claim to being one of the most faithful, traversing the story with some clarity and commendable sense of atmosphere. And its cast is distinguished enough to make one whet [*sic*] the lips a little.'

So will there be more Agatha Christie in the cinema? Certainly that is the hope of her admirers – and there are tentative plans for at least two films to mark the centenary. The first could be a new version of *Towards Zero,* the 1944 novel of Superintendent Battle's investigation into a psychopathic killer homing in on an East Coast seaside house, which Agatha had also dramatised for the stage with Gerald Verner in 1956. The interested producer is Simon Perry, who would like the highly rated French director and Hitchcock admirer, Claude Chabrol, to direct.

Death Comes as the End, Agatha's only mystery with a historical setting, about love and discord in an Ancient Egyptian family which culminates in murder, is the proposed second film. This ambitious project, which will require extensive location shooting in Egypt in order to remain faithful to Agatha's own on-the-spot research while writing the novel in 1945, is the dream of producers Alain Siritzky and Jeremy Thomas.

These two projects apart, there is still such a body of work available that many admirers hope it will not be too long before a few more movies are added to the existing roster of Christie classics. And, of course, the film rights of *The Mousetrap* are also being jealously guarded – though a prerequisite of any picture is that it must not appear until six months after the end of the stage run. However, as producers Victor Saville and Eddie Small, the original purchasers of the rights in 1956, have since died, and the rights have been assigned to others, quite who might produce such a film – and when – is a matter fraught with as much mystery as any Agatha Christie novel.

RADIO SERIAL MURDERS

here are a considerable number of admirers of Agatha Christie's stories who maintain that radio has come closer than any other medium of entertainment to presenting her work as she intended. Because it is known she preferred her characters to remain nebulous, thereby allowing readers to fill in the details in their own imaginations, the radio is claimed to be better suited to her aims than the theatre, films or television.

All Christie characters, their appearances and surroundings, are, of course, archetypes that can be recognised anywhere and at any time. The authoress developed these qualities in her very first novel and never had cause to abandon them. The potential drawback of radio therefore lies in the total dependence on the voices of those who play the characters. Nevertheless, from the Thirties onwards Agatha Christie not only wrote for the radio and liked the resulting productions, but even broadcast herself on a number of occasions, though it has to be admitted that tracking down the facts of Christie on radio is rather like following the tortuous path of one of her mysteries. The BBC archives for the early years of broadcasting are far from complete, and it is therefore only possible to present the highlights among her contributions – though these are just as fascinating as any to be found in the other fields of entertainment.

The British Broadcasting Corporation, with its famous call sign 2LO, began transmitting from Marconi House in London in 1922, offering those with 'wireless' receivers a mixture of live concerts, gramophone records, comedy sketches, news items and stories for children. In May of the following year, the embryo service moved to larger studios in Savoy Hill (next door to the famous hotel) and there remained for a decade until the opening of the custom-built Broadcasting House near Oxford Circus in May 1932.

The first BBC drama productions were either extracts from successful theatrical productions such as *Charley's Aunt*, scenes from Shakespeare's plays performed by leading actors, or short stories read by popular novelists of the day like W. Pett Ridge. When serials – those ever-popular features of the radio – were introduced in December 1925, the very first was *The Mayfair Mystery* which challenged listeners to be detectives and solve the mystery, offering a £100 reward for the first correct solution.

Appropriately, it was to be Inspector Hanaud, the first official policeman of importance in twentieth-century fiction, created by A. E. W. Mason in his 1910 murder mystery, *At the Villa Rose*, who became the first detective featured in a BBC serial in July 1926. The story of this rotund, middle-aged member of the Sûreté (whose similarities to Poirot have been commented upon by more than one critic) was actually introduced by listeners by his creator, and there then followed an account of his exploits recounted over five episodes by Campbell Gullan.

The reception for this series was encouraging enough for the BBC to decide to produce other tales of crime and mystery, and apart from the original creations of their own

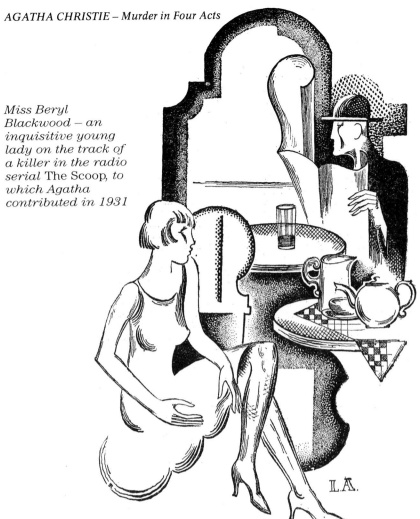

Miss Beryl Blackwood – an inquisitive young lady on the track of a killer in the radio serial The Scoop, *to which Agatha contributed in 1931*

scriptwriters (namely *Inspector Hornleigh Investigates*, 1937, and *The Gang Smasher*, 1938), the Thirties saw the debut on the airwaves of several other famous literary crime fighters including Sexton Blake, Edgar Wallace's Mr J. G. Reeder and Leslie Charteris's The Saint. The legendary Paul Temple also made his bow in 1938.

It was some years before this, however, that Agatha Christie made her first contribution to radio when, in the spring of 1930, she was invited by another leading crime novelist, Dorothy L. Sayers, to write an episode for a six-part serial entitled *Behind the Screen*. Agatha enjoyed the radio, and the idea of producing a round-robin mystery for the medium appealed to her – especially as the other contributors were the eminent detective-story tellers Hugh Walpole, Anthony Berkeley, E. C. Bentley, Ronald Knox and Dorothy L. Sayers herself.

Agatha's biographer, Janet Morgan, has explained how this pioneer serial about a man waking to find himself in a strange room beside the corpse of someone he has never met, was brought into being.

The idea had come from J. R. Ackerley, then an assistant producer in the BBC's Talks Department, and the contributors' task was complex, since each episode had to be dovetailed into the others. Each writer, nonetheless, sought to make matters difficult for those whose turn came later. Furthermore, despite the producer's efforts to make the story cohesive and coherent, each author succeeded in colouring the episode in question with his or her own idiosyncratic style (Agatha's introduced several false clues, a number of details as to timing and a great deal of conversation), and in giving it a special flavour by the way in which he or she read it aloud.

Opposite: *Agatha Christie's first weekly radio serial,* Behind the Screen, *was reprinted in* The Listener *during June and July 1930*

'Behind the Screen'—II

By AGATHA CHRISTIE

The following is the second instalment of the Serial Thriller, which will be continued in our next four issues, by Dorothy Sayers, Anthony Berkeley, E. C. Bentley and Ronald Knox. *See page 1109 for our competition in connection with this feature*

WITH Mrs. Ellis's shriek, Wilfred regained possession of his faculties. The numbing feeling of paralysis passed away. He was himself once more, cool, efficient, able to take command of the situation.

Crossing the room, he knelt by Dudden's body. He was vaguely aware of the others; of Mr. Ellis, half risen from the card table, his mouth open, his eyes staring; of Amy, of Robert, of Mrs. Ellis. They were all there behind him, waiting, peering, listening for the authoritative words he would soon speak.

He was careful not in any way to disturb the position of the body—a queer huddled position—he noted it automatically. The most cursory examination was all that was needed. Dudden was dead. The blood had welled from a wound in the neck, near the angle of the jawbone.

There was a curious expression on Wilfred's face as he bent over the dead man. Those eyes—those dead staring eyes—why surely ——. No, this wasn't his business. He mustn't imagine things. But it was odd—distinctly odd.

He rose to his feet. . . .

'He's dead', he said briefly.

'Oh!' It was a low moaning cry that broke from Amy's lips. She turned deathly pale, swayed, and clutched at her mother.

'Come, my dear, come'. The stout woman was compelling. 'Come, Amy love. . . .'

Putting her arm round the girl, she led her gently from the room. Her supporting arm kept the girl from falling.

Wilfred drew a sigh of relief as the women left the room. His eyes met those of Mr. Ellis. The latter seemed to be recovering from the shock.

'This is terrible—terrible', he ejaculated. 'What is it, my boy? Suicide, I suppose. A terrible thing to happen in one's house'.

'It's not suicide', said Wilfred.

'Not suicide—eh?'

'I'm not saying the wound couldn't have been self-inflicted. It could, though it's very unlikely. But in that case the weapon would have been still in the wound'.

'The weapon?'

'Yes. He's been stabbed—stabbed with a sharp, narrow blade and there's no sign of such a thing anywhere near him. This is a case for the police, Mr. Ellis.'

'You mean——'

'This is murder!' He repeated the word: '*Murder*. . . .'

'Murder? You can't mean it?'

'There's no doubt of it. You must ring up the police at once'.

'I—I——'

Mr. Ellis hesitated, swallowed nervously, then went shakily from the room.

Really, Wilfred supposed, he ought to have offered to telephone for him. The old man was so upset that he hardly knew what he was doing, whereas he, Wilfred, was perfectly calm and collected. Nevertheless, he had felt the strongest objection to leaving the room. His place was here.

His attention was suddenly drawn to Robert. The young man was standing by the edge of the screen. He was staring downwards with fascinated eyes. Wilfred could see the Adam's apple in his throat jerking up and down, while his long pale fingers twisted and untwisted themselves nervously. A thoroughly neurotic type, Wilfred thought rather disgustedly.

How strangely the boy was staring at Dudden. No—that was odd—he was not looking at Dudden at all. His fascinated gaze was elsewhere—on the tiny rivulet of blood. It seemed to fascinate him. He looked almost hypnotised. Suddenly, with a convulsive shudder, Robert seemed to come to himself. He turned abruptly and almost ran from the room.

Wilfred felt a sense of relief. He was alone. Once more, he bent over the body, examining it carefully. Curious attitude—the man might have been asleep, but for that tell-tale stream of scarlet. And his eyes—most peculiar! An unpleasant man, given to unpleasant vices, but all the same Wilfred had never noticed before — Oh! well, why think of it?

He raised a hand to brush the hair from his forehead and then started nervously.

There was blood on his fingers!

How did it come there? He had been most careful in his handling of Dudden. He had not touched the wound. He bent lower. There were dark smears on the cloth of Dudden's coat near its lower edge. He touched them — yes, they were faintly damp.

'You're wanted in the parlour'

They were smears of blood. How had they got there?

A slight sound made him turn his head. For a moment he saw nothing. The room was the same as usual—almost indecently peaceful. The patience cards still laid out on the table, Mrs. Ellis's book, a paper cutter between its pages, lying on her chair, a silk scarf of Amy's lying on the arm of the sofa. It was all as usual, as he had seen it a hundred times before.

The sound was repeated and now Wilfred recognised it for what it was. Someone was pushing the door very cautiously open. He waited. Suddenly the rubicund face of Mrs. Hulk came peering round the door, an expression of mingled fear and excitement animated her countenance. She seemed taken aback at the sight of Wilfred. Then she pushed the door a little further and came in. Her hands fingered her apron.

''E's dead, is 'e?', she asked, in a hoarse voice.

Wilfred nodded. He had just time to note that an expression of distinct satisfaction passed over her face when the doorbell rang. Mrs. Hulk went to answer it. There was a murmur of voices and Wilfred heard her say: ''E's in there. The young gentleman's there, too'. Two men entered the room. The first wore the uniform of a police inspector, the second Wilfred put down correctly as the police surgeon.

'Evening', said the Inspector. 'Are you Mr. Ellis?'.

The BBC's 'drama studio' in Savoy Hill consisted of a heavily curtained room, in the centre of which stood the large 'meat safe' microphone around which the broadcasters stood. Before reading her instalment of *Behind the Screen* – the second – Agatha had to undergo the somewhat unnerving experience of a voice test with J. R. Ackerley. The producer later recalled her voice as being 'A little on the feeble side – but quite adequate.'

Agatha was also given a stern warning about over-running her time, but nonetheless braced herself, put from her mind all thoughts of how unpredictable the huge microphone could be, and calmly read her episode. At the end, listeners were invited to send their solution to the mystery to the editor of *The Listener*, which was reprinting each episode in its pages.

No listener, in fact, got the answer completely right, though prizes were awarded to the nearest correct solutions. J. R. Ackerley was more than satisfied by the serial, and in the autumn asked Dorothy L. Sayers to repeat the experiment for transmission early the following year. This time, though, the producer wanted the story, provisionally entitled *The Scoop*, to run for twelve episodes.

Although by now Agatha was busy on another novel, *The Sittaford Mystery*, she accepted the invitation to match her wits again with Anthony Berkeley and E. C. Bentley as well as two other notable crime writers, Clemence Dane and Freeman Wills Croft. At a meeting of all the writers in December 1930, Agatha agreed to write the second and fourth episodes of the story about a newspaper reporter who is killed while investigating a murder case.

During their discussions, Dorothy Sayers told Agatha how much she had enjoyed *The Murder at the Vicarage* and Miss Marple in particular – 'Dear old Tabbies are the only possible right kind of female detective and Miss M. is lovely,' she had said. But although Agatha introduced an inquisitive female named Beryl Blackwood into *The Scoop*, she was an attractive young girl who set herself the task of bringing the journalist's murderer to justice.

However, with the Christmas holidays intervening, it was touch-and-go whether the contributors would complete their episodes before Dorothy L. Sayers read her first part on the air on 10 January 1931. In fact, unknown to the BBC, half of the serial *was* still incomplete at that moment, and in order to meet her own deadline, Agatha had to read her second episode from a relay station not far from her home in Devon.

By the skin of their teeth, the contributors to *The Scoop* met their eagerly awaited broadcast times, and once more the instalments were reprinted each week in *The Listener*, complete with evocative illustrations. For Agatha, though, it had been a rather traumatic experience, and when J. R. Ackerley approached her in September 1932 about a possible serial of her own featuring 'Mrs Marple' [*sic*], she declined as tactfully as she could.

'The truth of the matter is,' she wrote, 'I hate writing short things and they really are not profitable. I don't mind the odd one now and again, but the energy to devise a series is much better employed in writing a couple of books. So there it is! With apologies.'

But this was to be far from the end of Agatha Christie's association with the radio.

It was in March 1940, as Britain was emerging from the first winter of the Second World War, that a Christie character was first dramatised on the radio in a new weekly programme, *Crime Magazine*, produced by Bill MacLurg. The intention of the series was to introduce famous detectives from fact and fiction, and one of the main scriptwriters was the versatile Francis Durbridge.

Among the features in the first programme was a series entitled *Barton of the Yard* (no connection with the later famous Dick Barton!), played by a real ex-Scotland Yard detective inspector, Jack Henry; and a first 'Case for Sexton Blake' written by Francis Durbridge.

Two weeks later, following the publication of Agatha's new Poirot novel, *Sad Cypress*, an extract was broadcast on *Crime Magazine* in which Poirot began his cross-examination of those suspected in the poisoning of an heiress. The adaptation was by Francis Durbridge and Poirot was played by Lionel Gamlin.

In December 1942 another long-running series, *For the Armchair Detective*, was initiated on the BBC by Ernest Dudley, the well-known crime writer and critic. Dudley, who had a prodigious knowledge of detective stories, reviewed current fiction as well as including dramatised excerpts. He became widely known as 'The Armchair Detective' and listeners found his soothing voice a stark contrast to the murder, mystery and mayhem which he discussed.

Among the books Ernest Dudley recommended for Christmas stockings that year was Agatha's latest story, *The Body in the Library*, featuring Miss Marple. He read an extract from the book describing the finding of the body of a beautiful blonde in an evening dress in the library of Gossington Hall.

In January 1943, on the publication of *Five Little Pigs*, the Poirot investgiation into the murder of a famous painter, Ernest Dudley again scripted a dramatisation of the detective quizzing one of the female suspects. Billy Milton, a regular on *For the Armchair Detective*, read the part of Hercule Poirot.

Ernest Dudley's career on radio continued with a successful monthly quiz programme for armchair detectives entitled *Call Yourself a Detective*, which began in January 1946. Dudley was himself the quizmaster posing questions to an invited panel which included novelists such as L. A. G. Strong and the announcer, Bruce Belfrage.

Hercule Poirot was played by Lionel Gamlin in an extract from the novel Sad Cypress *on the radio programme* Crime Magazine *in 1940*

The popular programme, Armchair Detective, *featured Miss Marple in* The Body in the Library *in December 1942*

Belfrage, who also featured in a number of editions of *For the Armchair Detective* reading the parts of various sleuths, had the distinction of appearing in the very first television adaptation of a Christie play, *Ten Little Niggers*, shown in 1949.

Agatha was several times asked to take part herself in quiz programmes, in particular *Corner in Crime*, which the detective- and mystery-novelist John Dickson Carr inaugurated in August 1945. The programme was billed as a kind of criminal brains trust to answer listeners' questions, and among those who appeared were her former collaborators, Dorothy L. Sayers, Anthony Gilbert, E. C. Bentley and Freeman Wills Croft. But despite the blandishments of the chairman, Val Gielgud, elder brother of John, Agatha turned down the invitation.

The BBC, however, still continued to adapt extracts from her novels and short stories which were broadcast in *Corner in Crime* and Ernest Dudley's series during the middle and late Fifties. The long-running series, *Saturday Night Theatre*, which began in 1943 with one of Dorothy L. Sayers's Lord Peter Wimsey stories, 'The Man With No Face', also adapted Agatha's *Towards Zero* the following year, with Robert Holmes playing the redoubtable police officer, Superintendent Battle.

In 1945 the first radio series to be based wholly on Agatha's work was aired – not in Britain, though, but in America. There the CBS network in New York had negotiated with her American agent to produce a half-hour weekly series, *The Adventures of M Hercule Poirot*.

The show was also the first Poirot series and as such another important step in the use of

Christie characters in the broadcast media. The producer of the series – who was also the director, scriptwriter and star – was a stage and film actor named Harold Huber who until then had specialised in portraying villains.

The Adventures of M Hercule Poirot began transmission in the autumn of the last year of the war and soon attracted a faithful band of listeners for these dramatisations of Agatha's stories.

Another radio series to which Huber contributed was *Suspense*, a half-hour drama anthology programme which after its launch in 1942 became a fixture on CBS every Tuesday evening from 9.30–10.00 p.m. Its gripping mystery and crime stories not only enthralled listeners, but won for it the prestigious Peabody Award and a special cititation from the Mystery Writers of America, many of whose members' work was used on it.

In April 1946, Agatha joined the programme when *Suspense* dramatised her story 'Accident' from *The Listerdale Mystery*, in which the retired policeman, Inspector Evans, sets himself the task of unmasking an unnervingly charming woman he suspects of being a killer. Evans was played by a regular on the programme, the radio and TV veteran Ernest Truex, while the part of the woman he suspected was taken by his real-life wife, Sylvia Field.

It was not until 1947, having rejected several approaches from the BBC in the interim, that Agatha finally accepted a new commission from the corporation. It was to have the most far-reaching effects of any creation from her pen.

On 26 May of that year, the Queen Mother, Queen Mary, was celebrating her eightieth birthday, and to mark the occasion the BBC decided to offer an evening of her favourite

All the members of the royal family are Agatha Christie fans: here the Queen is seen meeting the authoress in 1974

programmes. When asked what she would like to hear, the grand old lady opted for music by the BBC Theatre Orchestra, a Gala Variety Show (starring her favourite entertainers, Tommy Handley, Eric Barker, Richard Murdoch, Kenneth Horne, and Elsie and Doris Walters) and a murder mystery by her favourite author, Agatha Christie.

The whole royal family, in fact, were and are enthusiasts of the Christie books, and the commission was obviously one the authoress could not refuse. Debating what she might write for a half-hour production, she remembered an idea that had come to her in 1945 when she had read in the newspapers of the death of a small boy, Daniel O'Neill, who had been horribly ill-treated while in the care of foster parents.

This, then, was the inspiration for *Three Blind Mice*, the play transmitted on that Friday evening in May. Afterwards, Agatha turned the play into a novella which was published in *Cosmopolitan* magazine in America, and then as the title work of a collection, *Three Blind Mice and Other Stories*, in 1950. Neither the story nor the collection has appeared in Britain to this day. The reason was that Agatha had yet another plan for the radio play: to expand it into a full-length drama for the theatre which would be called *The Mousetrap*.

Writing of this crucial decision in her autobiography, Agatha said:

> The more I thought of *Three Blind Mice*, the more I felt it might expand from a radio play lasting twenty minutes to a three-act thriller. It wanted a couple of extra characters, a fuller background and plot, and a slow working up to the climax. I think one of the advantages *The Mousetrap*, as the stage version of *Three Blind Mice* was called, has had over other plays is the fact that it was really written from a precis, so that it had to be the bare bones of the skeleton coated with flesh. It was all there in proportion from the first.

Agatha enjoyed listening to her play on radio as much as Queen Mary and her family did. And much of the credit for the excellent broadcast must go to its producer, Martyn C. Webster, who recruited a fine cast, all of whom deserve mention: Barry Morse (as Giles Davis), Belle Chrystal (his wife, Molly), Gladys Young (Mrs Boyle), Richard Williams (Major Metcalf), Raf de la Torre (Mr Paravicini), Allan McClelland (Christopher Wren), Lewis Stringer (Detective Sergeant Trotter) and Lydia Sherwood (Mrs Lyon). There were also three other small parts for a trio of now-familiar names: Marjorie Westbury, Duncan McIntyre and David Kossoff.

That week's issue of the *Radio Times* devoted a special feature to the birthday evening, but also had some very unhappy news for detective-story lovers: the final episode of *Dick Barton – Special Agent* was to be transmitted on the evening of 30 May. He was to be replaced by a family of circus trapeze artists, 'The Daring Dexters', written by Geoffrey Webb, the man responsible for many of the Dick Barton scripts. In fact, though, such was the outcry from listeners that the series was back on the airwaves by 6 October.

Two radio 'firsts' were produced in one in December 1947: the first 'Christie for Christmas' was broadcast on the evening of 27 December, when the 'Monday Matinée' programme presented what was the first radio adaptation of the 1943 stage triumph, *Ten Little Niggers*. Already filmed by René Clair in 1945, it became the first of Agatha's works to appear in all four entertainment media when it was adapted for BBC TV in 1949.

The 90-minute broadcast had been specially adapted by the producer, Ayton Whitaker, who assembled a strong cast of seasoned radio actors and actresses including Denys Blakelock (as Sir Lawrence Wargrave), Howard Marion-Crawford (Philip Lombard), Martin Lewis (General Mackenzie), Gladys Young (Emily Brent), Isabel Dean (Vera Claythorne) and film star Colin Gordon (Dr Armstrong).

Philip Hope-Wallace, the radio critic of *The Listener*, appeared to sense the coming of a seasonal tradition in his review of the play: ' "An Assassin for Christmas" – what more apropos?' he wrote. 'And Agatha Christie's *Ten Little Niggers*, a rather mechanical parade of slaughter, I have always thought, making Herod's little job look comparatively informal, though this defect – if defect it be for crime connoisseurs – seemed to matter less on the air than on the stage; since those assembled for murder in the studio already sound dedicated, not to say embalmed. Competent work.'

Hardly had the new year begun than listeners were in for another treat when Agatha provided a completely new half-hour play for a 'Mystery Playhouse' series entitled *The Detection Club*. This was another collaborative effort, though this time each writer was free to produce a self-contained mystery.

The man behind the project was none other than Martyn C. Webster, an urbane and

A Radio Times *illustration for Agatha's* grand guignol *tale, 'Butter in a Lordly Dish', which she wrote for the radio series,* The Detection Club, *in January 1948*

charming man whose care with Agatha's work in the previous year had made her trust and like him. He approached six crime writers and gave them a free hand to tantalise listeners. A feature in the *Radio Times* of 13 January before Agatha opened the series with her play, 'Butter in a Lordly Dish' explained Webster's idea:

> Many listeners may be wondering what the Detection Club is. They will not find its name and address in the telephone book, but it *is* a real organisation – a group of crime novelists who meet over a meal at regular intervals in London to discuss the latest news and gossip of their craft. Besides Agatha Christie, the following members will be represented in the radio series: Anthony Gilbert, Cyril Hare, E. C. R. Lorac, Dorothy L. Sayers and A. N. Other. Val Gielgud assures us that although he is a member of the club, the mystic pseudonym is not a cover for an example of his own work! [In fact, the other contributor was Christianna Brand.]

Agatha's contribution provided a striking opening to the series which must have unnerved many listeners sitting by their radio sets. Sir Luke Enderby, KC, a distinguished barrister and womaniser, contrives the hanging of an innocent man, but the victim is avenged when a nail is hammered into Enderby's forehead! An eerie musical score and some authentic sound effects added considerably to the impact of the play, in which Agatha used her characters to ponder the question of whether capital punishment allowed some men to play at being God, justly or unjustly. In the cast were Richard Williams as Sir Luke, Lydia Sherwood as his wife, Rita Vale as Julia Keene, Thea Wells as Susan Warren, Dora Gregory as Mrs Petter and David Kossoff as Porter.

The play was not as warmly received by Philip Hope-Wallace as its predecessor. In *The Listener* he described it as 'a perfectly straight bit of *grand guignol*, with Richard Williams and Lydia Sherwood enacting a latter-day Sisera and Jael – which, lacking any special feeling for radio, quite failed to excite'.

Listeners at home, though, may well not have shared this view, for 'Butter in a Lordly Dish' was repeated the following Friday, and Agatha herself was not discouraged by such remarks. Nor was she unduly disheartened a year later in 1949 when she learned that a plan by NBC Radio in New York to adapt her latest mystery-novel, *Crooked House*, had been dropped on grounds of morality. This story of a poisoned Greek restaurateur who is found dead in his London home in circumstances that suggest his much younger wife – who is rumoured to be having an affair with a young tutor – could be the murderer, was numbered by Agatha among her favourites. Yet NBC informed her agent that they would not be able to broadcast it as a Saturday evening serial, 'because of continuing complaints from the public about the number of murders being committed on the air'.

No such reservations about her books were to be voiced by the BBC's *Book at Bedtime* series which was inaugurated on the Light Programme on 6 August 1949, and which has – with a latter-day move to Radio 4 – continued to this day. The series divided novels into fifteen-minute episodes read by actors or actresses, and over the years has utilised a number of Christie books including *The Hollow* (1951) and *Spider's Web* (1954).

In the autumn of 1949, the BBC also sensed the potential of Agatha's short story, 'Witness for the Prosecution' and, two years before the play and seven before the film, adapted it for broadcasting. Ayton Whitaker was again the scriptwriter and producer, but remained faithful to the original tale by confining the courtroom drama to the climax of the 30-minute production.

The programme was broadcast on 28 January 1950 and featured J. Hubert Leslie as Mr Mayherne, the solicitor, and D. A. Clarke-Smith and Grizelda Hervey as Leonard and Christine Vole.

It was not until April 1953 that the very first dramatised serial based on one of Agatha's books was broadcast by the BBC – some eight years after Harold Huber's success with Poirot in America. In London, though, the choice fell on the cases of Tommy and Tuppence Beresford.

With hindsight, the reason for the partners in crime being chosen is not difficult to guess. For the couple cast in the title roles were Richard Attenborough and Sheila Sim, then very much in the public eye for their triumph in *The Mousetrap* which had opened the previous November and was already showing all the signs of being set for a long run. It was also no problem for the young husband and wife to record the thirteen-episode series for producer Audrey Cameron during the day before going on stage at the Ambassadors Theatre at night.

Two years after this successful series, an extract from *The Mousetrap* at the Ambassadors was used as part of a tribute to Agatha, 'the celebrated authoress and playwright'. The programme, *Agatha Christie in Close Up*, was written by Gale Pedrick and narrated by John Webster with contributions by a number of her friends and associates. The *Radio Times* announced the broadcast on 11 February, in these words:

The voice of Agatha Christie – most prolific of all best-sellers – has been heard on the

The original portrait of Hercule Poirot by W. Smithson Broadhead of The Sketch *in 1923.*
Among those who have portrayed the Belgian detective have been . . .

ALBERT FINNEY *in*
Murder on the Orient Express
(1974)

PETER USTINOV *in*
Death on the Nile
(1978)

IAN HOLM in Murder by the Book *(1986)*

Hercule Poirot meets his creator,
Agatha Christie —
a dramatic moment from
Murder by the Book,
with Ian Holm and
Dame Peggy Ashcroft

air at most half-a-dozen times in the past 25 years. Her book sales have been enormous. The pocket editions of her books alone in this country and in the United States are estimated to exceed fifteen millions. And as if this were not enough, she recently became the first woman playwright to have three successes running at the same time in the West End – to say nothing of a fourth in New York.

Yet less is known about Mrs Christie than about any other writer of her stature. Mrs Christie has been persuaded to overcome her distaste of the limelight and a Close-Up of her will be broadcast on Sunday. It will include a special recording made in her London flat.

Among those who appeared in the programme were Sir Mortimer Wheeler, who talked about her work for archaeology; Sir Allen Lane, whose uncle had been her first publisher; Peter Saunders, who had staged her plays; and the actors Richard Attenborough and Francis L. Sullivan, as well as Margaret Lockwood, then appearing in the West End in *Spider's Web*.

It has been suggested that Agatha was not altogether pleased with this broadcast, but certainly it did not prevent her writing another play for the BBC, *Personal Call*, which was transmitted in the run-up to Christmas on 29 November 1960.

This 30-minute play was warmly praised by its producer David H. Godfrey who said that it made full use of radio techniques in its telling of the death under a train of a woman who has either committed suicide or been pushed by her husband. The cast included Ivan Brandt (as James Brent), Barbara Lott (Pamela Brent), Vivienne Chatterton (Mrs Lamb), Beatrice Bevan (Fay), Michael Turner (Evan), James Thomason (Mr Enderby) and George Hagan as Inspector Narracott.

The new radio critic on *The Listener*, Frederick Laws, was one of a large and enthusiastic audience. '*Personal Call* by Agatha Christie,' he wrote, 'worked as neatly as those alarm clocks which also serve you with a cup of tea. It also did a bit of dodgy problem-solving of the sort psychologists allege that the mind does in sleep. And it only cheated, supernaturally, a little bit. It seemed, you see, as though a ghost was using the telephone service. Confident that neither the PMG [Postmaster General], the powers above, nor Miss Christie would permit this, one waited, and the disclosure was suitably remarkable.' Laws concluded his report: 'The detective story, against all probability, seems to be coming back to radio.'

For Agatha Christie it had never really gone away, and though *Personal Call* was to be the last story she wrote for radio, the tradition of regularly broadcasting her work has continued unabated to this day, as the following highlights will show.

The Unexpected Guest, Agatha's original stage production written in 1958, which had run for 604 performances, was adapted for the radio in 1982 and broadcast as a one-hour 'Afternoon Theatre' play on Radio 4 on 12 March. Scripted by Gordon House who also directed the production, it starred Alexander John as the stranger and Jill Meers as the woman he discovers in a fog-shrouded Welsh house standing with a gun in her hand beside the dead body of her husband.

Peter Davalle, reviewing the story in *The Times*, said it was, 'Agatha Christie on an off-day', but went on, 'the adapter/director Gordon House has somehow managed to conceal that fact . . . [and] a shoal of red herrings and the unmasking of the genuine killer made for an afternoon *divertissement*'.

The festive season of 1986 produced a memorable Poirot on British radio in the veteran actor Peter Sallis who starred in a 90-minute version of *Hercule Poirot's Christmas*. This 1938 novel about the wealthy practical joker, Simeon Lee, who brings his family together for an elaborate Christmas game and pays for it with his life, was dramatised by Michael Bakewell and directed by Enyd Williams.

Sallis, of course, is best known for his long running appearance as Clegg, the cloth-capped philosopher, in the television series, *Last of the Summer Wine*, but has also broadcast regularly and even written a number of radio scripts. Before playing Poirot he had starred as

Dr Watson in a Sherlock Holmes musical, as a solicitor in *The Moonstone*, the pioneer detective story by Wilkie Collins, and an evil archaeologist in the Paul Temple story, *The Quick and the Dead*.

'I have read a lot of Agatha Christie's books over the years,' Peter says, 'and I was delighted to have the chance to play Poirot as he is my favourite among detectives. I really do wish sometimes, though, I had those "little grey cells" of his!'

Among those who appeared in *Hercule Poirot's Christmas* were Cyril Luckham as Simeon Lee, with Richard Durden, Rachel Gurney, Gordon Reid, Avril Clark, George Parsons, Sheila Grant and Nicky Henson as the members of his family. Deryck Guyler was Tressilian the butler, and the two police officers were played by Manning Wilson and Edward de Souza.

The same partnership of Michael Bakewell and Enyd Williams was responsible for dramatising two more adventures of the little detective in 1987 and 1988: *The Murder of Roger Ackroyd* and *Murder on the Links*. In both of these 90-minute broadcasts, however, the distinguished stage actor, John Moffatt, took over as Poirot. Though he is actually tall and angular and possesses a deep, resonant voice, Moffatt generated a splendidly modulated accent that resulted in a very convincing Poirot.

In the story of the killing of Roger Ackroyd which draws Poirot into a chain of death, the case was narrated by John Woodvine as Dr Sheppard. Among the other leading players were Laurence Payne as Roger Ackroyd, Diana Olsson (Caroline Sheppard), Peter Gilmore (Raymond), Peter Craze (Kent), Simon Cuff (Inspector Davis), Richard Tate (Inspector Raglan) and Deryck Guyler as yet another butler, Parker.

Murder on the Links took Poirot to France only to find that the mysterious millionaire who had summoned his help was already dead, and the solution to his death lay in another crime committed twenty years earlier. Poirot's narrator this time was the faithful Captain Hastings, played by Jeremy Clyde. The cast also included Madeline Smith (Dulcie Duveen), Geoffrey Whitehead (Inspector Bex), David King (Judge Hautet), Stephen Tomkinson (Jack Renauld) and Joan Matheson (Madame Renauld).

To open 1990, the centenary year, Michael Bakewell chose to dramatise the 1931 novel, *The Sittaford Mystery*, in five half-hour episodes which ran through the month of January. This puzzling story set at a snowbound Dartmoor retirement home, where a seance brings a message of murder, features the quietly persistent Inspector Narracott, played by the excellent Geoffrey Whitehead. As a man familiar with playing sleuths – he had earlier appeared on the stage as a detective in Agatha's *The Unexpected Guest*, on TV in *Z Cars*, and in America as Sherlock Holmes – Geoffrey particularly relished the role.

'Detectives can be difficult to play on stage,' he said, 'because it's question, question, question and you can easily get your lines muddled. When you see actors who play policemen looking into their notebooks you know they're checking the script!'

And of Inspector Narracott, Geoffrey added, 'It's by being kind and courteous that he gets results. He's a fictional policeman from a different time – not hard-nosed like the modern ones.'

Also appearing in the serial (which Michael Bakewell directed as well as dramatised) were Norman Bird (Major Burnby), Barbara Atkinson (Mrs Curtis), Susan Westerby (Mrs Willett), Michael Graham Cox (Mr Duke) and the former Poirot, John Moffat, returning as the suspect Mr Rycroft.

The broadcasting of Agatha Christie mysteries is now an established tradition – the Poirot story, *The Mystery of the Blue Train* is to be aired as another serial – and the production of them has undoubtedly developed a long way from those early days in the Thirties at Savoy Hill. They also provide further proof that Agatha's amazing storytelling power shows no sign of going out of fashion in this medium, either.

Poirot seen as a mixture of Albert Finney and Peter Ustinov by Paul Dickenson for the Radio Times *of 24 December 1986, to mark the broadcast of* Hercule Poirot's Christmas *starring Peter Sallis*

DEATH ON THE SMALL SCREEN

gatha Christie's debut on television, the medium which has served her so well in recent years, was a most inauspicious one. The black-and-white live production of *Ten Little Niggers* in 1949 was light years away from the recent faithful, atmospheric and superbly colour-toned presentations which have made Poirot and Miss Marple household names and a variety of the other murder mysteries familiar to viewers on both sides of the Atlantic.

Admittedly, British television was still in its infancy – as well as recovering from the enforced austerity of the Second World War during which all screens had been blank for six years – when the BBC decided to present the multiple-murder thriller on the evening of Saturday, 20 August 1949. With no competition from either a second BBC channel or any commercial station, the potential audience of viewers with sets in southern England within range of the Alexandra Palace studios was under a million. Just how many of them watched what Agatha Christie later described as something close to a farce is now purely a matter for conjecture.

Television sets in 1949 had twelve-inch screens with grey, flickering pictures. They cost on average £40 and had to be viewed in rooms darkened by closed curtains. Programmes were only transmitted in the afternoons and evenings, and some – such as the news – were in sound only. Intermissions often occurred between programmes, and a typical day's viewing would consist of items such as a gardening programme, a light entertainment show, a current events round-up, and, as a highlight at the weekends, an outside broadcast of a major sporting event followed by a live drama presentation from the studios.

Ever since the BBC had become the world's first public television service in November 1936 (in America public transmissions did not begin until 1941), it had pioneered the broadcasting of plays using stage and film actors alongside a scattering of veterans from the radio. The work of such writers as George Bernard Shaw and J. B. Priestley was popular, and among the familiar names involved in these early dramas were Laurence Olivier, Cicely Courtneidge, Kenneth More and John Gielgud. Because they could not be pre-filmed and had to go out live from studio sets, these productions were prone to all manner of disasters. *Ten Little Niggers* had more than its fair share of these.

The man in charge of the 90-minute adaptation of the cunning mystery story was Kevin Sheldon, an accomplished stage director whom the BBC hired as guest producer. He was, in fact, a fan of murder stories and had seen the acclaimed stage version of *Ten Little Niggers* at the St James's Theatre.

Sheldon was determined to remain faithful to the original and used a slightly shortened version of Agatha's own script. By all accounts, she was initially quite enthusiastic about this television debut of the play which had so profoundly affected her career. And as it was a Saturday night production, she was told it had a bigger budget and a longer rehearsal period than most other programmes.

The setting of the play in an isolated mansion on a small island off the Devon coast was recreated in four sets designed by Richard Greenough, and Kevin Sheldon picked his cast with an eye to experience in the mystery genre. As Philip Lombard he chose John Bentley, who had made his name in the Thirties on radio and the stage, and in 1948 had starred in the first of what were to be a series of films about the famous radio detective, Paul Temple.

The important role of Dr Armstrong was played by John Stuart, who had been one of the most popular English film actors in the Twenties and Thirties, and the star of numerous crime films including *Enemy of the Police* (1933), *The Claydon Treasure Mystery* (1938) and *The Phantom Shot* (1947). Another familiar face was cast as General Mackenzie – Arthur Wontner, recognised by many viewers as the actor who had played Sherlock Holmes in a series of movies about the great detective made in the Thirties.

From the radio world came Bruce Belfrage to play Sir Lawrence Wargrave, Margery Bryce (Emily Brent), Douglas Hurn (Anthony Marston), Elizabeth Maude (Mrs Rogers), Stanley Lemin (Rogers) and Campbell Singer as William Blore. Singer later continued his association with Agatha Christie by appearing as Inspector Lord in the 1954 stage production of *Spider's Web*.

The 8.30 p.m. programme warranted a special item in the *Radio Times* in the 'Pick of the Week' column by 'The Scanner'. The credits of the leading actors were detailed along with an interesting reference to Arthur Wonter, 'who took the part of the sinister Sir Lawrence Wargrave when the play went on tour, but will be seen here as General Mackenzie'.

The broadcast began with a simple list of credits, and then, from behind the set of the lounge of a large house, came the sound of the sea and a boat landing, followed by the chatter of voices. One by one the cast of eleven arrived on the set, trooping before the cameras. There followed a mighty crash from off-camera, possibly caused by a piece of scenery falling down, and this was succeeded by a sound boom swinging into view over the actors' heads.

After this uncertain start, the drama continued smoothly enough, and for nearly half an hour was almost faultless except for a single actor speaking his lines to the wrong camera. Then came several out-of-focus shots, an inadvertent view of a camera crew wheeling their

The Radio Times *announcement of the first Agatha Christie story to be televised (on Saturday, 20 August 1949), starring John Bentley, the cinema screen's Paul Temple*

SATURDAY— August 20

8.30   ' TEN LITTLE NIGGERS '

A play by Agatha Christie
Produced by Kevin Sheldon

Setting designed by
Richard Greenough

Cast in order of appearance:
Rogers.................Stanley Lemin
Narracot................Barry Steele
Mrs. Rogers.......Elizabeth Maude
Vera Claythorne......Sally Rogers
Philip Lombard......John Bentley
Antony Marston.....Douglas Hurn
William Blore....Campbell Singer
General Mackenzie
                    Arthur Wontner
Emily Brent........Margery Bryce
Sir Lawrence Wargrave
                    Bruce Belfrage
Dr. Armstrong........John Stuart
The play opens on an August evening in the house on Nigger Island somewhere off the coast of Devon

3.45-4.0 **MOTOR-CYCLE HILL CLIMB**
A return visit to the motor-cycle hill climb at Readercott Hill

10.0   NEWSREEL
(Repeat of Friday's edition)

10 15-10.30 **NEWS** (sound only)

cumbersome equipment to a different set, and an even bigger gaffe by a supposedly 'dead' actor . . .

Ten Little Niggers did, though, run its course and its dramatic finale was, fortunately, executed without a mistake. Perhaps equally fortunately, there were no television reviewers to pick on the faults the next day.

Of course, living in the West Country far beyond the range of Alexandra Palace, Agatha Christie was not able to see the production. But she did receive a full report of the accident-prone transmission, and, in a letter a few days later to her agent, she commented sarcastically: 'Just as well I *didn't* see *Ten Little Niggers* on the television! I hear General Mackenzie, after being stabbed, got up and strolled away with his hands in his pockets, quite unaware he was in view. I should have been *livid.*'

It is perhaps not surprising afer such a debut that Agatha should declare herself 'distrustful' of television as a medium. Obviously, TV would have to do a lot to make amends . . .

Just two months after the BBC transmission, the first Agatha Christie story was shown on American television. Although across the Atlantic most TV dramas were also broadcast live and were just as subject to unforeseen hitches, there were already three major competing commercial networks. And as all programmes were sponsored, the companies involved demanded high standards and were inclined swiftly to withdraw support from shoddy or unsuccessful shows.

A great many of these drama series had hosts who introduced the stories and also promoted the sponsor's products. Many later famous performers started their careers on American television as hosts, including Orson Welles, Mary Tyler Moore and Ronald Reagan.

The first of Agatha's stories to be televised in the USA was 'Witness for the Prosecution' which was broadcast by NBC on the night of Hallowe'en, Monday, 31 October 1949, on the *Chevrolet Tele-Theater*, a big-budget live drama series that presented an original play or adaptation each week. This was not based on the famous stage and film adaptation, but on the original short story first published in Britain in the anthology *The Hound of Death* in 1933. Strangely, this particular book was not issued in America, and the story remained unknown there until it appeared in *Witness for the Prosecution and Other Stories*, published in 1948.

Agatha's stage adaptation of the story of 'Witness For The Prosecution' in 1953 has tended ever since to overshadow the original tale, but something of the impact it had on TV drama producers in America may be judged by the fact that it was to be featured in no less than three series in the five years which immediately followed the anthology's publication.

The essential plot of the short story differs little from the longer play and film. Leonard Vole is arrested for the murder of an elderly woman whose money affairs he has been managing and who has left him a fortune in her will. His solicitor, Mr Mayherne (changed to Mayhew on stage and in the movie), believes his only hope of an alibi lies with his wife, but she, instead, turns up in court as a witness for the prosecution.

In the half-hour adaptation for the *Chevrolet Tele-Theater*, however, Mayherne is the central character, meticulously building up a case for his client, with the trial and the commanding figure of the defence counsel (here a less flamboyant KC known simply as Sir Charles) restricted to the closing few minutes and the brilliant denouement of the story. Starring as Mayherne in this production was E. G. Marshall, one of the roster of top actors who appeared in the series.

Marshall, a forceful character actor who built his reputation on playing determined or morally indignant men on stage, TV and film, was ideally cast as the lawyer. Indeed, the part of Mayherne was to be an interesting forerunner to his much-praised later roles as a juryman in *Twelve Angry Men* (1957) and as the seasoned lawyer, Lawrence Preston, in the TV series, *The Defenders* (1961–5), which won him two Emmy Awards.

Charles Laughton and Tyrone Power in Witness for the Prosecution *(1957), which has been regularly reshown on British and American TV*

Just a year after this telecast (as television broadcasts were known at the time), a second version of 'Witness for the Prosecution' was offered to American viewers by another half-hour live drama series, *Danger*, on 7 November 1950. This Tuesday night series, which was transmitted from New York by CBS, ran for five years (1950–5) and featured psychological dramas and murder mysteries. It was hosted by Richard Stark.

The part of the lawyer was played by John Donovan, a stage actor who ran up a number of starring roles in *Danger*, including parts in 'Murder Takes the "A" Train' and 'Death Among the Relics'. Described as one of the less auspicious productions of the series, this 'Witness for the Prosecution' is perhaps only really notable for the fact that its director was a man later destined for Hollywood stardom, Yul Brynner, whose early years were spent as a TV director in New York. Interestingly, his successor on the series was Sidney Lumet, later the director of *Murder on the Orient Express* (1974).

The third 'Witness for the Prosecution' was shown on Thursday, 17 September 1953, on another big-budget live drama series transmitted from New York and sponsored by Lux toilet soap – *The Lux Video Theater*. This series had run on radio for sixteen years before moving to CBS TV in October 1950, and used major film stars as well as leading stage actors in half-hour stories which ranged from historical tales to contemporary dramas and situation comedies. With writers like William Faulkner and Maxwell Anderson being used on the *Video Theater*, it became a prestigious show for actors, and among those who starred were Veronica Lake, Celeste Holm, Broderick Crawford and Charlton Heston. The hosts, too, were familiar names, including Britain's James Mason.

Edward G. Robinson, the star of the CBS TV version of Witness for the Prosecution, *presented on* The Lux Video Theater *series in September 1953*

'Witness for the Prosecution' was the first of the Christie dramatisations on American television to rate a mention by *TV Guide*, and carried a note on its star, none other than the great Edward G. Robinson, playing what was announced as 'the role of an attorney in a gripping Agatha Christie murder story'.

At first glance, the charismatic and usually aggressive Robinson, who had come to fame in the Thirties in a string of hugely successful gangster movies, was an unlikely choice as Leonard Vole's lawyer. Yet he was an actor of enormous range, and despite a number of continuing problems in his personal life, worked successfully in films and television during the Fifties and Sixties. Following his death from cancer in 1973, he was deservedly honoured with a special Oscar in recognition of his achievements in film.

Although no review survives of Edward G. Robinson's performance in the 1953 'Witness for the Prosecution', the indications are that it was the most impressive of the three TV versions up to that point. Certainly there were no more adaptations until 1982, when the story again appeared on television. This time, however, the production was based on Agatha's stage script and ran for a full 120 minutes. It was filmed and not live, made in colour, and broadcast during prime time on the evening of Saturday, 4 December 1982.

In commenting on what it saw as the story's remarkable durability, the *New York Times* reviewer said: 'Clearly, television would have to come up with a very special package to justify still another version of the mystery thriller. It *has*.'

Although produced by an American company, Rosemont Productions, for the CBS series, *Hallmark Hall of Fame*, and directed by Alan Gibson, the leading roles were all taken by British actors: Sir Ralph Richardson as Sir Wilfred Roberts; Deborah Kerr as his nurse, Miss Plimsoll; Donald Pleasence as the prosecuting counsel; Wendy Hiller as the victim's elderly housekeeper; and Diana Rigg as Christine Vole. Only the part of Leonard Vole was played by an American, Beau Bridges, and the critics were unanimous in deciding he was 'too boyishly bland' for the role.

There was, however, universal praise for Sir Ralph Richardson's defence counsel.

'This is the kind of production that can almost play itself,' wrote John J. O'Connor of the *New York Times*, and went on:

> Just set the collection of devilishly clever actors loose, sit back and enjoy. Mr Richardson is splendid, both when he's being wickedly sly and when he's fulminating against the nincompoops of the world, not least of whom is his aggressively attentive nurse. The interplay between nurse and patient is overbroad at times in this adaptation by John Gay, but Mr Richardson and Miss Kerr make it work ... 'Witness for the Prosecution' still works wondrously well, its twists and turns devised to the point of perfection. It's still a great deal of fun.

How such a review would have delighted Agatha Christie! The production was similarly well received when it was shown on BBC1 two days later. (That same week, on BBC2, the original Charles Laughton film was also reshown, providing the ideal opportunity for comparison.)

In England, the major plaudits were awarded to Diana Rigg for her performance. *Variety* declared: 'Although Mrs Vole is less a character than a walking plot device, Rigg plays it to the hilt, her apparently icy disdain nothing more than the pose of a desparate woman who'll do anything to save her lover from the gallows. But, when rejected, she'll turn into a self-righteous avenging angel.'

Variety also spotted a blunder in the making of the film that would have made even a director of one of the earlier live telecasts, with their very much cruder techniques, blush. 'The director errs grievously at one point', the magazine's reviewer said, 'by not disguising Rigg well enough in a scene in which the viewer is not supposed to know that the cockney lowlife who's extorting money from the barrister in a dimly-lit flat is really Mrs Vole!'

Nor was this the only shortcoming. John J. O'Connor also pointed out: 'The direction was

Sir Ralph Richardson starred in the most recent television version of Witness for the Prosecution *on the CBS Hallmark Hall of Fame series in December 1982*

crisp and carefully focused, except for a brief but distracting tour of London that managed to plug a popular department store!'

But what all the critics on both side of the Atlantic were in agreement upon was – as *Variety* put it – 'there's now a new mass-media vogue for Agatha Christie . . .'

This vogue did not depend solely upon the various versions of 'Witness for the Prosecution', however. The second Christie tale to be shown on American television was 'Three Blind Mice' produced on Tuesday, 17 August 1950 as a live, half-hour drama on the dramatic anthology series, *The Web*. The novella which Agatha had written from her 1947 radio play had been published as the title story of a collection issued in the USA in 1950, and it was from the pages of this book that the producers of the series – Mark Goodson and Bill Todman of game show fame – had extracted it for transmission.

The Web, which ran on CBS for seven years from the summer of 1950, specialised in stories of everyday people suddenly finding themselves in extraordinary situations. Most of the teleplays were adapted from the work of members of the Mystery Writers of America, and achieved a standard of excellence which led to the show becoming the first television series to win the Edgar Allan Poe Award in 1951.

'Three Blind Mice' was one of the transmissions considered for the award. The atmospheric set of an old manor house and the haunting soundtrack featuring the famous nursery rhyme contributed to the suspense. Starring in the play was Richard Kiley, who had begun his career on the stage and radio, often playing heavies, and who later in the Fifties appeared in a number of crime films including *The Mob* (1951), *The Sniper* (1952) and *The Spanish Affair* (1958). Henry Hull and Mary Sinclair, who featured in other notable productions on *The Web*, were also in the play, which was narrated by the host, Jonathan Blake.

A little over two months later, the same story was adapted again for another live drama series, *Sure as Fate*, which had begun on CBS in July, but was destined to last for less than a year. Again the theme was people thrust into frightening situations not of their own making, and perhaps this similarity with *The Web* did not help its success, although it was initially well received by the critics.

The *Sure as Fate* plays were, however, an hour in duration and 'Three Blind Mice' had something of an advantage in being transmitted on the night of 31 October. The stars were two people much associated with the thriller genre, John Carradine and Marsha Hunt, and though the story was interrupted at every crucial moment by a commercial break, which did nothing to maintain the suspense, a *New York Daily News* review still called it 'a blood-curdling Hallowe'en trick or treat'.

The fourth presentation of the year was 'The Golden Ball' featured on Tuesday, 17 November on *Fireside Theater*, one of the earliest drama shows *filmed* especially for television.

Launched on NBC in April 1949, *Fireside Theater* began as a showcase for new programme ideas, but according to *TV Guide* it had switched by the autumn of 1950 to showing 'quickie' films, usually dramatic stories of 30 minutes each. These were made in two and three days at the Hal Roach studios in Hollywood by Frank Wisbar, the energetic producer of the series.

Always on the look-out for material, Wisbar had been working in Hollywood when Eagle-Lion had made the second version of *Love from a Stranger*, and he was prompted to search through Agatha Christie's work. In *The Listerdale Mystery*, the same book from which the movie of *Love from a Stranger* had originated, he found 'The Golden Ball', the story of a recently disinherited young man, George Dundas, whose apparently chance meeting with the beautiful Mary Montresor leads him into the clutches of a gunman.

The role of George was taken by George Nader, a Californian actor who after an extensive career in television graduated to action and adventure films; and Mary was played by Eve Miller, a pretty Hollywood starlet. Frank Wisbar later became the host of *Fireside Theater* in the autumn of 1952, and 'The Golden Ball' was published as the title story of a special collection of Agatha Christie tales issued in America in 1971.

The fifth and final story of 1950 was 'The Case of the Missing Lady', transmitted under the banner of the *Nash Airflyte Theater* on Thursday, 7 December. This telecast is of particular interest because it marks the debut on TV of Agatha's two young sleuths, Tommy and Tuppence, who, just as they had done in films, made their bow on television before either Poirot or Miss Marple.

Two years were to pass before another Christie mystery reached the small screen in America. On Tuesday, 22 January 1952, the long-running and highly rated series *Suspense* presented 'The Red Signal', adapted from the short story in *The Hound of Death*.

Suspense had transferred from radio to TV in the spring of 1949 and continued to exert its tremendous hold on the public's imagination. The stories which were dramatised varied from horror classics like *Dr Jekyll and Mr Hyde* to literary masterpieces such as Rudyard Kipling's 'The Man Who Would Be King'. Broadcast live from New York, the programme featured many Broadway and Hollywood stars including Basil Rathbone, Peter Lorre, Boris Karloff, Grace Kelly and Eva Gabor.

'The Red Signal' is one of Agatha Christie's most vivid supernatural stories, featuring Dermot West, a rather fey young man who admits to receiving warnings of impending danger by what he calls 'the red signal'. One night with some friends he takes part in a seance and is plunged into a horrifying situation when the medium receives a warning of bloody events to come.

Dermot was played by Tom Drake, a New York-born actor who was a regular on *Suspense* and who had starred in several films including *Scene of the Crime* (1949) and *FBI*

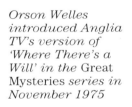

Orson Welles introduced Anglia TV's version of 'Where There's a Will' in the Great Mysteries *series in November 1975*

Girl (1951). This same story was filmed again in 1982 as one of the episodes in the ten-part Thames Television series, *The Agatha Christie Hour*, and this episode was shown in America as part of the CBS *Mystery!* series on 3 March 1983.

Though there was a considerable decrease in the number of television adaptations over the next ten years, both Miss Marple and Hercule Poirot finally made their long overdue debuts.

Miss Marple was the first, on 30 December 1956 in 'A Murder Is Announced', presented

LWT inaugurated a new era of Christie on television with their production of Why Didn't They Ask Evans? *in March 1980. The stars were (front row) James Warwick, Francesca Annis and Connie Booth, with (back row) Eric Porter, Madeline Smith and Robert Longden*

on NBC by the *Goodyear Playhouse*. The gentle lady sleuth from St Mary Mead was played by a long-time British favourite, Gracie Fields, and it was an important moment, not only for Miss Marple, but also because it marked the first Christie story to be televised in colour. Commercial colour transmission had begun in the US in 1953, pioneered by NBC whose parent company, RCA, manufactured the sets, and the number of receivers in homes across the nation by the end of 1956 ran into several millions.

Four years later, in 1960, Agatha Christie sold the rights to several of the Miss Marple books to MGM – hoping, as she said in her autobiography, that they would adapt them for television. Instead, the company used them as the basis for four Margaret Rutherford pictures for the cinema – and thereafter her disillusionment with both media became virtually complete.

The little Belgian detective made his small-screen debut in 1962 in a *General Electric Theater* presentation entitled simply 'Hercule Poirot', and starring Martin Gabel. This production, filmed in colour for CBS and screened on 1 April, was intended to be the pilot for a series featuring Poirot and was announced with some drum-beating by the host, Ronald Reagan. However, despite an engaging performance by Gabel and some solid support by the cast, no series ensued.

Another decade rolled on before the next adaptation of the 'Queen of Crime's' work was presented, this time in Britain, and with scant acknowledgement to the original. The story in question was 'Where There's a Will', another tale from *The Hound of Death*, where it had been called 'Wireless'. (The re-titling occurred when the story was included in the American anthology, *Witness for the Prosecution*, in 1948).

'Where There's a Will' was featured in the half-hour series *Orson Welles's Great Mysteries*, made by Anglia TV, and it was screened in Britain on 13 November 1975. Sole credit, though, was given to the adapter, crime writer Michael Gilbert. Admittedly the story had been somewhat altered from Agatha's original, and perhaps in the light of the rather inferior production anonymity was preferable.

Orson Welles himself introduced this story about a letter which is opened in error by a lawyer, Bruce Sexton, and which provides him with some rather dangerous knowledge concerning a murder case. The debonair Richard Johnson played Sexton, with the lovely Hannah Gordon as Phyllida Marjoram, and other members of the cast included Bill Maynard, Sheila Raynor, Bob Cartland and Norman Shelley. The programme was produced by John Jacobs and directed by Mark Cullingham.

'Where There's a Will' was the last television production made during Agatha Christie's lifetime, and might have seemed to suggest that there was little future for her work in the medium. In fact, the 1980s have proved the very opposite with a continuing series of outstanding productions from both Britain and America.

It was London Weekend Television who opened the new era of Christie adaptations in March 1980 – and appropriately so, for they have subsequently done as much as anyone to introduce her work to a whole new generation of viewers. The company was not above blowing its own trumpet in announcing the transmission of *Why Didn't They Ask Evans?* on the evening of Sunday, 30 March with these programme notes in the *TV Times*:

> A major coup for ITV drama, this is the first television adaptation of an Agatha Christie novel. Set and written in 1934, this crime story contains all the familiar Christie magic – mystery, suspense and suspects galore. As well as a star-studded cast, there are the added attractions of authentic period fashions, cars, trains and Thirties dialogue.

The LWT production was, in fact, to prove a prototype for subsequent dramatisations of Agatha's work on television, although the public had been prepared to some extent by the outstanding EMI films beginning with *Murder on the Orient Express*.

Interest in LWT's plan to make an authentic version of this 1934 story of two enthusiastic young amateur detectives, vicar's son Bobby Jones, and 'smart-set' member Lady Frances Derwent, began to develop as early as June 1979, with stories in the national press about location shooting.

Ken Irwin of the *Daily Mirror*, for example, found Francesca Annis, who was playing Lady Frances, practising on a golf course with a professional golfer.

'I've never played the game before,' explained the star, 'but a golf scene is an important part of the plot so I have had to learn how to handle a golf club. But it's great fun. Making the whole story is fun.'

Reports such as this underlined the intention of the producers Tony Wharmby and Jack Williams to present as faithfully as possible the two young sleuths' quest for the killer of a man found dying near a golf course and muttering the words, 'Why didn't they ask Evans?'

Francesca Annis, who the previous year had enjoyed great success playing the lead role in the TV series *Lillie*, the story of Lillie Langtry, the legendary beauty and mistress of royalty, was particularly attracted to the production because of the attention to detail in Pat Sandy's script.

'The particular tone of the people in the story was quite hard to catch,' she recalls. 'It was not just the accent, it was their belief that they were born to rule which permeated all aspects of their behaviour. Everyone was trapped in their own class.

'The upper classes were snobs. In no way were they liberal. Decades on from Lillie Langtry's life, the servants still didn't have separate existences. Nobody in "Evans" recognised the chauffeur. The maids and valets, around to meet every whim, were like shadows.'

Turning specifically to her own part, she went on: 'Women then were still changing from head to toe three times a day. Lady Frances would wear a casual outfit for the morning in the garden, change into a frock for lunch and then dress for dinner. She automatically accepted the ruling that the more money you have, the more clothes you have.'

Although Francesca admits that in her own life she hates class divisions and has always preferred casual dressing to being a dedicated follower of fashion, she was fascinated by the way her character accepted the way things were and had to continue to be.

'It would be shocking to offer any kind of alternative,' she smiles, 'and Lady Frances wasn't interested in being shocked. But she was very drawn to the villain, and maybe today she might go off with him because she wouldn't be afraid. In the film, of course, I found happiness with the good boy – which is what you would expect!'

Francesca enjoyed wearing the range of clothes provided for her by the LWT wardrobe department – although she actually bought some of the hats and shoes and other accessories herself during a tour of the West End.

'When I first read *Why Didn't They Ask Evans?* I thought it was very clever the way Agatha Christie only described Lady Frances by the outfits in which she was seen,' she says. 'But they tell you everything. They say, here, by and large, is an upper-class, conventional girl who constantly says, "Daddy will get us out of this."'

Co-starring with Francesca in the production, which took three months to film at a cost of nearly £1 million, was James Warwick as Bobby Jones. Though neither knew it at the time, it was to prove a fruitful partnership leading to a series of their own in 1983. Also appearing were John Gielgud as Bobby's father, plus Eric Porter, Bernard Miles, Connie Booth, Madeline Smith, Robert Longden, Doris Hare, and Joan Hickson as Mrs Rivington.

Initially, LWT planned to show the film as a mini-series, but subsequently decided on a three-hour special, which attracted a large audience and generally satisfactory reviews.

Sir John Gielgud – the man for all Christies! Opposite: *As the Reverend Thomas Jones with Francesca Annis (Lady Frances Derwent) in* Why Didn't They Ask Evans?
Left: *As the Marquess of Caterham with Cheryl Campbell (Lady Eileen Brent) in LWT's second major production,* The Seven Dials Mystery, *in 1981*

Cheryl Campbell as Lady Eileen 'Bundle' Brent at the wheel of a vintage Delage with co-star James Warwick (Jimmy Thesiger) in The Seven Dials Mystery

'Thirties throughout and nicely acted,' *The Times* decided, 'but twice as long as it should have been.' *The Daily Telegraph* agreed, and added, 'It was a pleasure to watch such a faithful adaptation of one of Dame Agatha's more perplexing mysteries.'

A year later, on 21 May 1981, the production was presented on American TV via the *Mobil Showcase* – introduced by the then-current Poirot, Peter Ustinov.

LWT was sufficiently encouraged by the reaction to the show to let Tony Wharmby set to work in the summer of 1980 on the adaptation of another of Agatha's novels, *The Seven Dials Mystery*. Five months' production work was allocated for this version of the 1929 story about some 'bright young things' who become involved in a death-by-poisoning in an old country mansion.

James Warwick was again cast in a leading role, as Jimmy Thesiger, this time opposite the delectable Cheryl Campbell as Lady Eileen 'Bundle' Brent. Among the luminaries were John Gielgud again (playing Lady Eileen's father this time), Robert Longden, Harry Andrews, Joyce Redman, Terence Alexander, Rula Lenska and Leslie Sands.

Cheryl Campbell now admits that she was not sure about taking the role when it was offered to her. 'I had some misgivings about the play,' she says; 'it seemed to be another period piece with a golfing, sleuthing, fast-driving aristocratic heroine just like LWT's previous Christie. It was a tried and tested formula with some of the same actors. So what was new? Lady Eileen Brent was new to *me*.'

Cheryl says that no one should imagine that Agatha Christie characters are easy to play. They can be glamorous, mysterious, brave and great fun, but, in her own words, 'like the Tin Man, they're a bit hollow'.

So how did she give life and credibility to Lady Eileen?

'I had no preconceived ideas. I had not seen the earlier film so I could let my imagination run riot. I suddenly saw "Bundle" driving through the countryside in this great big car (as I was destined to do), or battling with Superintendent Battle swathed in leather from head to toe – coat, helmet, gauntlets and goggles.

'Now, I realised I obviously couldn't turn up at social functions like that, so there had to be a compromise. But the image stayed and was my inspiration. That's how I made Bundle full of zest and curiosity with a good streak of the intrepid. I liked her a lot,' she adds.

Cheryl remembers the fun she had driving a vintage Delage car through the lanes of Sussex on location – and the drama which followed hard on the heels of their rehearsals in a drill hall in Hammersmith, when it was bombed by the IRA. She also loved working with John Gielgud.

'Sir John has such style, he achieves truth with a flourish,' she says. 'And that hauntingly beautiful voice! I remember at the end of one day's filming, he said to me, "You should never question Agatha Christie. Just say the lines and get off." He's right and he proved it.'

The exuberance of Cheryl Campbell's own performance when *The Seven Dials Mystery* was screened on Sunday, 8 March 1981, was warmly received by audience and critics alike, and the following month it too was screened in America on the *Mobil Showcase* hosted by Peter Ustinov.

LWT's belief in the appeal of Agatha Christie, authentically presented, had now been successfully justified. The plans for a mini-series were taken down from the shelf and refocused – the choice falling on the 'jazz age sleuths' Tommy and Tuppence Beresford, Agatha's 'partners in crime'.

A year later work began in earnest on *Partners in Crime*, the ten-part series of hour-long cases, to be preceded by a two-hour special of the young detectives' first novel-length adventure, *The Secret Adversary*. Francesca Annis and James Warwick, who had worked so well together in *Why Didn't They Ask Evans?*, were cast in the leading roles, and nine months and £2 million pounds later, the series was ready for screening in the autumn and winter of 1983.

Partners in Crime once more proved the television company right to have faith in Agatha Christie – a faith demonstrated even more emphatically in the most recent of all their series from her work, the cases of Hercule Poirot starring David Suchet.

But before that, other companies in Britain and America were encouraged by LWT's success to begin scrambling for the rights to other Christie stories.

In 1982, CBS presented a full-length Christie novel on American television for the first time with an adaptation of *Murder Is Easy* on the *Saturday Night at the Movies* series. This classic 1939 mystery tells of the gossipy village spinster, Lavinia Fullerton, who is killed by a hit-and-run driver while going to report a series of murders. However, her enquiries are taken up by a former colonial policeman, Luke Williams, and a nasty killer is eventually brought to justice.

The makers of the film, David L. Wolper and Stan Margulies, were fresh from their success with the series *Roots*, and sent director Claude Whatham to film on location in England. They also asked scriptwriter Carmen Culver to remain as faithful as possible to the original, though the period was to be updated to the present day and Luke Williams was to become an American computer expert on holiday in Britain.

Bill Bixby played the computer buff, and also in the cast were Olivia de Havilland as a friend of the murdered spinster; Leslie-Anne Down as Bridget Conway, the girl who catches Luke's eye; and Timothy West, Jonathan Pryce and Patrick Allen. Most intriguing of all, though, was Helen Hayes playing Lavinia Fullerton (a woman not unlike Miss Marple) and cultivating mannerisms she would later use to considerable effect as the lady sleuth.

It was she, in fact, who stole the best notices when the film was shown on 2 January 1982.

'Miss Hayes gives a delightful cameo as Lavinia Fullerton, a charming old gal who is on her way to Scotland Yard to report a series of murders, still unsuspected, in her quiet little village of Wychwood,' said the *New York Times*.

But the same reviewer was not very impressed with the production as a whole, adding: 'There are nice bits and pieces along the way – Mr West's harrumphing aristocrat and Miss de Havilland's mildly dotty museum curator – but it's easy early in the game to figure out who is the last person anyone would suspect, notwithstanding Miss Christie's predictable barrage of red herrings.'

Predictable or not, *Murder Is Easy* was shown in Britain on ITV on 3 June of that same year, and the BBC gave it a second British showing on 25 June 1986.

The year 1982 proved to be a bumper one for Christie fans with the presentation of the Ralph Richardson version of *Witness for the Prosecution*, and then the launching on 7 September of Thames Television's *The Agatha Christie Hour*, ten one-hour dramas based on a selection of her short stories.

Pat Sandys, who had previously scripted the two murder novel adaptations for LWT, was the producer of the series, with John Frankau as executive producer. Once again the series was enthusiastically greeted by the press, the *Daily Express* announcing: 'Agatha Christie, the "Duchess of Death", is back in business.'

Though taken primarily from those two old favourites, *The Hound of Death* and *The Listerdale Mystery*, the stories varied from gruesome puzzles to comedy thrillers and were filmed with close attention to period detail and location. The opening sequence to the programme was also memorable: a silhouette of Agatha in profile sitting by her typewriter, followed by the credits rolling across a piece of rumpled silk – a detail neatly reminiscent of the cinema credits of the Thirties.

The first story, 'The Case of the Middle Aged Wife', dramatised by Freda Kelsall, marked the debut on TV of another of the author's series characters, the mysterious do-gooder Parker Pyne, who comes to the aid of a dejected wife (Gwen Watford) whose portly husband (Peter Jones) is in the throes of an infatuation, by introducing her to a smooth-talking gigolo (Rupert Frazer).

The Times welcomed the appearance of Pyne. 'Maurice Denham brings the right kind of benevolent crustiness to the part, and Angela Easterling is excellently cast as Miss Lemon, his imperturbable assistant.' And Sarah Bond of the *Daily Express* also cheered, 'It is a charming 1930s flirtation that every woman and every sympathetic man will enjoy. Viewers were taken on a whimsical, nostalgic whirl back to the days of chintzy dance floors, satin nightgowns and crooners clad in white tuxedos.'

Maurice Denham returned as Pyne in the fifth story in the series, 'The Case of the Discontented Soldier', which T. R. Bowen dramatised. Pyne here helps a recently retired soldier find love by rescuing a girl from two burly attackers and then setting off with her on a hunt for buried treasure. William Gaunt played the soldier, Patricia Garwood the girl, and Lally Bowers made an appearance as the crime writer, Ariadne Oliver, Agatha's lighthearted version of herself!

The Times was less impressed with this return appearance, but drew a comparison with another of the author's famous sleuths. 'Parker Pyne, who puts things right (and spawned at least one literary descendant, Enid Blyton's Mr Pink Whistle), embodies a purely facetious worldliness. And as Poirot harped on the workings of the little grey cells, so Parker Pyne harps on statistics.'

The second story in the series, 'In a Glass Darkly', about a guest in a country house who sees a vision of a murder and then discovers the killer and victim are also guests, was dramatised by William Corlett. The play was atmospherically directed by Desmond Davis, and featured excellent performances by the two stars, Nicholas Clay and Emma Piper.

William Corlett was also responsible for adapting 'The Girl in the Train', the espionage drama of a playboy, George Rowland, accosted while travelling to London by a beautiful girl

A dramatic moment from the story of 'The
Fourth Man', one of the episodes in The
Agatha Christie Hour

who begs him to hide her and some secret papers. Directed by Brian Farnham, the story featured Osmond Bullock and Sarah Berger.

The *Daily Mail* found one of the supporting players in this story particularly worth mentioning. 'A comically cross-grained taxi driver is also added to the cast and the small part is given to Roy Kinnear, who knows how to make it memorable.' (Kinnear died tragically in September 1988 while filming in Spain.)

The fourth tale, appropriately titled 'The Fourth Man', was memorable for the performance by John Nettles of *Bergerac* fame. Patricia Craig in the *Times Literary Supplement* summarised the story thus: 'The fourth man (Nettles) collars his audience in a railway carriage and inflicts on them a thrilling account of a supernatural occurrence which ends in self-strangulation for the victim of the phenomenon. The prelude to this act, shown in a sequence of colourful flashbacks, calls for a great deal of overacting and gets it, especially from Prue Clarke as Annette Raval, the imperious young consumptive who declines to give

Agatha in elegant profile – the image which opened
Thames Television's ten-part series, The Agatha
Christie Hour, *in 1982–3*

up the ghost.' The adaptation was again by William Corlett, and the director was Michael Simpson.

'Magnolia Blossom', dramatised by John Bryden Rogers, told the story of a beautiful runaway en route to South Africa but suddenly halted in her tracks by the news of the collapse of her wealthy but uncaring husband's business empire. Ciaran Madden starred as the wife, Ralph Bates as her lover and Jeremy Clyde as the husband. Executive producer John Frankau himself directed this episode.

An antique Chinese jar which appears to be the source of a strangled cry of 'Murder!' was at the centre of the seventh story in the series, 'The Mystery of the Blue Jar', adapted by T. R. Bowen. The stars were Michael Aldridge, John Kermode and Isabelle Spade. Cyril Coke was the director.

'The Red Signal', which had been adapted for the US series *Suspense* in 1952, was given a new gloss by William Corlett and directed with some style by John Frankau. This account of a seance which brings a forewarning of doom was powerfully acted by Richard Morant, Joanna David and Christopher Cazenove.

The penultimate tale of the series, 'Jane in Search of a Job', provided Elizabeth Garvie with a fine acting challenge as Jane Cleveland, a young lady in straitened circumstances, who answers an advertisement for someone of her physical description, and finds herself on a dangerous mission masquerading as the Grand Duchess of Ostrova. Dramatised by Gerald Savory and directed by Christopher Hodson, the story also starred Amanda Redman and Andrew Bicknell.

Gerald Savory also scripted the last in *The Agatha Christie Hour*, 'The Manhood of Edward Robinson', the story of a mild-mannered competition winner who becomes involved with a beautiful adventuress and a stolen necklace, which bring about á complete change in his personality. The episode starred Nicholas Farrell, Cherie Lunghi and Ann Thornton, and was directed by Brian Farnham.

Curiously, when the series was shown on the American TV programme *Mystery!*, it was this last story which was screened as the opener on 17 February 1983. It was followed by just three more of the stories, 'Magnolia Blossoms', 'The Red Signal' and 'The Girl in the Train'.

If the impact of the series was less than expected in America, in Britain it undoubtedly found a large and appreciative audience. One viewer, A. C. Prior of Herne Bay, Kent, even took the trouble to write a special letter of tribute to the *Daily Mail*:

> The other night I watched one whole hour of television in which not one foul word was uttered, no violence done and no disgusting innuendo made. It was like turning the clock back 30 years. It was a dramatisation of an Agatha Christie story – of the days of decent and elegant behaviour and immaculate grooming.
>
> It is almost the only TV programme (apart from documentaries) my family has watched in years without one or other of us leaving the room in anger or distress at the unnecessary filth flung at us by directors and producers of most modern productions.

It was at Christmas 1982 that the BBC entered the new era of Christie on television when the corporation's second channel produced a new 90-minute version of Agatha's own original stage play, *Spider's Web*, with that engaging actress Penelope Keith as Clarissa Hailsham-Brown – a lady, to quote the *Radio Times*'s announcement of the screening on 26 December, 'used to weaving fantasies until she finds herself enmeshed in a real murder'.

Producer Cedric Messina and director Basil Coleman assembled an excellent cast of English character actors for the play: Robert Flemyng (as Sir Rowland), Thorley Walters (Hugo Birch), David Yelland (Jeremy Warrender), Elizabeth Spriggs (Mildred Peake) and John Barcroft as Inspector Lord. The *Radio Times* devoted a sizeable photographic spread to *Spider's Web* and also included a parody short story 'Murder with Mistletoe' by 'Agatha Woddis', offering a £10 book token to the first reader to spot the vital clue and name the murderer of Neville Drapes, the fictitious drama critic of *The Sentinel*!

The real drama critics of the national press were divided in their opinions about *Spider's Web*. Maureen Paton of the *Daily Express* was enthusiastic:

> Nervous wrecks everywhere must have lifted up their hearts and rejoiced at this splendidly corny and cosy Agatha Christie whodunnit to help them unwind with a surreptitious hair of the dog after the festive overkill. The fine cast including TV's favourite bossy boots provided just perfect escapist entertainment.

But Michael Poole of *The Listener* was obviously less convinced:

> As LWT discovered when they attempted to blockbuster Agatha Christie's *Who Killed Evans?* [*sic*] a few years ago, the lady's not for playing straight – not any more, anyway, and certainly not on TV. Happily director Basil Coleman seems to have recognised this because *Spider's Web* was played strictly for laughs. Penelope Keith led the rest of the cast over the top and back again. No question of a *literary* adaption – a respectful attempt to recreate the world of Golden Age detective fiction – rather an entertaining romp that honestly reflected its place in the Christmas schedules.

Undoubtedly, though, the nostalgia this play and the earlier independent television productions had evoked for viewers was not lost on other producers, either, and the following year, 1983, saw four more major Christie adaptations: *A Caribbean Mystery* and *Sparkling Cyanide* from America, and the Tommy and Tuppence adventures, *The Secret Adversary* and *Partners in Crime*.

A Caribbean Mystery was another two-hour Stan Margulies production which introduced Helen Hayes as the fifth actress to play Miss Marple in the famous West Indies-based case of intrigue and death. The story, which co-starred Bernard Hughes and Maurice Evans, was transmitted on 22 October 1983. (Six years later, on Christmas Day, 1989, the BBC transmitted their own adaptation with the sixth Miss Marple, Joan Hickson.)

Sparkling Cyanide, also produced by Stan Margulies and shown on 5 November 1983, was less of a success, probably because the compelling Thirties tale of a beautiful heiress mysteriously poisoned in a London restaurant was relocated to the present day and a lakeside community near Pasadena in California. This was the handiwork of the director, Robert Lewis, and the scriptwriting team of Robert Malcolm Young, Sue Grafton and Steven Humphrey. And despite starring Anthony Andrews, Deborah Raffin, Christine Belford, June Chadwick, Pamela Bellwood, Nancy Marchand, David Huffman, Josef Sommer and Harry Morgan, the 120-minute adaptation was poorly received on both sides of the Atlantic.

The *New York Times* wrote on 4 November, 'One of the more glaring weaknesses of this mystery is that nobody bothers to ask the private investigator Tony (Anthony Andrews) what it is, precisely, that he is investigating until the final scene. That's not cricket, even in a mystery novel!'

Julie Davidson in the *Glasgow Herald* was even more caustic when ITV showed the story on 26 April 1984:

> What on earth are the Americans doing to Agatha Christie? Their TV version of this whodunnit is recognisable only by name and denouement. Thus *Sparkling Cyanide* was lacquered with transatlantic *Dallas*-style gloss (although of inferior quality) which rendered indistinguishable the various female suspects, all mane-like hair and pearly teeth, and propelled the dialogue into lines like this: 'The last time you saw Victor he was still a long-haired surfer living in cut-offs and wet suits.' Whatever would the little Belgian and the old pussy-cat make of that?

It was a question well worth the asking – and not long in the answering. For the very next year, 1984, brought the arrival of the definitive Miss Marple as played by Joan Hickson in the first of her BBC serials, *The Body in the Library*, which was screened on the three nights immediately following Christmas Day. For fans of the lady sleuth, who have waited so long for a wholly convincing portrayal, the rest has become history as Joan has confirmed her reputation in another nine stories. (Helen Hayes also followed up her interpretation of Miss Marple with another well-received performance for CBS in *Murder with Mirrors* in 1985.)

Poirot, too, has found his definitive interpreter in David Suchet, now with two series behind him and more cases to follow. Nevertheless, no one should forget Ian Holm who gave a single excellent performance in *Murder by the Book* in 1986, or Peter Ustinov, who also has many admirers and at the time of writing has appeared in three productions specifically made for TV, *Thirteen at Dinner* (1985), *Dead Man's Folly* (1986) and *Murder in Three Acts* (1987).

Granada Television has provided viewers with an outstanding production of Agatha's *Hound of Death* short story, 'The Last Seance', as part of their major paranormal drama series, *Shades of Darkness*, transmitted on 27 September 1986. The hour-long adaptation by Alfred Shaughnessy was something of a coup for the Manchester-based company and its producer/director June Wyndham-Davies, for it lured the distinguished French film actress Jeanne Moreau, star of the internationally acclaimed movie *Jules et Jim* (1962), to appear on television.

'A long time ago I made a vow never to appear on television,' Jeanne explains. 'I am a film person, you see, and working in TV didn't interest me at all. That is until June sent me the script and I was immediately fascinated by the role of Madame Exe.'

Madame Exe is the catalyst in the story of a great French spiritualist medium, Simone

The celebrated French actress Jeanne Moreau, who starred in Granada Television's outstanding version of 'The Last Seance' in 1986

(played by Norma West), who is growing increasingly worried about her powers but is promised by her overbearing fiancé, Raoul (Anthony Higgins), that she can stop after one more dramatic seance.

Filming the story provided a quite different kind of drama behind the scenes, as June Wyndham-Davies has explained: 'It was a tricky period for Jeanne. She had to cope with a personal trauma right in the middle of filming. She flew back to Paris to be with her close friend Francois Truffaut, the great French film director who had directed her in *Jules et Jim*, hours before he died tragically of cancer. She returned to Manchester deeply upset, but she never let it affect her performance.'

The *Daily Express* was just one of the papers with high praise for 'The Last Seance', which it thought the best in the series and called a 'superior drama'. TV critic Louise Court added, 'With Norma West as the doomed psychic, Anthony Higgins as her ambitious lover, and Jeanne Moreau as the devious and eerie mother desperate to reclaim her dead child at any cost, it was a joy.'

What Jeanne Moreau, David Suchet, Joan Hickson and all the other fine actors involved in the recent productions have undoubtedly helped to create is a huge, appreciative audience for the works of Agatha Christie on television, not only in this country and America, but in the many other countries of the world where they are now being shown. It is all a far cry indeed from those flickering grey pictures which first brought *Ten Little Niggers* to a small English audience huddled around its tiny sets forty years ago.

THE LITTLE GREY CELLS OF M POIROT

Ten actors who have starred as the great Belgian detective

CHARLES LAUGHTON

'The fat and sentimental ratiocinator'

The first actor to transform the figure of Agatha Christie's imagination into a character of flesh and blood was the redoubtable Charles Laughton. On the night of 15 May 1928, on the stage of the Prince of Wales's Theatre in London, Hercule Poirot, at that time the hero of seventeen cases (three novels and a collection of fourteen short stories) emerged into the spotlight as a somewhat rotund young man in a dinner jacket and bow tie with slicked-down hair and a little moustache. Laughton's Poirot may not have been how the authoress, or indeed her growing number of readers, had envisaged the Belgian detective, but it was none-theless an impressive entrance for a man destined in time to be bracketed with those other immortals of the detective genre, Sherlock Holmes and Inspector Maigret.

The play was called *Alibi* and it had been adapted from Agatha's novel, *The Murder of Roger Ackroyd*, by the veteran playwright Michael Morton. The producer was Gerald du Maurier and Laughton himself was both star and director. Apart from introducing Poirot to a new medium, *Alibi* was also to prove an important stepping stone in Laughton's own career, for as a *Sunday Express* feature on his life written in 1935 commented, 'Laughton found fame in London as Hercule Poirot in *Alibi*, and then the gangster Tony Perelli in Edgar Wallace's *On the Spot*.'

Though there is no doubt about the time and place of Hercule Poirot's stage debut, a legend persists that Laughton was also the first man to play the detective on film. For during the highly successful run of *Alibi* at the Prince of Wales's Theatre (lasting for 250 perform-ances), Charles Laughton and his actress girlfriend Elsa Lanchester (who was later to become his wife) made a number of short, two-reel comedy movies. In one of these, rumour has it, Laughton appeared in a scene as a detective looking precisely as he had done on stage as Poirot. Such an appearance could have breached Agatha Christie's copyright in her char-acter, and for this reason the scene may well have ended up on the cutting-room floor – if it was ever intended for inclusion in the first place, of course.

In fact, the mystery of Laughton's film impersonation has proved impossible to solve, although research has established that he did make three movies in 1928 for the versatile producer, Ivor Montagu. Entitled *Bluebottles*, *Day-Dreams* and *The Tonic*, the films were little more than sketches on contemporary life and art, and would probably have escaped all record had not the distinguished writer H. G. Wells been responsible for the scripts.

Although these short stories were Charles Laughton's first experience of film-making, his place on the London stage was already well established. Born in 1899, the son of a Scarborough hotelier, he had been a gold medal winning pupil at RADA before making his debut in the West End in 1925. His heavy-set build and crumpled features made him ideal casting in sinister and mysterious roles such as the sadistic *Man with Red Hair*. With *Alibi* and Poirot he was, though, trying for something different.

In an interview in 1953, Laughton recalled, 'The late Twenties were the time for thrillers on the stage and producers everywhere were on the look-out for new stories and characters. Edgar Wallace, who was later to write a play about a gangster for me called *On the Spot*, was very popular with the public

'It was Gerald de Maurier who read *The Murder of Roger Ackroyd* and thought it would make a good play,' Laughton continued. 'He asked Michael Morton to adapt it for the stage. At first Morton wanted to make the character of Poirot a bit of a ladies' man with lots of girls falling in love with him. He was even going to make him twenty years younger than in the books and call him Beau Poirot! Apparently Agatha Christie wouldn't allow this, although she did let them change an old spinster lady in the book into a bright young thing so that Poirot could have a little romance!'

Laughton read the original book before immersing himself in the script. 'I interpreted the character the best way I knew how – which is the way I play every part,' he explained. 'My

Left: *Charles Laughton's Hercule Poirot takes his bow on the London stage at the Prince of Wales's Theatre in* Alibi, *May 1928*

Above: *Poirot and Dr Sheppard (J. H. Roberts) viewing the body of Roger Ackroyd (Norman V. Norman) in* Alibi

The Punch *theatre cartoonist, Haselden, captures Charles Laughton's mannerisms as the Belgian detective in a scene from* Alibi *with J. H. Roberts*

idea of things may be wrong in the minds of some purists, but on stage I can only give forth my own ideas.'

Charles Higham, Laughton's biographer, has written of this particular production, 'Charles gave an excitingly detailed performance, his Belgian accent flawless, his cross-examination of the various witnesses quietly deadly, his final pointing at the killer electrifying in its impact on the audience.'

Laughton was also impressive in the closing scene where he gave more than a hint that Poirot might return – if not for the girl, whose hands he had kissed as she left the stage, then perhaps because his services in the pursuit of justice might be needed again. It was a piece of clever presentiment: though no one could possibly have appreciated then just what kind of a career in all the entertainment media lay ahead for Poirot.

The national newspaper reviews of *Alibi* were almost universally favourable – *The Times*, for instance, commenting on the star's ability to make 'a personality out of the fat and sentimental ratiocinator' while *The Sketch* said Laughton 'admirably impersonated Poirot' – but Agatha Christie herself was not altogether satisfied.

'Mr Laughton is a good actor,' she said after attending a performance, 'but entirely unlike Hercule Poirot.'

This was a verdict she was to repeat several times more during her lifetime as other actors wrestled with the problem of portraying the little Belgian.

In 1932, Laughton was asked to introduce Poirot to a new audience across the Atlantic in New York, where the play was adapted for American audiences by John Anderson, retitled *The Fatal Alibi*. This time, however, at the insistence of the Broadway producer, Jed Harris, the star had to change his interpretation of Poirot, and though his performance was both witty and relentless, the show was doomed. It closed after just 24 performances. Laughton had not been able to put into practice his dictum of following his own ideas on the stage, and the *New York Times* probably correctly surmised just what he had objected to when the paper's critic wrote, 'Laughton's poster portraiture of Poirot diverts attention from the play.'

This was not, though, Charles Laughton's last association with the work of Agatha Christie – or even with stories of crime. In 1949, already an international star following his memorable performances in movies such as *The Private Life of Henry VIII* (1933), *Mutiny on the Bounty* (1935) and *The Hunchback of Notre Dame* (1939), he became the first non-

Frenchman to play Georges Simenon's famous Inspector Maigret, in *The Man on the Eiffel Tower*. Made by RKO in Paris, the picture was directed by co-star Burgess Meredith, though Laughton himself directed the scenes in which Meredith appeared.

Then, in 1957, Laughton gave another brilliant performance in what was to be his last major film, as Sir Wilfred Roberts, the defending counsel, in *Witness for the Prosecution*. This courtroom drama of a murder trial had originally been adapted by Agatha Christie for the stage in 1953 from one of her own short stories, before being brought to the screen by director Billy Wilder.

But even before Charles Laughton left England and began his immensely successful film career in Hollywood – eventually becoming an American citizen himself – he saw the play he had made famous turned into a movie. He was never approached about the screen role, and indeed may well not have wanted it even if it had been offered, so concerned was he about becoming typecast. In fact, he was still playing the role of Poirot on the stage while an actor named Austin Trevor, even less like the detective than Laughton, was busy shooting *Alibi* at the Twickenham Studios outside London.

By making *Alibi*, Austin Trevor became the actor who officially first brought Poirot to the screen – and though there is no record of any comment by Laughton on his successor's performance, one can guess it would have been scathing and quite probably unprintable.

AUSTIN TREVOR

'A clean-shaven young detective'

A tall, handsome young Irishman with the strange name of Trevor Schilsky was the unlikely actor first to portray Hercule Poirot in a feature film in 1931. Better known by his professional name of Austin Trevor, this accomplished character actor played the Belgian detective as a typical clean-cut Thirties hero adept at charming the ladies and outsmarting the criminals.

Indeed, a more vivid contrast between Austin Trevor and Agatha Christie's description of her detective would be hard to imagine: yet the fact remains that both the first Poirot movie, *Alibi*, and its successor, *Black Coffee*, made in the same year, were popular with the general public and helped get their star mentioned in film magazines and newspaper gossip columns.

Trevor, who was born in Belfast in 1897, enjoyed a long and successful acting career. In the theatre he ranged from Shakespeare to musical comedy ('I made my debut as the ghost in Hamlet,' he once remarked), and he made appearances in films directed by Alexander Korda and Alfred Hitchcock, as well as working on radio and television in a variety of broadcasts and drama presentations. Undoubtedly, though, the strangest role that ever came his way was that of Poirot.

In a radio interview given a few years before his death in 1978, aged 80, Trevor explained how this extraordinary piece of casting came about.

'Those Hercule Poirot films? They were the idea of the producer Julius Hagen. He was on the look-out for thriller material and saw *Alibi* with Charles Laughton and decided to buy the film rights. I never saw the play myself, but I believe that Laughton was very good in the part.

'I think that Julius Hagen and the director Leslie Hiscott decided that a film with a fat, foreign detective for a hero would never appeal to British audiences, so they turned him into a typical Thirties sleuth – you know, felt hat, raincoat and a dinner jacket when necessary.

'I had only recently started to get into films after years on the stage and so I was happy to play the character any way I was asked,' Austin Trevor said. 'I was never quite sure why they cast me as Poirot. It was probably because I had played a French detective the previous year – Inspector Hanaud of the Sûreté in the film *At the Villa Rose.*'

Interestingly, at this time the actor was already beginning to build a reputation for his fluency in several languages as well as his ability to portray various ethnic types in English – which naturally poses the question as to just how he might have interpreted Poirot had he been given the chance to play the character a little closer to the way Agatha Christie had created him. As it was, Leslie Hiscott, who also adapted Michael Morton's play for the screen, made him into a lean, very English sleuth without even the merest trace of the famous Poirot moustache.

Charles Laughton's powerful characterisation of Poirot which was still running on the stage no doubt influenced the film-maker's attitudes while making the picture, and indeed the casting of the other roles differed considerably from the characters who had been seen in the London production. Among those who appeared in the film were Elizabeth Allen, Clare Greet and the venerable thespian, Franklin Dyall.

Perhaps helped by the reputation of *Alibi* on the London stage, the film was well received in the cinemas, where audiences were less demanding over accuracy in adapting literary figures for the screen than they are today.

Before the end of that year, the same team of Hagen, Hiscott and Austin Trevor had brought another of the Poirot cases to the screen, this time *Black Coffee*, based on Agatha Christie's play of the same name which she had written specially for the theatre. It had opened at the Embassy Theatre in December 1930 and had run for 100 performances. Starring as Poirot was another bulky actor in the Charles Laughton mould named Francis L. Sullivan.

Once again, so that there should be no confusion between stage and screen, Trevor retained his dashing, clean-cut Poirot for cinema audiences. His co-stars were Richard Cooper, Adrienne Allen and C. V. France.

The star himself was more assured in the role in this second appearance, and took particular pleasure in the dramatic scene where he pretended to drink poisoned coffee in order to unmask the murderer. Cinema audiences cheered with delight as he revealed the criminal, who hissed at him in very un-Christie like tones, 'You cunning swine!' Reviewing the series for the first time, *The Times*, while making no comment on Poirot's appearance, concluded, 'The film nowhere departs from the beaten track of detective stories, and is, in its own kind, a reasonable and competent piece of work.'

However, despite such acknowledgement, albeit muted, the second Poirot movie was not as successful at the box office as its predecessor. Nevertheless, in 1934, Julius Hagen went ahead with a third picture. This time, though, he decided upon a direct adaptation of Agatha Christie's latest book, *Lord Edgware Dies*, which had been published in 1933. A new director, Henry Edwards, was recruited, and Austin Trevor (who in the interim had been acclaimed for his roles in two other thrillers, *The Chinese Puzzle*, 1932, and *On Secret Service*, 1933) reprised the role of Poirot. Appearing with him were Jane Carr, John Turnbull and Richard Cooper.

For this picture, however, the publicists at Hagen's Real Art Studios actually boasted about the differences between their man and the 'real' Poirot.

'The detective is described by the authoress as an elderly man with an egg-shaped head and bristling moustache,' a press release announced: 'Austin Trevor is a good-looking young man and clean-shaven into the bargain!'

The case, in which Poirot tracks down the murderer of the husband of a vain American actress, proved the last of the series, and Austin Trevor thereafter left the small-time British film companies for richer pastures on the London and Broadway stages as well as some major roles in later films such as *Goodbye Mr Chips* (1939), *The Red Shoes* (1948) and

Left: *Poirot as a clean-shaven ladies' man, played by Austin Trevor in* Black Coffee *(1931) with Adrienne Allen*

Above: *Austin Trevor as Poirot* (centre) *examines a body in the film version of* Alibi, *also made in 1931*

opposite Alec Guinness in his outstanding performance as G. K. Chesterston's famous detective *Father Brown* (1954).

'At the time, the three Poirot films were just steps in my career,' Austin Trevor recalled. 'No one, myself included, had any idea how famous Agatha Christie and Poirot were to become. I did read some of her books, including most of the Poirot stories. It has always made me smile to think just how unlike the little Belgian I was in those three pictures!'

By one of those curious twists of fate that Agatha Christie herself would probably have appreciated, this was not to be quite the end of Austin Trevor's association with Poirot. In 1965 he made what was to prove his final appearance on the cinema screen in *The Alphabet Murders*, the MGM film which starred Tony Randall in the role that Trevor had originated.

'It was only a bit part, really,' Austin Trevor said, 'but it was interesting for me watching someone else trying to be Hercule Poirot. There was another nice touch, too. Margaret Rutherford who had played Miss Marple on the screen also made a brief appearance in the film!'

FRANCIS L. SULLIVAN

'The most talkative of detectives'

The second Poirot to be seen on the London stage, in *Black Coffee*, was Francis L. Sullivan, an actor whose career was similar in many ways to that of Charles Laughton. Despite Sullivan's fame on the screen playing villains – in particular the first of the great megalomaniac criminal masterminds, Carl Petersen in the Bulldog Drummond movies – it was for his stage performances as Hercule Poirot that both *The Times* and *The Daily Telegraphe* remembered him in their obituaries.

After his death in a New York hospital at the age of 53 in November 1956, *The Times* commented, 'Corpulent, his sharp eyes embedded in florid features, . . . a deep, plummy voice suited Sullivan admirably for the part of the suave but foxy lawyer. He was an obvious choice for Bottom and perhaps for Mr Bumble, but not for Hercule Poirot; yet, though his appearance offended some preconceptions about that dapper detective, he played the part with good success in two of Agatha Christie's plays on the London stage.' *The Daily Telegraph* concurred with this view, adding, 'He weighed nineteen stone, and one of his best-known parts was the dapper Hercule Poirot in several Agatha Christie plays.'

What none of the obituaries mentioned about the rotund figure, with his special ability to create a sinister presence on stage or screen, was 'Larry' Sullivan's close friendship with Agatha Christie. Though the authoress was on a trip abroad and did not see him in *Black Coffee*, a Poirot story she had written specially for the London stage in 1930, they did meet the following year and subsequently spent many happy days together sharing their joint passion for criminology. Agatha acknowledged this friendship by dedicating her later Poirot novel, *The Hollow* (1946) to Sullivan and his wife, 'with apologies for using their swimming pool as the scene of the murder'. (*The Hollow* was adapted for the stage in 1951, though the Belgian detective was omitted entirely from the play.)

Francis Sullivan was born in London in January 1903. Like Charles Laughton he utilised his unprepossessing looks to carve a place for himself in the world of entertainment, and, also like Laughton, he became an American citizen. Sullivan made his debut at the Old Vic in 1921 and afterwards joined the Manchester Repertory Company where he played a variety of roles from comedy to grandiloquent villainy. By 1929 he had appeared on both the London and New York stage, but it was his performance as Poirot in *Black Coffee* (which opened at the Embassy Theatre on 8 December 1930) that earned him widespread recognition and led to important stage roles as well as a film career on both sides of the Atlantic.

It was only to be expected that his appearance in this spy thriller about the murder of a scientist and the theft of a secret formula for making dangerous weapons should earn him comparison with his predecessor. He did, though, come out rather better, as this typical review from *The Daily Telegraph* demonstrates: 'Mr Sullivan's rendering of the part of Poirot is preferable to the one that Mr Charles Laughton gave us in *Alibi* . . . Mr Laughton's Poirot was a diabolically clever oddity. Mr Sullivan's is a lovable human being.'

The following April, the play moved to the St Martin's Theatre, where it ran for 100 performances – the same St Martin's which was later to become home to that all-time record-breaking play, *The Mousetrap*. Of the cast, John Boxer, who had played Captain Hastings at the Embassy, was replaced by Roland Culver, while Dino Galvani took over the role of Dr Carelli from Donald Wolfit.

Although Agatha Christie once again found the man cast as Poirot far from her conception, she and her husband Max became firm friends with Francis Sullivan and his wife, Danae, a theatrical designer, and frequently spent time with them at their country home at Haslemere, surrounded by Spanish chestnut woods.

'I always found it restful to stay with actors in wartime,' she wrote years later in her auto-biography, 'because to them, acting and the theatrical world were the real world, any other world was not. The war to them was a long drawn-out nightmare that prevented them from going on with their own lives, in the proper way, so their entire talk was of theatrical people, theatrical things, what was going on in the theatrical world, who was going into ENSA – it was wonderfully refreshing.'

In May 1940, Sullivan donned the role of Poirot a second time at the Vaudeville Theatre in *Peril at End House*, which Arnold Ridley (author of the comedy-thriller *The Ghost Train* and, much later, star of BBC TV's *Dad's Army*) had adapted from Agatha's 1932 novel about the death threats to a young girl. A third Captain Hastings appeared with Sullivan in the person of Ian Fleming.

Again the reviews for the star were laudatory, and the measure of Francis Sullivan's own enthusiasm for the part can be judged from this review by *The Times*'s theatre critic: 'Though Hercule Poirot is the most talkative of detectives and the greatest part of this intricate story comes to us through his perpetual ratiocinative talk, Mr Sullivan conspicuously enjoys Poirot's eloquence and handles it skilfully.'

During the winter of 1942, Francis Sullivan used his own eloquence to try to persuade Agatha Christie to let him put on a third Poirot play. He had read a script entitled 'Moon on the Nile' which she had written some years earlier after a journey through Egypt in 1933. It had, though, subsequently been confined to her bottom drawer in favour of the full-blown detective novel, *Death on the Nile*, published in 1937, and later ranking among the most famous of her books as well as becoming the basis of one of the most successful of all British films.

Agatha Christie and the ebullient actor discussed the project over several entertaining luncheons, at which the authoress explained her growing dislike of Poirot and her wish to

Right: *The plump and imperturbable Poirot of Francis L. Sullivan as he appeared on the stage in* Peril at End House *in May 1940*

Above: *The master criminal who turned master detective: Francis L. Sullivan as Carl Petersen in the Bulldog Drummond films – the role that made him famous on the screen*

replace him in the play – if it was indeed going to be staged. She would, she said, create an entirely new central role for the actor as Canon Pennefather, 'a kind of budding Archbishop of Canterbury and Sir William Beveridge rolled into one', to quote her own words.

Sullivan, reportedly, finally agreed to the idea when he began to visualise himself on stage as a splendid figure in a purple silk costume with a huge cross hanging on his chest. At this, thoughts of Poirot disappeared from his mind.

Sadly, though, fate was to be against *Moon on the Nile*. Though it was previewed in Dundee in January 1944 with Sullivan as the canon (his wife, Danae, having produced the costumes and props) and was well received by the audience (including Agatha herself, who hid up in the balcony), efforts to find a London theatre came to nothing. Finally Sullivan had to take himself off to film the coveted part of Mr Jaggers in David Lean's *Great Expectations*. Perhaps, in the light of what happened when the play *did* finally open two years later, he was glad of the way events had turned out.

Murder on the Nile, as it was now called, opened on 19 March 1946 at the Ambassadors Theatre with David Horne as the flamboyant clergyman. This was followed in September by a Broadway production – retitled *Hidden Horizon* – with Halliwell Hobbes as Archdeacon(!) Pennyfeather and Diana Barrymore as Jacqueline de Severac. The reviews on both sides of the Atlantic were equally dismissive and neither production survived more than a few weeks.

The friendship of Francis Sullivan and the authoress continued beyond the war years, however, and in 1954 the actor was reunited with her work when he appeared in what was to be his last major performance in the American stage production of *Witness for the Prosecution*. It was perhaps ironic that a man who had become famous for villainy should suddenly find himself playing an honourable man, for like the other actor to whom his career had been compared, Charles Laughton, Sullivan played Sir Wilfred Roberts QC. He gave a triumphant performance and the play won the New York Drama Critics' Circle award as the best foreign production, running for 22 months including a transfer to Chicago, all despite his claim on the opening night that 'The public will *never* believe I'm innocent.'

For Francis Sullivan, Hercule Poirot remained his favourite role – just as his friendship with Agatha Christie was among the warmest of his life. 'We had some fascinating times together,' he once said, 'and we both owed it all to villainy!'

HAROLD HUBER

'A comical French detective'

Though Hercule Poirot appeared first on the stage and in films in Britain, his radio debut took place in America in 1945 as the clouds of war were at last dispersing. Despite the fact that a substantial amount of Agatha Christie's work had already been dramatised for the radio in Britain, it took an American enthusiast to introduce the detective to the air waves on the other side of the Atlantic.

The programme, *The Adventures of M Hercule Poirot*, holds the dual distinction of being the first to feature the little Belgian and also the first *series* to be made from the work of Agatha Christie. And it was all due to the efforts of a determined actor-cum-scriptwriter who was best known to the public for 'portraying dozens of squint-eyed, scheming villains on radio and in films', according to media critic, Tim Brooks.

Harold Huber was born in New York in 1910, and became a fan of crime and mystery stories in the famous pulp magazines of the Twenties such as *Black Mask* (which first

DAVID SUCHET:
the latest Belgian detective in
Agatha Christie's Poirot

Poirot at work – a scene from 'The Peril
at End House', with (l. to r.) co-stars
Philip Jackson (Inspector Japp),
Hugh Fraser (Capt. Hastings)
and Pauline Moran (Miss Lemon)

ANGELA LANSBURY, an outstanding Miss Marple in The Mirror Crack'd *(1980)*

JOAN HICKSON, the most recent Miss Marple, in '4.50 from Paddington' (1987)

*JEANNE MOREAU in the superb television version of
one of the best of Agatha Christie's short stories, 'The Last Seance', made in 1986*

published Dashiell Hammett and Raymond Chandler) and *Detective Story Magazine*. His insatiable thirst for such stories in time led him to the novels of other writers in the genre, including Agatha Christie.

As a young man, Huber displayed precocious intelligence and while at college qualified for three degrees, including one for the law. Instead of taking up a career in the legal profession, however, he was drawn to the stage and films. His dark features and deep voice made him ideally suited to play sinister or criminal types, and he claimed to have appeared as the villain in over 100 films during the 1930s.

Among his best roles in this era were parts in the suitably titled *Lawyer Man* (1933), *The Defence Rests* (1935), *The Trunk Mystery* (1935) and *A Slight Case of Murder* in 1938. In 1940 he had something of a foretaste of playing Poirot when he was cast as a comical French police inspector in *Charlie Chan in the City of Darkness* with Sidney Toler.

During the Second World War, Huber worked on the New York stage and also began writing for radio. He became a regular scriptwriter for the highly popular CBS radio series, *Suspense*, from 1943; and in 1945 enjoyed his biggest success in the theatre when he appeared in *The Assassin* on Broadway.

The success of this play plus his work for *Suspense* encouraged him to take to CBS an idea he had been nursing for some time. He had become a great admirer of Agatha Christie's Poirot cases, and with the current vogue for detective stories on radio he believed a popular series could be made, based on the various short stories and novels.

Huber proposed himself as producer, director, scriptwriter and star of the series, and having convinced CBS got a sponsor, the Mutual Insurance Company.

The Adventures of M Hercule Poirot were half-hour stories on Wednesday evenings. Huber played fair with his audience by retaining the British settings for most of the stories, though his own accent was closer to pidgin French, and his pronouncements were often ended by an irritating chuckle as if he was still the comical French policeman from the Charlie Chan film.

The first adventures in the series were drawn from the three collections of Poirot stories that Agatha had published by 1945: *Poirot Investigates* (1924), *Murder in the Mews* (1937) and *The Regatta Mystery* (1939). From the 21 novels which had appeared, the series presented four-part adaptations of *Murder on the Links* (1923), *The Big Four* (1927) and *Poirot Loses a Client* (1937), the last of which was known as *Dumb Witness* in the UK.

Among the best remembered dramatisations were, perhaps naturally enough, those with an international flavour to them, like the movie-world case of 'The Adventure of "The Western Star"'; the big business mystery of 'The Million-Dollar Bond Robbery'; 'The Lost Mine' with its Chinese fortune hunters; 'The Incredible Theft', a tale of missing secret bomber plans; and the Mediterranean card-sharping puzzle of 'Problem at Sea'.

Agatha, who was paid the princely sum of £65 per week for the use of her material, never heard the broadcasts, and Janet Morgan believes that with the reservations she had about the impersonation of Poirot by this time, it was perhaps just as well. A phoney French accent on the radio might have been quite as hard to take as the Laughton, Sullivan and Trevor impersonations on the stage and cinema screen.

Be that as it may, *The Adventures of M Hercule Poirot* was a success in America, and the forward-thinking Harold Huber sensed there were even wider fields to conquer. In 1949 he wrote to Agatha seeking her permission to make a television series about Poirot.

Huber was convinced of the enormous potential of television in the United States – in which he was right – and believed there would be a sizeable market for a detective series. In this he was right, too, but Agatha refused, apparently fearful of what might happen to the personality of Poirot in American hands. Huber wrote several times more to Agatha's American agent hoping to change her mind, but she remained adamant and he was denied his ambition to become the first actor to portray Poirot on television.

Huber's career continued with further stage productions on Broadway and several films

Harold Huber, like Francis
L. Sullivan, played sinister
villains on the screen
before becoming Hercule
Poirot

Huber playing a comical French police
inspector in Charlie Chan in the City of
Darkness (1940) with Sidney Toler

including the 1950 musical *Let's Dance*, with Fred Astaire. That same year he also achieved
his ambition of producing a television show, and again it was a far cry from his early image as
a villain. He starred as Johnny Warren in a half-hour weekly series, *I Cover Times Square*,
about a crusading journalist whose beat was the seamy side of show business, and who was
said to have been based on the columnist Walter Winchell. The series ran for two years.

Huber's busy life ended in September 1959 when he was just 49. His death merited short
obituaries in several film and theatrical papers, including *Variety* which paid tribute to his
pioneer radio series.

'Huber also portrayed Hercule Poirot, Agatha Christie's sleuth, in a popular CBS radio
series for several years,' the magazine said. It was a brief acknowledgement of another piece
of Agatha Christie history.

MARTIN GABEL

'The celebrated Belgian gumshoe'

The actor who did eventually being Poirot to the television screen in 1962 was, like Harold
Huber, an American. Though Britain had led the world in TV broadcasting, it was once
again the producers at CBS who first attempted to exploit the potential of the little detective
in a television series.

The man who portrayed Poirot was the award-winning character actor, Martin Gabel.
And the story in which he featured on the Sunday-night *General Electric Theater* drama
series transmitted on 1 April 1962 was introduced to the nation by an actor for whom the

future held the greatest 'starring role' in America, Ronald Reagan.

The *General Electric Theater* series, which had run for almost a decade from 1953, included a wide range of stories in each half-hour presentation, from Biblical tales to contemporary spy dramas and from light comedy to Westerns. For the first year, many of the productions were screened live, but by 1962, when the Poirot case was broadcast, the whole series was pre-filmed and featured many leading actors including Tony Curtis, James Stewart, Broderick Crawford, Burgess Meredith, Alan Ladd, Bette Davis and Sir Cedric Hardwicke. Ronald Reagan hosted each show, reading the commercials and introducing the plays. He even appeared with his wife, Nancy, in some of the productions.

Martin Gabel, born in Philadelphia in June 1912, was arguably the first actor to be cast as Poirot who substantially resembled Agatha Christie's original conception. Aged 50, he was just a little over 5 feet 4 inches tall, with a rounded face, dark, thinning hair and strong, piercing eyes. Always a smart dresser, Gabel required little more than a well-cut English suit and a small moustache to make him a more than passable Poirot.

A *TV Guide* special feature on Gabel in 1962 affirms the aptness of the casting:

> He is a solidly built, compact man whose sonorous voice resounds from a chest like a bourbon barrel. His wide interests continually compounded by his ceaseless reading make his conversation not only absorbing but instructive for his companions, for he has an encyclopedist's memory and is capable of injecting into casual barside chatter some such fact as, 'Did you know that Lionel Rothschild was refused admission to the House of Commons five times because he wouldn't accept the wording of the oath?'

The star's wife, the actress Arlene Francis, confirmed his suitability for playing Poirot by adding, 'He cares about taste, presentation of self, and he's very analytical.'

Martin Gabel had started his acting career in the early 1930s with small character parts on Broadway which earned him recognition as an 'all-around man'. He next appeared in several of the prestigious productions of Orson Welles's Mercury Theater company, and earned critical acclaim for his work on radio as the narrator of the Second World War drama, *On a Note of Triumph*. In 1952, he played the first of several detective roles in the film, *The Thief*, and in 1961 won a Tony award and a New York Drama Critics' Circle citation for his role in the stage comedy, *Big Fish, Little Fish*.

In a *New York Times* TV column announcing Poirot's debut on television on April Fool's Day, Martin Gabel said, 'He's a very smart detective, both in the way he dresses and the way he figures things out. Not your average American private eye, but one of those British sleuths who solves crimes in country houses rather than skyscrapers. Over the years I've played quite a number of detectives – about the only one left is Sherlock Holmes. But I'm a bit too short for him!'

The half-hour production on the *General Electric Theater* at 9 p.m. was announced simply as a 'drama' entitled 'Hercule Poirot', but a precis in *TV Guide* provides more concrete facts as to its origin:

> Martin Gabel and Nina Foch star in 'Hercule Poirot' adapted by Barre Lyndon from one of the mystery writer Agatha Christie's many novels about her famous sleuth. When Mrs Davenheim's husband disappears, she hires the best help she can get – the celebrated Belgian gunshoe, Hercule Poirot. Confident as ever, Poirot announces that he will solve the case without even leaving his hotel room.

This description clearly indicates the story upon which the drama was based as being 'The Disappearance of Mr Davenheim' from Agatha's 1924 collection, *Poirot Investigates*, in which the detective outsmarts Inspector Japp in tracing the missing wealthy banker.

Left: *Martin Gabel was the first actor to play Poirot on television, in the* General Electric Theater *drama series in April 1962*

Right: *Peter Sellers as Poirot? How the Belgian detective might have been played in the musical version of* Hickory Dickory Dock *if it had ever reached the stage in the Sixties*

Nina Foch, the chic, cool blonde playing Mrs Davenheim, was a Dutch-born actress who had appeared on Broadway and in numerous films (including several crime and detective movies), making a speciality of portraying aloof, sophisticated ladies, sometimes a little neurotic. Like Martin Gabel, she was excellently cast.

Two major changes were made by scriptwriter Barre Lyndon for the television broadcast. The setting was moved from a London flat to a New York hotel, and Inspector Japp was replaced by two US police officers, Chief McManus (Philip Ober) and Detective Floyd (James Callahan.) Even so, hopes were high for the production – for a footnote in *TV Guide* informed viewers that the drama was 'a pilot for a proposed series'.

Options had already been secured on the other stories in *Poirot Investigates* and a successful launch would have resulted in a series for Martin Gabel. As it was, the selection of such a 'confined' story – more than likely on financial grounds – did not give the star the chance to develop his character, and public and critical indifference to the production doomed any further plans. It was not helped by having to compete with the popular Western series, *Bonanza*, in colour on Channel 4, and an hour-long variety special, *At This Very Moment*, on Channel 7, hosted by Burt Lancaster to raise money for cancer, featuring Bob Hope, Jimmy Durante, Lena Horne, Rock Hudson, Paul Newman, Harry Belafonte, Edward G. Robinson and President John F. Kennedy! (*General Electric Theater* in fact only ran for another five months.)

Martin Gabel appeared in several more films during the Sixties, but from then until his death in May 1986, he worked mainly on Broadway as a director, producer and impresario. Among the highly successful shows with which he was involved were the Gloria Swanson revival of *Twentieth Century*; Jean Giraudoux's *Tiger at the Gates*; and the smash hit musical *Once More with Feeling*.

He never forgot his association with Poirot, however, and in the Sixties was one of several Broadway managers who expressed an interest in staging a proposed British musical version of Agatha's novel, *Hickory Dickory Dock*, to be called *Death Beat*. The idea to turn this story of several murders in a youth hostel into a lavish musical had been proposed by the British entrepreneur, Sir Nicholas Sekers, who with Agatha's blessing had recruited the entrepreneurs Peter Daubeny and Bernard Delfont. They, in turn, had asked John Wells to write a script and Alex Weissenberg to prepare a musical score, and had suggested the versatile comic, Peter Sellers, who had played Inspector Clouseau in the first of the successful 'Pink Panther' films, as Poirot.

In New York, Gabel indicated his enthusiasm for the project, and said that if Sellers would not cross the Atlantic in the event of a transfer, he might well play the maestro himself. Sadly, despite the names of Sean Kenny as designer and Johnny Dankworth as orchestrator, the musical has never been produced in either Britain or America. (There has, though, been one musical loosely based on an Agatha Christie story; *Something's Afoot*, inspired by *Ten Little Niggers*, which ran briefly at the Lyceum Theater, New York in the summer of 1976. It starred the heavyweight English actress Tessie O'Shea as a Miss Tweed in a musical mystery spoof written by James McDonald, David Vos and Robert Gerlach about ten guests marooned on an island.)

Although Martin Gabel's obituary notices in 1986 remembered him only for his films and his Broadway productions, to American fans of the work of Agatha Christie he will always be the first man to have brought Hercule Poirot to the TV screen.

TONY RANDALL

'An egocentric creep'?

There was to be a gap of over thirty years from the last of the trio of Austin Trevor/Poirot movies before the Belgian detective once more returned to the cinema screen. Again the casting was unusual – with the American comedy actor Tony Randall being signed up to play Poirot in the 1966 version of *The Alphabet Murders*, based on Agatha Christie's 1935 novel, *The ABC Murders*. Randall had not, though, been the first choice for the role.

This mystery tale of an apparently motiveless series of murders linked only by the victims' initials being successive letters of the alphabet is widely regarded as one of the most ingenious of the Poirot cases. It is notable, too, for the important role Captain Arthur Hastings takes, departing from his previous practice of describing only the events at which he was present, and instead – Watson-like – recounting all the important occurrences in the development of the story. Because of this, a major role in the film was created for the well-known English character actor, Robert Morley, as Hastings.

MGM, who had already brought four of the Miss Marple stories to the screen in the early Sixties with Margaret Rutherford in the title role, were now hoping to do the same thing with Poirot – though their initial plans were to change both the character and personality of the detective (making him tougher) as well as introducing more violence into the script. If all went well as the box office, it was planned that Poirot would likewise feature in his own movie series.

The first star the producers lined up to play the detective was the exuberant American former stand-up comic, Zero Mostel (1915–77) who was fresh from award-winning stage performances on Broadway in *A Funny Thing Happened on the Way to the Forum* (1963) and *Fiddler on the Roof* (1964).

Mostel was, apparently, ready to begin work on the movie with the English director Seth Holt when production was abruptly halted. According to Janet Morgan, this was brought about when the authoress learned what MGM planned for Poirot – including a bedroom scene, no less! All this was so out of character, she believed, that she objected in the strongest possible terms.

'I will not have him turned into some sort of gorilla or private eye,' she insisted to her agent. 'Anyway, if people have liked Poirot for about forty years as an egocentric creep they would probably prefer him to go on that way.'

Better, she thought, if the film was going to be made that it should be without Poirot at all. Somewhat chastened, MGM backed down.

Mostel with his huge bulk and larger-than-life acting style would have doubtless turned the detective into a caricature; as it was, Tony Randall, who replaced him when MGM agreed to a complete re-write of the script, did his utmost to play the role 'straight'.

MGM also brought in a new director, an American, Frank Tashlin. Purists immediately had their doubts about him, as his reputation had been made with comedy – in particular the zany Jerry Lewis movies and Bugs Bunny cartoons. The script, though, was entrusted to David Pursall and Jack Seddon who had written the Margaret Rutherford films, and out went the violence and the suggestions of Poirot the lover, though some of the comedy was retained and elements of the surreal added. Shooting at last took place at Elstree Studios with some location work in London.

Above: *Tony Randall as Poirot in an unusual publicity still for* The Alphabet Murders *(1966)*

Right: *Tony Randall and Robert Morley as Hastings discover another body and a vital clue in* The Alphabet Murders

Tony Randall remembers the picture with a mixture of nostalgia and amusement. During the filming he felt that the army of Poirot fans might well not like his interpretation of the detective though he made a conscientious effort to be true to the hero of the books.

Born in Tulsa, Oklahoma, in 1920, Tony established himself as an urbane character actor able to switch from comedy to melancholy with ease, and there are several critics who believe his talent has been much underrated. He was certainly more than willing to match his skill against the difficulties of playing Poirot. He has the advantages of being small, inquisitive by nature, and with an oddly featureless quality that can be moulded to suit any role.

'Frank Tashlin who I had worked with in 1957 on the big success *Will Success Spoil Rock Hunter?* sent me the script of *The Alphabet Murders*,' he recalls. 'He is one of my favourite directors, so I sat down and read it straight through. Then I read the original book.

'I knew Poirot had been played before, but not very well. It seemed to me I should find out how Agatha Christie had described him. In one of the early books there is a portrait of him – exactly like her description: he's bald, has a big nose, moustache and a pot belly. The clothes, too, he's very careful about those, so it was important to make him look debonair. I felt comfortable in the picture, it was fun. It may not have been terribly good, but I enjoyed it,' he added.

Aided by Robert Morley as a bowler-hatted and rather accident-prone Hastings, *The Alphabet Murders* turned out to be a stylish film which certainly offered the best film portrayal of Poirot so far. With a nice touch of humour, Frank Tashlin found small roles for both Austin Trevor and Margaret Rutherford – the great dame sweeping into one scene with the memorable line, 'This is as simple as ABC!'

Interestingly, it was decided against releasing the picture in Britain under the familiar title of the novel as it was felt that the string of murders it contained might cause the public to shun the chain of ABC cinemas that were going to show it!

Tony Randall also remembers that his sense of humour got the better of him in some of the interviews he gave at the time, telling one journalist with a conspiratorial smirk that Agatha Christie 'would definitely *not* approve' of his Poirot. Several of the British newspaper film critics did approve, however, even if they thought he looked a little on the young side.

By contrast, the *New York Times* felt the picture had missed a great opportunity. 'What MGM and the cast have failed to do is to make Poirot and his intriguing gallery of friends and foes the classic characters that have genuinely fascinated millions of Agatha Christie readers all these years,' it declared.

Fair criticism or not, what *The Alphabet Murders* had actually done was to demonstrate what a durable character Hercule Poirot now was, and to suggest that some day, perhaps, *someone* would impersonate him exactly . . .

ALBERT FINNEY

'*A fat, oily-haired fellow*'

The year 1974, in which the famous Poirot novel *Murder on the Orient Express* (1934) was filmed, can be seen with hindsight as the turning point in the history of the adaptations of Agatha Christie's work for the cinema. The huge success of this accurate version of the railway melodrama with a major star at last attempting a faithful representation of the Belgian detective pointed the way to a future in which the authoress's brilliant creations might be seen as she had intended them.

It had, though, been a long haul to reach this point, for Agatha Christie had always retained a special fondness for this book which had been sparked by an actual journey she had made on the Orient Express in 1928. Indeed, almost from the day of its publication she had resisted the blandishments of entrepreneurs and writers on both sides of the Atlantic who had been trying to get her permission to adapt the story for the stage or screen.

The great American scriptwriter Ben Hecht, for one, had wanted to prepare a stage version of *Murder on the Calais Coach* (as the book was entitled in the USA), while in England in 1963 MGM hoped to build on their success with the Miss Marple movies by adapting the dramatic railway mystery. Agatha, though, objected to both proposals: she told Ben Hecht she hoped to adapt the book for the stage herself; while to the MGM proposal she replied: 'To have it [the novel] possibly transformed into a rollicking farce with Miss Marple injected into it and probably acting as the engine driver, though great fun, no doubt, would be somewhat harmful to my reputation.'

In fact, it was not until ten years later, and thanks to the persuasive powers of Lord Mountbatten, an admirer of Agatha Christie's works since her earliest days, that she gave permission to Mountbatten's son-in-law John Brabourne and his co-producer Richard Goodwin to bring *Murder on the Orient Express* to the screen. Though the authoress was once again to have her reservations about the man who played Poirot, there could be no denying the impact of the film. Shot in colour, filmed in a railway compartment constructed from parts of the actual Orient Express and on location in snow-bound Yugoslavia, it was to become not only the most ambitious British film to date but also the most successful, in time reaping profits in excess of £20 million.

Attention to detail was the hallmark of the picture, from Paul Dehn's screenplay, through Sidney Lumet's direction, to the magnificent ensemble playing by the galaxy of stars brought together to play the stranded passengers. But Albert Finney, a Lancashire bookie's son, born in 1936, who had taken the entertainment world by storm as *Billy Liar* (1960) as well as proving himself a superb classical actor in various Shakespearean roles, was still an unlikely and, at first, unwilling Poirot.

'There were several good reasons for not doing that picture when it was offered to me,' he recalls today. 'I have never been that keen on pictures with lots of other star names, and at the time I was fully committed to a long run in the West End with the play, *Chez Nous*. Because both parts demanded me being around for virtually every line of dialogue it meant working around the clock. In the end it was the fact that Sidney Lumet, a director I have always admired, was going to direct the picture that made me agree to do it.

'Right from the start Sidney had a sort of rapacious keenness to get it done. He has a reputation for bringing in a film ahead of schedule. He does it very efficiently, and is particularly suited to a film with a strong narrative line like *Murder on the Orient Express*. He was clear about what he wanted and it was a marvellous way to work. Everybody stayed sharp and quick-witted during the shooting.'

There was, perhaps, also an omen in Finney's past that indicated he *would* take the role. For the first man who had given him a supporting part in a London production when he was still fresh from RADA was none other than the very first Poirot, Charles Laughton.

When the first discussions about the film took place, both Sidney Lumet and Albert Finney were agreed that the actor must be made to look as much like the famous detective as possible. No easy task for a man then just 38 years old and in the peak of physical condition. But as Albert was to discover, he would be very glad of his fitness when the demanding weeks of filming began.

In order to achieve the authentic look, Finney spent hours with Charles Parker, a leading make-up artist, researching the Poirot books and experimenting with different methods of altering his face and body before arriving at what everyone connected with the film believed to be the most satisfactory resemblance.

'It took me two hours in make-up every morning for two months to play Poirot,' he recalls. 'According to the books, Poirot is precisely five feet four inches tall. He has an egg-shaped

Albert Finney in his memorable interpretation of Poirot in Murder on the Orient Express *(1974), with Sir John Gielgud as Beddoes*

head with he carries a little to the left on not too robust shoulders. He wears black patent shoes and is always impeccably dressed.

'Facially, the transformation was achieved with a false nose – my own is too tilted for Poirot – and padded cheeks to achieve the egg-shaped look. But by far the most important part of the make-up was the gleaming black hair and the meticulously trimmed and waxed period moustache. For if you remember, his moustache is always ferociously waxed into points at the end, and he uses a certain "tonic" – not a "dye" – to keep his hair perennially young looking.

'Now because I was doing the play each night and was appearing in it as a kind of older version of myself, I could not have my own reddish brown hair permanently tinted for the film. But the hairdresser Ramon Gow solved this problem by applying lashings of hair cream mixed with black powder. The effect was amazing – but it took four shampoos to get rid of it every time!' he says with a smile.

'In order to get a short, solid look I wore body padding – a T-shirt draped with cotton wool. I also had to have padded thighs to make me look wide so that my own height appeared less. By the time I got on the set I looked about twenty years older and thirty pounds heavier!

'It also got really tough physically shooting in the crammed interior of the train under the lamps,' he continues. 'I would get so hot by lunchtime I'd leave my padding in the fridge during the break. It was nice and cold when I put it on again!'

As a thoroughgoing professional, Finney also wanted to get into the mind of Poirot the detective.

'He made his first appearance in literature as far back as 1920 so the early years of this century must have had a lasting effect on him,' Finney explains. 'I don't know how he would cope with a crime today because he relied more on his brain than on equipment of any kind. The psychology of the murderer was more important to him than his finger prints. He is obviously a great respecter of law and order both in his work as a detective and in his private life as a neat, dapper, tidy man who would arrange all his personal belongings in perfect

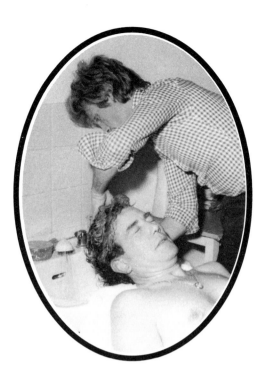

Finney before and after: (left) *on set as Poirot, ready for bed; and* (right) *after filming, regaining his natural hair colour*

order before donning his pyjamas, his hair net and his moustache protector.'

Finney was also particularly intrigued by Poirot's use of broken English.

'It is generally accepted that his English was deliberately imperfect and liberally interspersed with phrases literally translated from the French. For example, "Do not derange yourself, I pray you, monsieur." The reason he does this is because he realised that the English as a nation could be tricked into saying things heedlessly through their disparaging attitude towards anything foreign, in an Alf Garnett sort of way. This was particularly true before the war in 1935 when travelling on the continent was still something of an adventure.

'So the general reaction to his interrogations was that anyone who looked and spoke as Poirot did in the Twenties and Thirties could be easily outwitted. But suddenly when he has solved his case and the denouncement of the guilty party is about to be made, generally in front of the suspects, Poirot's English improves as if his accent has been sharpened along with his wits during the stimulating mental exercise of solving a crime through the logical process of deduction,' he adds.

Interestingly, the French accent that Finney actually spoke as Poirot was the result of coaching from his then wife, Anouk Aimée – though he still jokes that his French must have horrified any native Parisians who saw the picture!

He also admits to having enjoyed every minute of making *Murder on the Orient Express,* even overcoming his dislike of working with a lot of star names.

'Actually all those stars in the cast were not just a gimmick,' he says, 'but a real set of characters. A lot of people obviously got a lot of pleasure from the picture.'

The performances of the other leading players indeed nicely complemented Albert Finney's – and among the best performances must be mentioned those of Sean Connery, Martin Balsam, John Gielgud, Anthony Perkins, Richard Widmark, Lauren Bacall, Rachel Roberts, Vanessa Redgrave, Wendy Hiller and Ingrid Bergman.

So, at a stroke, the earlier, cheaply made Poirot films were surpassed, and even Agatha Christie herself, who attended the premiere, was impressed by the lavish production. She had, though, one major reservation about Albert Finney.

'I wrote that my detective had the finest moustache in England,' she said, 'but he *didn't* in the film. I thought that a pity. Why shouldn't he have the best moustache?'

Notwithstanding this small quibble, Albert Finney was nominated for an Oscar for his performance as Poirot in what critics everywhere agreed was a great train melodrama in the same tradition as Alfred Hitchcock's *The Lady Vanishes* and Graham Greene's *Stamboul Express.* Though he did not win an award, the picture did have two interesting repercussions on his career. The first was a decision not to make any more films for several years.

'At that time, two of my biggest roles had been as Scrooge and Hercule Poirot,' he says. 'In both I was in heavy disguise. I was going through a period of not knowing what I represented on screen. So I decided to go back to the National Theatre and live audiences.'

It was six years, in fact, before he returned to filming, and it was on his arrival in Hollywood to make a horror movie entitled *The Wolfen* that he had an amusing demonstration of just how convincing his portrayal of Poirot had been. The memory still makes him laugh today.

'When my name came up for the picture one executive said, "He is that oily-haired fellow, isn't he? The one that's rather fat?"', Finney says. 'Apparently, the man had seen *Murder on the Orient Express* and thought that was the way I really looked!'

PETER USTINOV

'*A difficult chap to fathom*'

Peter Ustinov, the actor selected in 1978 to step into Poirot's neat little shoes for EMI's second film, *Death on the Nile*, following Albert Finney's decision not to repeat the role, soon learned about the difficulty of the task facing him. Although Agatha Christie had died in 1975, her daughter Rosalind was endeavouring to be even more careful that no liberties were taken with her mother's inimitable detective.

'At the premiere of *Death on the Nile* I was introduced to Agatha Christie's daughter,' Peter recalls with the hint of a smile creeping across his face. 'She was quite blunt. "You are not Poirot, Mr Ustinov," she said. To which I replied, "I am *now*, madam. I am now!"'

This was a line the engaging Mr Ustinov was to use thereafter with any and every Christie purist who might take him to task.

Since that meeting, however, the attitudes of many people towards Ustinov as Poirot have changed from an initial uncertainty to a genuine admiration. For Peter has played the Belgian detective no fewer than six times: three adaptations for the cinema; *Death on the Nile* (1978), *Evil Under The Sun* (1981) and *Appointment with Death* (1987), and three times for television; *Thirteen at Dinner* (1985), *Dead Man's Folly* (1986) and *Murder in Three Acts* (1986). With the exception of David Suchet, he has now played the Belgian detective more times than any other screen actor.

Ustinov, born in London in 1921 to a Russian father and French mother, is a multi-talented man – an actor, director, playwright, screenwriter and raconteur *par excellence*. But he has confessed rather shamefacedly that despite his wide range of interests, crime fiction is not one of them.

'I had never read a detective story or even any of Agatha Christie's books before taking on the role of Poirot,' he says. 'But the idea of playing a detective did appeal to me because it was such a relief from my usual casting as either a victim or a suspect.'

This enthusiasm for the part was no doubt part of the reason why he made a success as Poirot, although the quite different approach he adopted from that of his predecessors was also crucial. A prime reason for this was, as he says, because he is physically quite unlike the little Belgian, being bulky with a full head of hair. Neither is he as methodical or analytical in manner.

Discussing his initial approach to the role, Peter explains, 'Much as I admire Albert Finney, I think he was too conscientious in trying to be what the book said the man was. My interpretation had to be different. You only have to look at us to see that it would have had to be different!

'I am sure that Albert suffered playing the part. I have – it is a very exhausting part. You see, the character is so important to the films that you have to be on the set virtually every day. I'm used to sustaining long parts on the stage, of course, but the trouble with Poirot is that he is a difficult chap to fathom.

'Even Agatha Christie's biography doesn't help too much about his character. It seems he was created by a process of elimination. She wanted to create a detective and was very conscious of the success of Sherlock Holmes. So she didn't want him tall and thin. She thought he ought to be on the bald side and probably small. Then she thought he should be French, but decided that was too obvious and made him Belgian. She also made him absolutely cold and calculating . . .'

Peter pauses and twirls the ends of an imaginary moustache just as his Poirot might do, and then slips into a slightly accentuated voice to illustrate what he means.

'Poirot is so terribly accurate and tidy in his mind and habits. So meticulous. That's quite a strain on someone who isn't particularly gifted in that direction. I mean I do clip my nails every third day, but I'm not an ordered person.

'In fact, I'm the sort of man who likes to sit on the floor a lot. I just feel more comfortable there. Even in other people's houses, after about twenty minutes I get restless on the sofa and finish up on the floor. Poirot would *never* do that!' he laughs.

'Poirot is the sort of man who has a little sewing kit with him at all times so that an offending button on his underwear – that nobody could actually *see!* – can be replaced at a moment's notice. He is a very engaging character, but quite awful really.

'Actually I should hate to know him. He's so vain, self-contained and finicky. Do you know, people have asked me why he never married. The reason is simple. There is no room for more than himself in his life. If he did marry he'd have to solve the reason why. Another reason is that he's actually rather in love with himself. I sometimes think his real first name should be Narcisse, not Hercule.

'I'm sure he has been quite true to himself over the years. I don't think he's ever cheated on himself!' Peter adds.

This kind of insight into the character and attention to detail was to be a highlight of *Death on the Nile*. The original book, written in 1937, had evolved from trips Agatha Christie had made to Egypt, first as a teenager with her mother, and later with her husband, Max, and it always retained a special place in her affections. 'I think, myself, that the book is one of the best of my "foreign travel" ones,' she wrote years later. 'I think the central situation is intriguing and has dramatic possibilities.'

Co-producer John Brabourne agreed with the authoress's high opinion, though he decided to recruit one of the best playwrights in the business, Anthony Shaffer (author of the widely acclaimed play, *Sleuth*) to produce the screenplay, with John Guillerman to direct. Again a galaxy of stars was recruited to enact this story of a series of murders aboard a Nile steamer, including Bette Davis, David Niven, Maggie Smith, Mia Farrow, Jack Warden and Angela Lansbury (playing a woman novelist and destined two years later to play Miss Marple). It was decided to shoot as much of the picture as possible on the actual Egyptian locations – the first time any film company had worked in the unsettled country for years.

Peter Ustinov recalls vividly the six weeks spent on location between Aswan and Cairo as well as at the Sphinx, the pyramids and the ruins of Karnak and Luxor. 'Although I don't particularly like hot countries, I enjoyed exploring the place with my wife, Helene. Whenever the Egyptians saw me coming they'd start shouting, "Farouk! Farouk!". It was rather like a triumphant homecoming!'

He also remembers that the heat in Egypt was as much a problem for him as the studio lights had been for the padded and heavily made-up Albert Finney.

'But a steamboat is not like a train,' he says, 'It's not like a tube of toothpaste. There's more freedom of movement and it was possible to have a lot of flashbacks to break up the voyage.'

Peter thinks that the steamboat was as much a star of this film as the Orient Express had

Peter Ustinov in an enigmatic pose as Poirot in Death on the Nile *(1978)*

been in its predecessor. The boat was actually an adapted 138-foot-long Egyptian cruiser specially painted in brilliant blue and white.

The twelve cabins of the steamer were recreated at Pinewood for the remainder of the filming, and these were kept under tight security with no visitors allowed on the set in order to preserve the mystery of 'who-dun-it'. Peter still jokes that there was no chance of him giving the game away because he had found a highly original way of keeping an edge on his performance.

'Although I read the script I could never actually remember who did the murder,' he says. 'I have no interest in who did what to whom and why. I deliberately blocked the name of the culprit out of my mind. It was a good thing, probably, because it helped keep my perform- ance fresh – and it's something I've done ever since.'

Ustinov's performance as Poirot was certainly fresh, and it earned him the accolade of 'Best Actor of the Year' from the Variety Club of Great Britain. Four years later, in 1982, he was happy to accept the offer from John Brabourne to play the detective again in *Evil Under the Sun*. This movie was to be given a Royal Command Premiere at which Peter met the Queen and discovered that Poirot was one of her favourite fictional detectives.

'Her Majesty told me that she particularly wanted to see this film as she had liked the way I played Poirot in *Death on the Nile*. I was very pleased and flattered.'

In his second appearance as Poirot, Peter deliberately made the detective a wittier and more flamboyant figure. He also made the detective's accent a little more extravagant. Explaining these changes, Peter says:

'Agatha Christie only made Poirot a Belgian because someone told her there were far too many French detectives around. With another stroke of the pen she could easily have turned him into a Luxembourgeois. On the printed page Poirot is no more Belgian than Major Thompson is English.

'In language terms we probably see him as one of those foreign schoolmasters whose English is too correct – all very fluent and fluid and quite artificial. Remember that Poirot only puts the simplest words into French, the complex ones are always left in English.

'But I did develop a genuine Belgian accent for him,' he adds. 'It came from listening to the Belgian Ambassador to Paris. He does not drop his aitches but instead adds them where they are not supposed to be! So you get words like "halibi" which is how a Belgian might talk.'

Poirot confronts the awful Salome Otterbourne (Angela Lansbury) in Death on the Nile. *Two years later Angela was to become an impressive Miss Marple*

Peter in the swimsuit he devised specially for Evil Under the Sun *(1982)*

Peter also contributed to the actual making of the film by adding lines to Poirot's dialogue and inventing a swimsuit for one of the crucial sequences.

Anthony Shaffer was again responsible for scripting the picture, but this time decided to shift the location of the original 1941 novel about a woman found on a beach, originally set by Agatha Christie on her native Devon coast. Instead, the beach became a dazzling resort on the Adriatic and the typically English hostelry, the Jolly Roger, became a luxurious hotel fit for a king. Against this background, Guy Hamilton, famous for his work as the director of four James Bond movies, fashioned a glossy and exotic picture. It was he who suggested that location filming should take place on Majorca after the producers had combed the Mediterranean for an unspoiled holiday resort. As a resident of the island he knew precisely where to film.

Peter also enjoyed working on Majorca, though he again emphasises that no great liberties were taken with Agatha Christie's work.

'The form of the original story was preserved exactly,' Peter says; 'what we did was to put a little flesh on the bones and give it a more colourful setting. I think Poirot also had some better lines – some of which I put in myself!'

Agatha Christie was herself a keen swimmer and loved modern bathing costumes – a fact which inspired Peter Ustinov's other contribution to the picture: an invented scene in which Poirot, normally unhappy on a beach, let alone in the water, actually goes into the sea. For this Peter devised a two-piece costume.

'I wanted one of those pre-war bathing suits which were so absorbent that wearing them wet was like being slapped across the skin with a Dover sole!' he recalls with a laugh. 'We also wanted a break in the film – the form is as rigid as an interview, with Poirot asking all the questions and not being able to put on a bravura performance until the very end.'

Once again a star-studded cast played out the mystery, this time including James Mason, Sylvia Miles, Diana Rigg, Maggie Smith, Jane Birkin, Roddy McDowall and Colin Blakely. Peter Ustinov finished the filming convinced there would be more Poirot films in the future.

In fact, though, the actor was to come face to face with a real murder before playing the detective again. In November 1984 he was in New Delhi to record an interview with the Indian Prime Minister, Mrs Gandhi, when she was assassinated only yards away from where he was waiting to meet her.

There is still a note of sadness that creeps into his voice when he speaks of that terrible event. 'As she came towards me I heard several shots. I heard three individual shots followed by the rattle of bren-gun bullets. Then there were two more bursts of an automatic weapon. That would have been the end of at least one of the assassins.

'After the shooting the film team and I were held by police and questioned at length, but we were released after five hours. It was an awful experience – I had never expected to be quite so close to death as I was during those moments.'

Peter had to put these events behind him when he returned to London early in 1985 to film *Thirteen at Dinner*, the first of what were to be three Poirot cases made especially for television. Behind this project was the American company Warner Bros TV.

Thirteen at Dinner was a 90-minute updated version of *Lord Edgware Dies*, scripted by Rod Browning. In this new story, Poirot appears on the David Frost TV show and meets a blonde American actress who is supposed to be Jane Wilkinson, the wife of Lord Edgware. In fact she is Carlotta Adams, a professional impersonator, and the real Jane is so impressed with the 'act' that she invites Carlotta and Poirot to dinner. During the course of the meal, Jane announces that because her husband will not give her a divorce she would like to get rid of him. When he is later found dead, she naturally heads the list of suspects . . .

Starring in the production with Peter were Faye Dunaway, as both Jane and Carlotta; Lee Horsley, as an actor whose he-man image is created by stunt men; Jonathan Cecil as a faithful and zanily humble Hastings; and David Suchet getting his first taste of Christie on TV, playing Inspector Japp!

In reviewing the show on 19 October 1985, John J. O'Connor of the *New York Times* said of Japp and Poirot:

> The Inspector gives M Poirot endless opportunities for delivering pompous lectures: 'A good crime is like a fine omelette – it is plain on the outside and you only discover the first clue when you put your fork in.' Mr Ustinov, of course, rarely leaves centre stage and he manages to keep the action percolating nicely as, a splendid wardrobe draping his considerable girth, M Poirot sets about revealing his very special talents, which include, at one point, an ability to speed-read upside down.

A nice touch in the film which amused both Peter and David Suchet is the moment when an American producer at a cocktail party turns to Poirot and wonders if, as a famous detective, 'you've got a mini-series in you?' To which Poirot responds, 'I doubt it – I don't even have my tonsils any more!' (*Thirteen at Dinner* was later shown in Britain on LWT in June 1986.)

Less than six months later, Ustinov played Poirot a fourth time in *Dead Man's Folly*, a two-hour adaptation of Agatha's 1956 mystery in which the Belgian detective is teamed up with Mrs Ariadne Oliver, a parody of her creator. Rod Browning again wrote the screenplay and the director was Clive Donner.

The story centres on a chance meeting between Poirot and Mrs Oliver at Harrods when she invites him to a country weekend at which she has arranged a fictitious murder hunt complete with carefully planted clues. Poirot accepts – but the fake murder turns out to be a real one, the victim being a rather common local girl.

Dead Man's Folly featured Jonathan Cecil as Hastings again; Jean Singleton as Ariadne

Oliver; Tim Piggott-Smith as the country house owner; and Constance Cummings as the former owner of the estate now living in a small lodge.

The *New York Times* thought the production 'a laboured romp', but when it was screened in Britain by ITV on Christmas Day, 1986, the *Daily Mail* described Peter's performance as 'twinklingly gracing our screens'. The impetus of the series continued, and for their third television special, Warner Brothers decided on rather more exotic locations than England, and travelled to Mexico and Acapulco to make *Murder in Three Acts*.

This 105-minute movie – also billed as 'Agatha Christie's Three Act Tragedy' – was directed by Gary Nelson and based on the 1935 novel, *Three Act Tragedy*. Adapted by Scott Swinton, it brought Poirot to Acapulco intent on beginning work on his memoirs only to be coerced into attending a cocktail party in a hill-top mansion belonging to a very successful, but now retired character actor named Charles Cartwright. As the assorted guests, mostly Americans living in the surrounding area, are drinking a toast, one, a harmless looking priest, suddenly falls over dead, and Poirot realises he will have to use his 'little grey cells' for solving a new crime rather than writing about old ones.

Cartwright was played by Tony Curtis, making his second Christie movie, having earlier appeared in the Miss Marple case, *The Mirror Crack'd* (1980). Also in the cast were Emma Samms, as a young amateur detective somewhat besotted by Cartwright; Dana Eclar as neurologist Dr Strange; and Jonathan Cecil once more the devoted Hastings.

After the screening on 30 September 1986, John J. O'Connor wrote:

> Mr Ustinov's Poirot is kept busy offering unsolicited wisdom ('The truth must be respected at all times') or being terribly cute – trying to filch a piece of fruit at an open market or falling asleep in front of his beeping data processor. Miss Christie, you see, has been brought up to date for these TV adaptations.

This was not to be the case the following July when Peter Ustinov again found himself in a hot location – this time Israel, for the third and latest of his EMI big-budget Poirot movies, *Appointment with Death*. As with its predecessors, a line-up of top stars was assembled by director Michael Winner including Lauren Bacall, Jenny Seagrove, Michael Sarrazin, Piper Laurie, Carrie Fisher, Hayley Mills and the Christie regular, Sir John Gielgud.

Adapted from the 1938 novel in which Poirot, while on holiday in Jerusalem, overhears a conversation planning the murder of a woman, *Appointment with Death* was kept firmly in its original period by the scriptwriters, Anthony Shaffer, Peter Buckman and Michael Winner. Despite all this to-ing and fro-ing in time periods between TV and film, Peter continued to play Poirot very much as he had done from the beginning, though he did once confess to a journalist during filming that his character 'must now be a hundred and forty-two or a hundred and forty-three because he only took up detective work when he retired from the Belgian police!'

He continued, 'Playing Poirot has become a little like Bach on the violin, you have to say the same thing all the time, but do it differently. You have to relax in the part.'

In fact, it was not easy for him or any of the cast or crew to relax in the intense heat of Israel, and there were two car crashes while on location – one so badly injuring the actor Michael Sarrazin that he had to be replaced by David Soul.

Yet, despite such problems and the fact he is approaching 70, Peter told the press after completing the film that he still has plans for his Poirot.

'It's not my ambition to spend my life playing him,' he said with a grin, 'and after the next one I'd probably have to play the part in a wheelchair, like Raymond Burr. I have said I'd like to do a Poirot set in wartime with Hercule measuring out his ration of powdered egg and assessing the quality of the Spam! I'd be a little annoyed if anyone else did him now.'

But of course David Suchet, the man who followed so dumbfoundedly in his footsteps playing Inspector Japp in *Thirteen at Dinner*, has done just that.

IAN HOLM

'An object of wrath!'

It was in 1986 that the English television producer and scriptwriter, Nick Evans, had the unusual idea of devising a confrontation between Hercule Poirot and Agatha Christie: a meeting of the creator and the creation whom she ultimately came to resent for 'hanging round my neck like the old man of the sea'.

Nick's hour-long television drama, *Murder by the Book*, not only provided an intriguing story, but also one of the best portrayals of Poirot, this time by Ian Holm. Nick Evans himself explains how the unique story was conceived.

'I got the idea after reading a biography of Dame Agatha which mentioned her resentment of Poirot. I thought: "I wonder what would have happened if Poirot had actually met his maker?" Mind you, my imagined confrontation between the humourless detective and his creator was not intended as a send-up, but it does contain a lot of the ingredients which are to be found in Christie. A country house, a bottle of poison, old revolvers, a maid and a gardener – even a dog like hers that used to bite everyone!'

Nick's story brings Poirot to a splendid but sinister country house just as night is falling. He knows he is about to face the most vital case of his career. A murder is to be committed – and he is the intended victim.

The house is, of course, the home of Agatha Christie, who is intent on killing him. There follows a battle of wits involving Arabian daggers, an old army revolver in a chest of drawers, a bottle of deadly mole poison and a final, murderous chase along moonlit corridors . . .

'There was an element of comedy about Nick Evans's script which made it such fun to do,' Ian Holm recalls, 'plus the challenge of trying to play Poirot as Dame Agatha had intended him. I knew she disliked all the screen and stage portrayals during her lifetime, so it was

Ian Holm brilliantly impersonated Poirot in the TVS production of Murder by the Book *(1986)*

Poirot (Ian Holm) with the tools of his trade in Murder by the Book

obviously important that the figure who confronted Agatha should be Poirot to a T.'

Ian, a doctor's son born in Goodmayes in 1930, who has played many of the leading Shakespearean roles with great panache, as well as proving himself one of the country's best character actors, looked at all his predecessors before deciding how he was going to play Poirot. A perfectionist by nature, he knew his own diminutive build (5 feet 6 inches) and oval-shaped head were an immediate advantage.

His research led him to the one source that all the other Poirots had missed. Not the original books, but a drawing which had appeared in *The Sketch* magazine in the spring of 1923 illustrating the serialisation of twelve Poirot short stories.

'It appears that Agatha Christie thought this drawing was the closest to the mental picture she had of him in her mind,' he says. 'The *Sketch* drawing proved absolutely vital to me. It showed the real Poirot was short, extremely dapper and with a most elegant moustache. He was certainly *not* fat.'

Ian had, though, to suffer for his art. His make-up as Poirot stretched his features and to achieve the little detective's high-domed forehead, he had to have his own hairline shaved back by three inches.

'I would like to think Agatha Christie would have approved of my Poirot,' he says, 'because she could be quite an old battle-axe when things weren't right. She had a wicked tongue and vented a lot of her wrath on Poirot.'

Ian must, therefore, have taken pleasure from the *Daily Mail* which headlined its review of the production transmitted on 28 August: 'At last . . . a Hercule Poirot that even Agatha would like!'

Agatha Christie was played by the formidable Dame Peggy Ashcroft who presented a stunning likeness to the late 'Queen of Crime'. Also appearing were Richard Wilson as her husband, Sir Max Mallowan; Michael Aldridge as her literary agent, Edmund Cork; and Dawn Archibald and John Atkinson as two servants.

'I have a shrewd suspicion that if Hercule Poirot could have chosen his own end it would have been while he was still vigorous and upright rather than crippled in a wheelchair,' says Ian Holm recalling the death Agatha Christie actually inflicted on her hero in the novel *Curtain: Poirot's Last Case* (1975). 'But the truth is, of course, that he's now one of the immortals up there with Sherlock Holmes and the rest of the great figures of literature.'

DAVID SUCHET

'The greatest lateral-thinking detective ever created'

David Suchet, whose playing of the character in LWT's *Poirot* series has led to him being dubbed the 'definitive' Hercule Poirot by several critics and a large number of Christie fans, had long nursed an ambition to play the part, especially after appearing as the Belgian detective's foil, Inspector Japp, in the 1985 television version of *Thirteen at Dinner*.

'Of the various fictional characters I've read, Poirot's always been one I wanted to play,' David says. 'I knew it meant stepping into the shoes of other well-known actors like Albert Finney and Peter Ustinov, but I have played plenty of other familiar roles like Shylock, Iago, Caliban and even the Fool in *Lear*, so it was a feeling I was rather used to.

'I especially wanted to play Poirot after appearing in the Peter Ustinov film. I enjoyed Peter's Poirot, but it was never as I envisaged him. It wasn't rooted in Christie, in that he never attempted to become physically like him, or indeed pick up the personal eccentricities of the character.

'You see we've now got a generation who knows Poirot visually rather than through litera-

*The definitive Poirot: a characteristic portrait
of David Suchet in the LWT series*

Hugh Fraser as Captain Hastings and David Suchet as Poirot in a scene from 'Double Sin', in the second LWT series

ture, so what Agatha Christie wrote became my anchor point for playing him,' he says.

David has, of course, a considerable advantage over his predecessor in that he is almost the same height as Poirot, has his egg-shaped head, receding hair and brightly searching eyes. Only his figure needed padding to achieve the required transformation for the cameras.

'I have to wear a large amount of false padding on my tummy, chest and back and shoulders to get the right shape,' he explains, 'and the wing collar helps make my face look fatter. I'm actually fairly slim in reality – I normally weigh eleven stone two pounds, but I have to look fifteen stone. It's all an illusion – but then that's the story of my life!'

David Suchet was born in 1948, the son of an eminent Harley Street gynaecologist, and originally had no intentions of becoming an actor. As a small boy he wanted to be a cowboy!

He did, though, argue ferociously with his brothers about how the part should be played. (David has two brothers, John Suchet, who is a television newscaster, and Peter, who works in advertising.)

'I was meticulous even then,' he says, referring to his childhood. 'I wanted the right gun for the right holster!'

It was almost as if he was beginning to prepare for his role as the fussy and precise little Belgian detective.

David had his first taste of acting at school in Somerset when he was selected to play the part of a girl, Mary Bohum, in *Richard of Bordeaux*. He was even asked to have his legs shaved so he could wear a pair of tights, but refused.

Initially, he thought of following his father into the medical profession, but in his teens preferred being a jazz drummer and the centre of attention.

'Strangely, one of the things I have found happening to me as I have got older is that I've become more introverted.'

It was a visit to the National Youth Theatre at the Royal Court when he was eighteen that made him decide on a career on the stage, and after training at LAMDA, he joined the Gateway Theatre in Chester. Since then, with the exception of a brief spell out of work in the 1970s, his painstakingly developed skills have kept him busy in the theatre, in films and in television, as well as on the radio.

Though David's work in the classical theatre with the Royal Shakespeare Company earned him good notices, it was undoubtedly his portrayal of Sigmund Freud in the 1984 BBC2 series, *Freud*, followed by the enigmatic Blott in Tom Sharpe's uproarious farce, *Blott on the Landscape*, that thrust him into the limelight. The latter also won him the 'Best Actor of the Year' award from the Royal Television Society in 1986.

Like Poirot, David is a perfectionist where his work is concerned, and when the producer Brian Eastman – who had worked with him on *Blott on the Landscape* – offered him the role of the detective in 1988 he promptly read all 40 short stories and studied every word that Agatha Christie had written about her creation.

Brian Eastman says of his star, 'David is an actor I have always admired, particularly in the role of an anglicised foreigner. He has a wonderful ability to pick on the idiosyncrasies of the British character and turn them to use as a foreigner. He was perfect for Poirot.'

Describing his preparation for the role, David continues, 'I wanted to be as truthful to the original as I could be. I was not going to play Poirot as a caricature. The result is that I am playing him with all the facets which I believe Christie gave him in her books.

'Do you know, I even found out Poirot's telephone number,' he smiles. 'If anyone wants to give him a ring it is Trafalgar 8137!'

David also spent a lot of time developing a soft French accent – and sometimes found it hard to shake it off at the end of a day's shooting.

'I had to keep up the accent all day – even when I was not on the set,' he explains, 'because if I had to keep going in and out of the voice it added up to an hour to my day.

'I once arrived home still talking Poirot-speak – as I used to sit in the car learning my lines on the way home for the next day's filming – and it caused much hilarity to my family.'

David believes Poirot's moustache is a crucial key to understanding the man.

'In the books the moustache is variously described as being stiff and military, or alternatively small, tight and very finely curled. But what is more important is what Poirot *himself* says about it. He says it has to be a thing of beauty and must suit his face because he is a very vain man.

'I had to find the look to find the man. The moment I put the moustache on I took on his personality. Then, and only then, did I really feel I had *become* Poirot. But the more I have become Poirot, the more I have enjoyed him,' he says.

David has the same eye for order as the little detective. 'I like things to be symmetrical. If I put two things on the mantelpiece they have to be exactly evenly spaced, that sort of thing.

But I am nowhere near as fanatical as Poirot – I don't need exactly the same sized eggs for breakfast, as he did.'

The actor does admit, though, that the parts he plays do have a habit of taking him over.

'My wife Sheila quite likes living with Poirot. She says I have become much more tidy as a result. She wasn't so keen on Freud, because he was a manic depressive. He became the sitting tenant I couldn't evict. But those who know me say that as Poirot I'm good fun to be with.'

After he had played Poirot in the first ten stories, David had reached these conclusions about the role: 'He is a man of supreme intelligence, a walking brain. He is the greatest lateral-thinking detective ever created in literature, far greater than Sherlock Holmes.

'One of the things I wanted to bring out about him was his love of life, which very much includes his work. He is a workaholic and neurotic when not working. I'm like him there, in that I don't like not working.

'He also loves people and he is a great twinkler, especially with the opposite sex. He is a confirmed bachelor, of course, completely non-sexual, but he does flirt. I'm told by people that I'm a twinkler. I don't see myself as a flirt, although I am capable of being one!

'Poirot is, though, quite different to me in that he is a loner and I am not. I am a family man – my whole life is centred around my wife and the two children, Robert and Katherine, which I regard as incredibly important.'

Right from the moment LWT decided to make the series, it was agreed that this should be a faithful recreation of the suave, brainy and egotistical Poirot and his world. It was also decided to set all the episodes in 1935 rather than range across the years as do the original stories. This put special demands on Clive Exton who was the main adapter, as well as the designer, Rob Harris, who had to find locations still much as they were in the Thirties.

But this eye for the architecture and fashions of that era, matched with the acting of David Suchet and his co-stars, helped earn the series the highest accolades. *The Sunday Times*, for instance, declared, 'David Suchet is well on the way to becoming the screen's most accurate Poirot so far,' while Alan Coren in *The Mail on Sunday* enthused, 'David Suchet's Poirot is an immeasurable improvement on Peter Ustinov's . . . by homing in unerringly on the most telegenic of Poirot's quirks, he has succeeded in making the character entirely his own. He has given us a Belgian dandy, meticulous of cuff and spat, as much obsessed by sartorial detail as forensic.'

Playing Poirot's assistant, Captain Hastings, actor Hugh Fraser has enjoyed appearing as a likeable character after several villainous roles in recent TV productions such as *Edge of Darkness* and *Jack the Ripper*. He sees parallels between his partnership with Poirot and that other famous pair, Holmes and Watson.

'Watson asks the questions that the audience want to ask,' he explains. 'Poirot, like Holmes, is a lateral thinker and one of Hastings's functions is to elucidate what is going on in Poirot's mind for the audience. I am certain it is a working relationship and that Poirot actually employs him.'

And of his own character, he adds: 'He's a likeable chap – he's not a great brain but then he's not a fool either, although he certainly isn't in the same league as Poirot as regards the "little grey cells"!'

The first hour-long episode, transmitted on 8 January 1989, was Clive Exton's adaptation of 'The Adventure of the Clapham Cook' in which Poirot tackles the mystery of a missing cook and a bank clerk who has absconded with £50,000. The story introduced Pauline Moran as the detective's equally fastidious secretary, Miss Lemon; and Philip Jackson as the down-to-earth policeman, Chief Inspector Japp. Also appearing were Brigit Forsyth and Dermot Crowley, and the director was Edward Bennett.

Clive Exton also dramatised 'Murder in the Mews', the story of a very unusual death on Guy Fawkes night, again directed by Edward Bennett, and co-starring Juliette Mole, David Yelland and James Faulkner. The third case, 'The Adventure of Johnnie Waverly', again adapted by Exton, had Poirot unable to prevent the kidnapping of a rich man's son but deducing that the culprit must surely be a relative. Renny Rye was the director, and the co-stars were Geoffrey Bateman, Julia Chambers and Patrick Jordan.

Russell Murray was the scriptwriter of 'Four and Twenty Blackbirds' in which the over-hearing of a chance remark during a quiet meal put Poirot on the trail of a murder and an ill-gotten inheritance. Renny Rye again directed, and the co-stars were Richard Howard, Holly de Jong and Tony Aitken. The fifth case, 'The Third-Floor Flat', dramatised by Michael Baker, produced a murder in Poirot's very own block of flats. It was directed by Edward Bennett and co-starred Suzanne Burden, Amanda Elwes, Josie Lawrence and Captain Hastings's treasured Lagonda car.

A change of location to the exotic Greek islands made 'Triangle at Rhodes', adapted by Stephen Wakelam, one of the highlights of the series. The story of a mysterious poisoning

The new Poirot has become a favourite of the cartoonists: this sketch is by Gary of the Daily Mail

among the guests at the hotel where Poirot was staying called for the most astute use of his 'little grey cells' to unmask an unlikely killer. The co-stars were Peter Settelen, Annie Lambert and Frances Low; the director was once more Renny Rye.

A Mediterranean cruise provided the background to 'Problem at Sea', again scripted by Clive Exton. The murder of an obnoxious guest while her husband is ashore in Alexandria called for the special investigative skills of Poirot once again. Renny Rye was the director, and the co-stars were Sheila Allen, John Normington and Ann Firbank. Exton worked jointly with David Reid on 'The Incredible Theft', which had Poirot setting out to recover the missing plans for a secret aircraft. Edward Bennett returned to direct this story which co-starred John Stride, John Carson and Phyllida Law.

'The King of Clubs', adapted by Michael Baker, took Poirot into the world of film-making and the murder of an unsavoury impresario. The co-stars were Niamh Cusack, David Swift and Gawn Grainger, and the director was Renny Rye. Concluding the first series was 'The Dream', again scripted by Clive Exton, which presented Poirot with the puzzle of a man who has been dreaming of suicide and is then found dead, apparently by his own hand. As always, though, there was a more murderous explanation to be brilliantly discovered by Poirot. The director was Edward Bennett, and the co-stars were Alan Howard, Joely Richardson and Mary Tamm.

The end of the series brought praise both from viewers and the press. Writing to the *TV*

Left: *Hugh Fraser, David Suchet and Philip Jackson (Inspector Japp) in 'Double Sin', and* (right) *the three actors on location for 'The Cornish Mystery'*

Times, Amy Cotsford of Sittingbourne in Kent said, 'I was convinced that here was the definitive Poirot.' And Margaret Forwood of *The People* echoed the widespread view that 'LWT have followed the BBC's superb casting of Joan Hickson as Miss Marple with David Suchet just the way Poirot should have been all along.'

The success of the series deservedly led to a second to mark the centenary year, consisting of eight one-hour episodes and a special two-hour version of the classic mystery, *Peril at End House*. The team of David Suchet, Hugh Fraser, Pauline Moran and Philip Jackson again reprised their central roles.

The start of the new series on 7 January was widely covered in the press, *The Sunday Times* in particular welcoming the return of David Suchet's 'definitive, understated portrayal of the Belgian detective'. It was announced, too, that the series was to be shown in the USA, where the star for one was sure it would succeed.

'The Americans will find Poirot old-fashioned, but I think that will be a big point in his favour,' said David. 'They will find it like *Upstairs, Downstairs* with clues!'

Talking about continuing in the role, he added, 'I think the second series has slightly broadened his character. I've tried to make him light, humorous and witty; although you must take his brilliance seriously, you can still smile and laugh with Poirot.'

Also appearing in the prime-time showing of *Peril at End House*, dramatised by Clive Exton, and directed by Renny Rye, were Polly Walker, John Harding, Jeremy Young and Mary Cunningham.

The second story, 'The Veiled Lady', again scripted by Clive Exton, was taken from the first collection, *Poirot Investigates* (1924), and dealt with the recovery of a love letter which threatens the marriage of Lady Millicent Vaughn. The co-stars were Frances Barber, Terence Harvey and Carole Hayman, with Edward Bennett directing.

'Double Sin', about a stolen case of miniatures, and the title story of Agatha's 1961 American collection, provided the third story in the series. Clive Exton was the dramatiser, Richard Spence the director, and the co-stars were Adam Kotz, Paul Gabriel, Caroline

Milmoe, Gerard Horan, David Hargreaves, Michael J. Shannon, Amanda Garwood and Elspet Gray. 'The Lost Mine' (also from *Poirot Investigates*), about Poirot's possession of valuable shares in a Burmese mine by virtue of having solved the murder of a Chinese businessman in London, was the fourth case, with co-stars Vincent Wong, Richard Albrecht, Anthony Bate and Julian Firth. The script was by Michael Baker and David Renwick, and Edward Bennett directed.

A suspected case of poisoning provided the background to 'The Cornish Mystery', a somewhat gentler case for the Belgian detective which co-starred Amanda Walker, Tilly Vosburgh, Jerome Willis and Derek Benfield, with a script by Clive Exton and Edward Bennett as director. The sixth episode, 'The Adventure of a Cheap Flat', written by Russell Murray, in which Poirot's suspicions were aroused as to why a particular flat in an expensive block of apartments was being rented at a ridiculously low sum, co-starred Samantha Bond and John Michie, with Richard Spence again directing.

Another *Poirot Investigates* case, 'The Kidnapped Prime Ministers', about the disappearance of the leader of the government on the eve of a crucial conference, dramatised by Clive Exton and directed by Andrew Grieve, co-starred Timothy Block, Jack Elliott, David Horovitch, Ronald Hines and Lisa Harrow.

The penultimate story, 'The Adventure of the Western Star', scripted by Clive Exton, involved Poirot in a society scandal about some diamonds belonging to two rival beauties, and co-starred Caroline Goodall, Rosalind Bennett and Bruce Montague. The director was Richard Spence.

Then by an interesting twist of fate that old favourite, 'The Disappearance of Mr Davenheim', which had launched the first television Poirot, Martin Gabel, back in 1962, provided David Suchet with his bow in the second series. It was scripted by David Renwick and directed by Andrew Grieve. Co-starring with David in this formidable display of the powers of Poirot's 'little grey cells' which again hinted at more cases to come were Mel Martin, Fiona McArthur, Ken Colley and Tony Mathews.

A LADY WITH MURDER TO REPORT

Six actresses who have portrayed the famous sleuth of St Mary Mead

---

BARBARA MULLEN

'*A woman who is so adventurous*'

Barbara Mullen, the actress with the distinction of having first played Miss Marple, crowned her career as one of the best-known and best-loved characters on television, Janet McPherson, the white-haired, softly-spoken housekeeper to the doctors in the long-running BBC series, *Dr Finlay's Casebook*. Originally intended to run for only six episodes – with Barbara allocated just two lines in one episode – the stories of young Dr Finlay (Bill Simpson) and his crotchety older partner, Dr Cameron (Andrew Cruikshank), quickly became compulsive Sunday evening viewing and the programme ran from 1962 to 1971. Thereafter it continued as a radio serial with the same trio of actors until 1978.

The heart-warming tales of the medical practice based in Arden House, Tannochbrae made Barbara, who seemed the epitome of the selfless Scottish gentlewoman, a star in the later years of what had been an amazing life and career. Yet she had, in fact, been born in poverty in 1914 in Boston, USA, where her parents had emigrated from Aran Island.

Barbara's fame as Janet McPherson has, not surprisingly, rather obscured her achievements as Miss Marple, a part which she played on the London stage in two productions, over a quarter of a century apart, of *The Murder at the Vicarage*. She always remembered the role with pleasure, just as she did her contact with Agatha Christie.

'I met her when the first production was being put on at the Playhouse in London in the winter of 1949,' Janet recalled in one of the last interviews she gave before her sudden death from a heart attack in 1979. 'We got on very well, but she didn't try to tell me how to play the part, though I know she had her own ideas. She was a very reticent lady – an acute observer of human nature, much like Miss Marple: she just watched all the time.

'To play Miss Marple you have to study Agatha Christie. Though she was a very shy person and talked very little about herself, I think the part is as near a self-portrait as you can get.'

An an author herself – Barbara wrote a revealing autobiography, *Life Is My Adventure*, in 1938 – she understood Agatha Christie's reticence. 'I know that a bit of yourself creeps into everything you write, but as a writer I never talk about myself. As an actress, yes – acting is giving out in public all the time – but writing is lonely and alone: it's between yourself and your brain and your heart and your pen. That's all and nobody can come into that.'

Her book is full of the rich detail of her life which began in the horrors of the American Depression in South Boston. She was one of ten children raised by her mother in a home over a Chinese restaurant. She remembers vividly that her mother made money during the Prohibition years by running a speakeasy in their home and making moonshine whisky in the cellar below.

From her infancy, dancing was Barbara's great passion and she made her stage debut at the age of three. By the time she was a teenager she had won numerous dancing trophies and a career in show business seemed inevitable. (One of the trophies which Barbara kept all her life bore a bullet hole made by a police revolver used in a raid on the speakeasy!) In the years which followed she worked hard at dancing, singing, reciting and taking small parts in plays. She was prepared to travel anywhere around Boston to find work.

'There were no other jobs, except entertainment,' she recalled. 'When times are bad people want to be entertained. But they expect you to be good – it was great training.'

Barbara developed her skills in this demanding school for almost twenty years before coming to Britain in search of more work. Her vast experience made her invaluable to repertory companies and from there it was a short step to the London stage, films and television. Among her stage appearances were the West End hit, *Jeannie* (1940; filmed the following year), *What Every Woman Knows* (1943) and *Arsenic and Old Lace* (1947). Her films included *Thunder Rock* (1942), *A Place of One's Own* (1945) and *Corridor of Mirrors* (1948), while she made her debut on television – the medium which was to bring her lasting fame – as early as 1938, dancing in an Irish programme transmitted by the BBC from Alexandra Palace.

It was on 14 December 1949, however, that – according to *The Daily Telegraph* – she 'scored a great success as Miss Marple in *The Murder at the Vicarage*'.

Although Agatha Christie had intended to adapt her novel for the stage, it was the dramatists Moie Charles and Barbara Toy who wrote the two-act play. The authoress did, however,

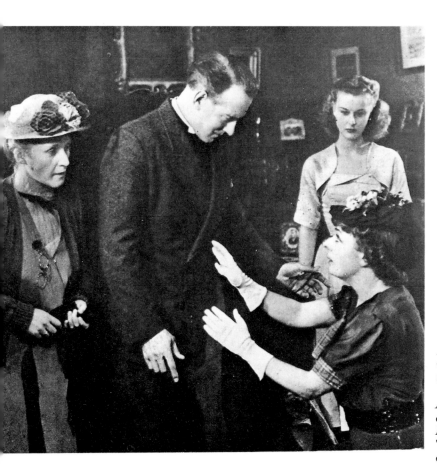

Above: *The young Barbara Mullen, who was transformed on stage into the first Miss Marple in 1949*

A rare photograph of Barbara Mullen as Miss Marple at the Playhouse, London, in the 1949 production of The Murder at the Vicarage. *With her are Jack Lambert, Genine Graham and Betty Sinclair*

take a keen interest in the adaptation and flatly refused to allow one liberty: Miss Marple fainting at the end of the play. 'It really is corny,' she told Barbara Toy, 'just done for the curtain – and absolutely untypical of her!'

The producer of *The Murder at the Vicarage* was Reginald Tate, who also took a leading role as Lawrence Redding. Among the cast were Michael Derbyshire as the curate, Revd Ronald Hanes; Francis Roberts as Dr Haydock; Genine Graham as Griselda; and, of course, Barbara.

Talking in 1975 about the play and her part in it, Barbara said: 'It was a very difficult role then – as it still is. I was thirtyish playing sixtyish and it was Miss Marple's first detective case. So there was very little to go on in the book for her character.'

Such modesty disguises the measure of her achievement in transferring the detective to the stage – an achievement which *The Times*'s reviewer acknowledged by reference to Agatha Christie's other famous sleuth who had already made several appearances in the theatre and cinema.

'There is perhaps a certain piquancy in the fact that Hercule Poirot's place is taken by an inquisitive village spinster, but she uses the master's methods and is immediately ratiocinative . . . Barbara Mullen is Miss Marple, and once she is allowed to take a firm, practical hold on the story she manipulates it with all possible skill.'

The Murder at the Vicarage proved one of the hits of that winter season and ran for 1,776 performances, after which Barbara moved on to other work. She was both surprised and delighted when, some 26 years later, she was asked to appear in a revival of the same play at the Savoy Theatre in July 1975, with Derek Bond and Carolyn Moody as her co-stars.

In the intervening years, Miss Marple had been featured in some twenty cases and Barbara, at 61, was almost precisely her character's age. On the evening of the opening night she had this to say:

'It is not until now, when I've studied all the other books, that I've found out Miss Marple's idiosyncracies. It's only by studying what she grows into that you find out what she was in that first case. Now, after thirty years, I see her quite differently.

'I know she's a gentlewoman of reduced means, but she's indomitable as an avenging fury. She believes absolutely in good and evil, and fights evil tooth and nail. But that doesn't diminish her sense of fun – she has a subtle, sly, round-the-corner sense of humour which creeps up on you unbeknown.

'I know now that she has excellent taste in clothes – few clothes, but in the sharpest possible taste for an elderly lady. She's a slight figure of a woman, which I like because she has such courage. And later on she has a lady to look after her who fusses, which irritates her – it would me! – for a woman who's been so adventurous.'

Though the revival proved a success with the public – actually running for two years and more performances than the original – few of the national newspaper critics liked the play, *The Times*'s Charles Lewsen calling it an 'exhibit from the Agatha Christie museum'. But Barbara's understanding of the character only slightly softened Lewsen's otherwise damning prose.

'Of course, everyone has a motive for killing nasty Colonel Protheroe – and must be questioned by the slow-witted professional detective and shrewd, intuitive Miss Marple who, like the heroine of a Victorian melodrama, has been in danger of having her land appropriated by the villainous colonel. As Miss Marple, Barbara Mullen opens her eyes winsomely and narrows them shrewdly . . . and to demonstrate the intuitive undercurrents that give life to her intellectual shafts, she has invented a series of staccato semaphore tics that suggest Imogen Holst conducting the Rolling Stones!'

Throughout her life, Barbara Mullen maintained that 'a bit of oneself rubs off on to every part you play, and a bit of the part rubs off on to you'. In the case of Miss Marple, a little of her can be seen in all her successors, just as she has admitted that there was some of the detective's indomitable character and calm resolve to be seen in Dr Finlay's housekeeper, Janet.

GRACIE FIELDS

'A quiet lady with a nose for murder'

Although America was the country in which Miss Marple made her television debut in 1956, it was an English actress who actually brought her to the small screen. The choice, though, was as extraordinary as any to be found in the annals of Christie casting – none other than the 'Lancashire Lass', Gracie Fields.

Gracie, the vivacious former music-hall performer turned comedienne, singer and actress, was almost the opposite in every respect from the gentle little spinster detective. Perhaps only her age, 58 at the time of the TV production, was close to that of Miss Marple.

The story which brought Jane Marple to the screen was an adaptation of the novel, *A Murder Is Announced*, first published six years earlier, and widely acclaimed as a masterpiece of crime. It was also heralded by Agatha Christie's publishers on both sides of the Atlantic as her 50th book. The story marked the return of Miss Marple after a seven year absence and introduced Chief Inspector Craddock who would help her in the unravelling of three mysterious murders in the typical English village of Chipping Cleghorn.

The TV show on which this adaptation was shown was the *Goodyear Playhouse* which had been launched in October 1951 to present hour-long dramas to a nationwide audience every Sunday evening. By 1956 it was one of the most highly rated drama series on US television, utilising both original plays and adaptations from other mediums, as well as attracting top stars. The stories were broadcast live from New York which is why, tragically, no recording exists of Miss Marple's television debut.

Left: *Gracie Fields made an unlikely Miss Marple in the lady sleuth's first appearance on television in America in 1956*

Above: *Roger Moore, later famous on the screen as James Bond, featured in Miss Marple's American debut*

It was the show's producer, Fred Coe, a detective story enthusiast, who decided on the adaptation of *A Murder Is Announced* and scheduled it for 30 December 1956. The dramatisation was prepared by one of the show's regular writers, William Templeton, and though restricted to studio sets it still managed to create a more-than-passable impression of an English village of the Fifties.

Among the actors used in Goodyear productions were several who have subsequently been associated with films of Agatha Christie stories – in particular Martin Balsam *(Murder on the Orient Express)*, David Niven *(Death on the Nile)*, Roddy McDowall *(Evil Under the Sun)* and Tony Randall, who played Hercule Poirot in *The Alphabet Murders* in 1966. However, the director of *A Murder Is Announced*, Paul Stanley, cast none of these, opting for Malcolm Kuin as Inspector Craddock and Jessica Tandy as the stylish central character, Letitia Blacklock, the host of a game of Murder which goes terribly wrong. (Jessica Tandy was, of course, already famous for her Broadway performance as Blanche Dubois in *A Streetcar Named Desire* by Tennessee Williams.)

For two other roles he chose English actors: Gracie Fields as the lady detective, and a young man named Roger Moore as a guest, Patrick Simmons. The role was one of the first parts Moore landed in a career which was to culminate in playing the third James Bond.

Gracie was an effervescent girl who had risen to unprecedented popularity on the stage and in films in Britain in the years leading up to the Second World War, becoming the highest paid actress in the business. After the declaration of war she rebuilt a new career for herself in America. (She had left England to join her husband, the Italian-born actor-director Monty Banks, when he was declared an alien by the British authorities and deported after Italy entered the war on the Axis side.)

Gracie made a number of films in Hollywood and then in the Fifties began to work in television. Even though she was an enthusiast of detective stories, and a particular fan of Agatha Christie's work, she was nonetheless an unusual choice as Miss Marple. Although her hair was carefully streaked with grey and pulled back on her head and she was dressed in traditional English tweeds, Gracie found it difficult to disguise her Lancashire accent in the rather formal lines of dialogue that the script provided her with.

Though the actual murder scene in the darkness, in which the killer shoots two people and then turns the gun on him- (or her-) self, was effectively played and there was some nice character acting from Betty Sinclair, Josephine Brown and Pat Nye as other guests, the production did not live up to its pre-publicity: 'An edge-of-the-seat murder mystery featuring The Queen of Crime's famous Lady Sleuth.'

In a programme note in *TV Guide*, Gracie was quoted as saying: 'Miss Marple is very popular with Agatha Christie's readers all over Britain and America and it is a rather daunting task to try and play her on television. I have always imagined her as a rather quiet lady with a quick mind and a nose for murder.'

If crime story fans enjoyed the show, most of the newspaper television critics did not. The *New York Times*, for instance, declared on 31 December: 'The mystery on the *Goodyear Playhouse* last night was not whodunnit – but rather why. Why, for example, did Jessica Tandy and Gracie Fields ever get involved in such an inferior melodrama? It was murder from beginning to end.'

As there are no copies of *A Murder Is Announced* to view today, it is impossible either to agree with or dispute this verdict. What is certain is that, while *Goodyear Playhouse* ran a number of series based on characters and writers who proved popular with their audience, there was no such return for either Miss Marple or Agatha Christie's stories.

Gracie Fields herself remained a fan of the authoress's work until her death in 1979, the library in her home on Capri containing an almost complete set of the works of Agatha Christie. Fate also linked Gracie in one other strange way with our story.

For her husband, Monty Banks, died in her arms when they were travelling across Europe in . . . the Orient Express.

MARGARET RUTHERFORD

'An indomitable sleuth one jump ahead of the police'

The first actress to create a lasting impression as Miss Marple with the general public was undoubtedly the third woman cast in the role – the redoubtable Margaret Rutherford of the bulging eyes and indignant, wobbling chins. Indeed, for many years she was regarded as the definitive Jane Marple by millions of fans. The fascinating truth is, though, that not only was Margaret reluctant to play the role, but Agatha Christie herself considered her a far cry from her tall, thin, acidulated detective.

When MGM initially bought the rights to a number of the Miss Marple stories in 1960, they were provisionally intended as the basis of a television series, but with a sudden demand in America for British comedy movies, plans were changed. Two years later, after an extensive search to cast Miss Marple, the first of what were to be four pictures with Margaret Rutherford in the lead were filmed at the company's Borehamwood Studios.

Margaret, born in London in 1892, had been a teacher of speech and piano before turning to acting and utilising her long, lined face and jutting chin plus her natural eccentricity to become a very popular, and ultimately much loved, star of the screen. Although she gave several memorable performances in films in the Thirties, it was as the bicycle-riding medium in *Blithe Spirit* (1945) that she won the hearts of British audiences.

That same year, Margaret had her first encounter with the work of Agatha Christie when she appeared in a touring company version of the stage hit, *Appointment with Death*. The author herself had adapted this exotic mystery, set in the Holy Land, in which Hercule Poirot solves the murder of a tyrannical American widow, Mrs Boynton. For the theatre,

Margaret Rutherford, the first screen Miss Marple, searching for clues in Murder Ahoy! *(1964)*

however, Poirot had been replaced as the murder investigator by Colonel Carbury.

The play opened in London on 31 March 1945, with Owen Reynolds as the colonel and an excellent performance from Mary Clare as the evil Mrs Boynton. A quiet little spinster named Miss Pryce was played by a young actress called Joan Hickson, whose future also lay entwined with Agatha Christie and, ultimately, Miss Marple. According to the theatre historian, J. C. Trewin, an even better company than this took the play across the Channel in May of that year. Trewin has written: 'Led by Ivor Novello (as the homicidal maniac), Diana Wynyard and Margaret Rutherford, this was the first play sent, with a portable theatre, to the Normandy front.'

It was to be over fifteen years later that Margaret Rutherford was approached by MGM to star in their first Miss Marple picture, *Murder She Said* (1962). Discussing this in the late Sixties at her country home in Gerrard's Cross – almost a duplicate of Miss Marple's house in St Mary Mead – she explained her initial reluctance to take the part with which she has ever since been associated.

'I never really wanted to play Miss Marple,' she said. 'I have always hated violence of any kind and murder in particular. I turned down a number of film parts over the years because I did not feel they had the right moral value for me. Besides, I thought my public expected something better of me – they might well not approve of Rutherford playing Sherlock Holmes!'

In fact, it was some while before she was inveigled by the combined efforts of her family, her agent and the film's director, George Pollock, into reading the script by David Pursall and Jack Seddon based on the Christie murder mystery, *4.50 from Paddington*. Margaret explained:

'George Pollock was perhaps the man who most convinced me I should play the part. He explained to me that Miss Marple was a fine woman and she was not so much concerned with crime – even though she was an indomitable sleuth always one jump ahead of the police. He persuaded me that she was more involved in a game – like chess – a game of solving problems rather than murder.'

What may also have helped clinch the actress's decision was the suggestion that there would also be a part in the picture for her husband, the character actor, Stringer Davis, as Miss Marple's trusted assistant, the village librarian. Stringer was, in fact, to appear as the librarian in each of the four Miss Marple films Margaret made. (Miss Rutherford has further admitted in her autobiography, written just before her death in 1972, that there was a certain degree of financial necessity about making the film as she was 'hopeless' with money and was at that moment being relentlessly persued for back taxes by the Inland Revenue.)

Margaret Rutherford also recalled how Agatha Christie had reacted to her casting. 'I didn't know it at the time, but she was not at all keen on me playing Miss Marple. It was not a question of my acting, just that I didn't look at all like her idea of the detective. She saw her as a kind of fragile, pink-and-white lady, not physically like me at all!

'But when we met face to face on the set of *Murder She Said*, we instantly clicked and became friends. We became admirers of each other's work – hers is the world of observation and the pen, and mine is speech. Agatha even dedicated to me one of her Miss Marple books, *The Mirror Crack'd from Side to Side*,' she added.

Margaret took great care in researching her character as well as deciding on the outfit she would wear. 'I see her as a dear spinster lady,' she told an early interviewer, 'living in a small country town, who is able to apply her knowledge of human nature to any conceivable crime and come up with a solution ahead of the police. She is eccentric, but her passion for justice is very real.'

For her costume as Miss Marple, the actress plumped for a sweater and tweedy skirt plus a deerstalker hat. She was particularly amused when a journalist visiting the film set later described her as looking like 'a warmly bundled English bull-dog'.

The film's major difference from the book was the removal of the character of Elspeth

McGillicuddy, who sees a murder in a passing train. Instead Miss Marple becomes the eye-witness and is thus propelled into her investigations. Several of the railway scenes were shot at the level crossing near her home at Gerrard's Cross and had to be filmed early in the morning before the trains came by.

Among her co-stars were several well-known English character actors, including Charles Tingwell as Inspector Craddock (who also appeared in all four movies), James Robertson Justice, Thorley Walters, Muriel Pavlow, and, by another curious twist of fortune, Joan Hickson playing a charlady, Mrs Kidder.

Reviewers were generally kind to the film, most singling out Margaret Rutherford's larger-than-life performance. Alexander Walker in the *Evening Standard* wrote:

> Margaret Rutherford fills the spinster's tweeds of the renowned detective Miss Marple splendidly. She is hugely enjoyable. With chin wagging like a windsock on an airfield and eyes that are deceptively guileless, she clumps her way through lines, situations and disguises that would bunker an actress of less imperial aplomb.

The American press also enjoyed this latest example of English eccentricity, the *New York*

Margaret Rutherford and her husband, Stringer Davis, on location in Gerrard's Cross for Murder She Said *(1962)*

Times reporting: 'It is mainly Miss Rutherford's show: she dominates most of the scenes with a forceful characterisation that enhances the humour of her lines and the suspense in the murder.'

When Agatha Christie saw the film, on the other hand, she found it poor, lacking in suspense and excitement. But, as she wrote to her agent: 'Don't think I'm upset by *Murder She Said*. I'm not. It's more or less what I expected all along.'

For Margaret Rutherford the picture brought quite unexpected success. In a matter of months her money worries had disappeared and MGM were busy telling the press that she was now the highest paid actress in the country. She also began to receive an increasing amount of fan mail – not a little of it addressed to 'Miss Marple' and seeking her aid in solving all manner of problems from simple domestic upsets to missing jewellery!

Because her home was not far from the MGM studios, Margaret and Stringer Davis would often drive to work in a pony and trap – a fact which delighted visiting journalists looking for examples of the actress's by now well-known eccentricity.

In 1963, Margaret filmed her second Miss Marple picture, *Murder at the Gallop*, with the same director and scriptwriters. She was particularly pleased to have her old friend Robert Morley playing a riding school proprietor, Hector Enderby. (Three years after this, Morley co-starred in another Christie movie as Hercule Poirot's assistant, Hastings, in *The Alphabet Murders*.)

For the purist, this film was something of a shock. David Pursall and Jack Seddon had based the story on Agatha's 1953 novel, *After the Funeral*, which was actually a Hercule Poirot case, but now it was Jane Marple who investigated a riding academy to discover how an elderly recluse had died. Talking about the movie, Margaret Rutherford said:

'Here again Miss Marple got her man after some delicious romps in the hunting set, which also involved me having to mount a horse! I didn't actually ride it. The only time I ever rode was when I was two or three in India. I had a white pony then. But they managed to find a nice quiet horse for the film and the shot was quickly in the bag without mishap!'

For members of the cast and crew, one of the best memories of that film was Margaret Rutherford's determination to create a happy working environment with little comedy routines. She would often break into a jig on the set – and when it was suggested that she should do a waltz in one scene, she insisted on doing the dance of the moment, the twist, instead!

Though once again Agatha Christie was upset by the travesties that had been visited upon her story by the scriptwriters, the press and public liked the picture. MGM promptly put the same team together the following year to make *Murder Most Foul*, based on another Poirot tale, *Mrs McGinty's Dead* (1952). (Presumably, no one among the production team at MGM was aware that in one of Agatha Christie's short stories, 'Mr Eastwood's Adventure', written in 1934, the gentleman of the title, an author, had actually complained about publishers changing the titles of his short stories to just such things as 'Murder Most Foul'!)

Miss Marple now found herself on a jury disagreeing with her fellow jurors in the case of a blackmailing actress who has been murdered. Among the stars in the picture were Ron Moody, Megs Jenkins, James Bolam, Andrew Cruikshank and Francesca Annis. The venerable Cruikshank was then also co-starring with the first Miss Marple, Barbara Mullen, in the successful BBC TV series, *Dr Finlay's Casebook*; while Francesca Annis was to star in 1983 as Tuppence Beresford, half of Agatha Christie's dynamic pair of detectives, Tommy and Tuppence, in the long-running LWT series, *Partners in Crime*.

Agatha Christie was again horrified at what had been done with her characters. But one final indignity remained – the last picture in the series, *Murder Ahoy!*, released in 1964.

This time, David Pursall and Jack Seddon abandoned any pretence of adapting an existing Agatha Christie story and produced a wholly invented plot in which Miss Marple investigated murder and blackmail on a naval training ship. When the authoress learned of these plans, she objected strongly, but MGM went ahead nevertheless.

However, despite the enthusiastic direction of George Pollock, a resourceful performance by Margaret, and some good support playing by Lionel Jeffries, William Mervyn, Derek Nimmo and Miles Malleson, the film proved a failure at the box office and brought the series to a rather undistinguished end. Even the press sensed the decline, *The Times* commenting, 'Margaret Rutherford makes a brave attempt to make this murder bright, but it is rarely exciting, intriguing or even comic.'

MGM's preliminary plans for the fifth picture, *The Body in the Library* – this one actually based on a novel featuring Miss Marple – were immediately shelved.

Margaret herself best remembered her last Jane Marple film for the celebration of her 80th birthday on the set and for having to fight a fencing duel with the murderer – something she did not enjoy because of her hatred of violence, but which she agreed to do in the interests of her art. Curiously, she never saw the finished film, according to one of her relatives.

Agatha Christie made no secret of her pleasure at the demise of the series. '*Murder Ahoy!* was one of the silliest things you ever saw!' she said later. 'It got very bad reviews, I'm delighted to say.' Even so, this did nothing to harm her friendship with Margaret Rutherford.

The actress, her fortunes completely restored by the four films, went on to other things – not least a wonderful part as the redoubtable Duchess of Brighton in the Elizabeth Taylor-Richard Burton movie, *The VIPs*. This had come about as a direct result of the popularity of the Miss Marple pictures in the USA, where they had been seen by the director of *The VIPs*, Anthony Asquith. The picture won Margaret Rutherford her one and only Oscar.

She made one final entrance in an Agatha Christie film, *The Alphabet Murders*, in 1966, and a year later she was made a Dame of the British Empire in recognition of her services to the theatre and films.

Depite their somewhat inauspicious demise, the Miss Marple films had unquestionably helped establish the detective with a world-wide audience, and there are overseas fans like the American cinema writer, Jon Tuska, who hold them in the highest regard. In 1978 he wrote in his exhaustive study, *The Detective in Hollywood*, 'Margaret Rutherford's four Miss Marple films in the Sixties are among the finest detective films in general and those featuring female investigators in particular . . . I cannot help but suspect that with books like

Margaret with her friend and co-star, Robert Morley, in a scene from Murder at the Gallop *(1963)*

The famous duel from the finale of Murder Ahoy!, *Margaret's last Miss Marple film*

The Mirror Crack'd, which Dame Agatha dedicated to Margaret Rutherford, the screen interpretations effected subtle changes in the fictional characterisation, especially in terms of Miss Marple's attitude toward the on-coming of old age, her indomitable will, her inflexible determination, and her eccentric but insatiable curiosity about human nature.'

Be that as it may, Margaret Rutherford certainly retained the warmest memories of the character to the end of her days, recalling in 1972:

'I completely overcame my first tentative prejudices about Christie crime and became fond of Jane Marple. She was of course so right for the period when directors like George Pollock were producing low-budget, lightweight comedies that sent people home from the cinema feeling warm and happy with life. This was in the days before brutal realism became a fashion.

'Perhaps I am old-fashioned', she added, 'but I think the Miss Marple films did a great service in winning us friends all around the world. And this is important too.'

ANGELA LANSBURY

'A woman who abhors violence'

The jowly features of Margaret Rutherford were still familiar with a great many people fifteen years after her last picture when the British-born, American-based actress, Angela Lansbury, became the fourth screen Miss Marple in an adaptation of the very book Agatha Christie had dedicated to her predecessor, *The Mirror Crack'd*. Angela knew as soon as she was offered the part she would have to exorcise the ghost of Margaret Rutherford – who, like the authoress, had died in the intervening years – to have any chance of success.

While filming was taking place in May 1980 at St Clere House, a red-brick seventeenth-century country house in the rolling farmland of Kent which was doubling for St Mary Mead, Angela explained just how she had approached the part. First, she said, she had 'read her way through' all the Miss Marple books. These had helped give her some ideas about the character of the detective.

'There are two kinds of preconception about Miss Marple,' she said. 'From the people who remember dear Margaret Rutherford, and from people who have their own ideas directly from reading the books. I see her as she is described: a tall, china-blue-eyed, slender spinster. A kindly rather than a domineering person.

'I know there are always those who will associate Miss Marple with Dame Margaret. I admired her tremendously, loved her as a performer – but I never saw her play Miss Marple, oddly enough. From the descriptions I've read she was simply wonderful.

'But,' Angela continued, 'I'm also aware that Agatha Christie wasn't too happy about the visual aspects of Dame Margaret for the role. Well, I have the height, I have the eyes, and I'm trying to be willowy. The complexion and the hair can be fixed!'

She also knew that there was a lot of slapstick comedy in the Rutherford films – which, she agreed, was what audiences then came to expect – but there was actually none in the Christie books.

'I decided I wanted the character to emerge as she was written,' Angela continued. 'This puzzled me very much because there isn't a tremendous amount on the printed page. I learned more about Miss Marple from things that Agatha Christie wrote in her own autobiography, and I did a great deal of other research into what she is all about.

'Her secret of detection was that she would reconstruct the crime by using parallels from her village of St Mary Mead. She knew that human beings responded basically the same way in stress, passion or crime whoever they were. Her village was a microcosm of the world.

'She does have the odd blind spot, though,' Angela went on. 'She is very rigid in her code of ethics. She expects people to behave in a certain way and if they don't she really berates them. The class thing is a bit dodgy. One opinion is that she was a terrible right-wing snob, a maiden lady who lived an unreal kind of existence in this little village and lorded it over all the little girls she trained and sent out to big houses. But I think of her more as a kind of back-water remnant of Edwardian life that lingered on in the Thirties in England. She doesn't exactly look down her nose at people, but they have to know their place. Actually, in

Angela Lansbury, an imposing Miss Marple
in The Mirror Crack'd *(1980)*

Angela in the Kent village which doubled for St Mary Mead in The Mirror Crack'd

Christie's later Marple books she does get a bit more broadminded.'

Thus Angela Lansbury's Miss Marple became a neatly formal lady in a jersey twin-set and matching grey felt hat. Her age was set at about 70 and her manner was a mixture of the iron hand and the velvet glove. By the time shooting began of the story of a Hollywood film crew descending on the village to shoot an epic version of *Mary, Queen of Scots* and rapidly descending from bitchiness to cold-blooded murder, Angela could claim, 'I am beginning to know the character so well that I am fearfully protective of her. If the writers give me a line that makes me uncomfortable, I change it.'

This was to be an attitude she would adopt again when her screen career took another turn into television . . .

Determination and strength of character are very much a part of the life of Angela Lansbury, who was born in London in 1925. While still a teenager, she was taken to America by her recently widowed mother along with her twin brothers, Bruce and Edgar, and half-sister, Isolde, to escape the German blitz which fell on the capital during the Second World War.

As the granddaughter of the Labour Party leader, George Lansbury, and the daughter of an actress, she felt destined to become a perfomer. As a child, she was a dreamer, too, playing out in her imagination the characters from the movies she saw – in particular the crime story hero, Boston Blackie.

In Hollywood, where her mother knew many of the members of the British film colony including Basil Rathbone (the star of the 1937 version of *Love from a Stranger*), she began her film apprenticeship with a small role as Elizabeth Taylor's sister in *National Velvet* in 1944. These two actresses were to be reunited again as stars on the set of *The Mirror Crack'd* when Elizabeth played a bitchy American film star called Marina.

After *National Velvet*, Angela worked in films and on the stage for many years, though her unusual features – narrowed lips and large, menacing brown eyes – tended to get her parts as domineering women often much older than she actually was. Though these rarely earned her top billing, they made her much respected in the profession and popular with the public.

In 1978 she was offered what was to prove her first significant contact with the work of

Agatha Christie when she was cast as the drunken authoress Salome Otterbourne in John Brabourne's *Death on the Nile*, starring Peter Ustinov. Fate might almost have meant these two to appear together in the film, for Ustinov's first wife had been her sister, Isolde, and she and Peter had spent happy hours improvising conversations in funny accents when she was seventeen.

Several reviews maintained that Angela stole the picture from her galaxy of co-stars, and she certainly admits she hammed her part up unmercifully. 'The director wanted me to play it larger than life,' she says. 'I knew exactly what I was doing. I went way overboard. She was such a lush, that woman!'

Angela also remembers the film for the oppressive heat of Egypt and her two co-stars, Bette Davis and Maggie Smith, with whom she had to share a dressing room in the Nile steamer while they were on location.

'We all had to dress and undress in this tiny, stifling-hot space, which had two bunks to make matters more crowded,' she says. 'It was a real test of our professionalism. We didn't bat an eyelid. In the end, two of us would wait outside while the other changed. I suppose no one will believe we didn't have a fight!'

Angela's professionalism stuck in the mind of John Brabourne – and when EMI films decided to follow their successful Poirot movies with one featuring Miss Marple, everyone was in agreement that Angela was the only one who could play the part. She had both an English accent and an American reputation. The only problem for the film producers was that, when they wanted to begin shooting in the autumn of 1979, Angela was starring on Broadway in a very successful musical, *Sweeney Todd*, to which she was tied by contract.

She remembers the surprise she felt when she was offered the role – although Miss Marple was a part she had coveted for a number of years.

'John Brabourne called me and said, "We're going to do a new Agatha Christie movie and we would like you to be our Miss Marple." Well, I nearly fell off the end of the phone – I really *was* amazed – in the first place that they'd thought of me, and in the second place because it happened to be something I'd thought perhaps one day I might play. I just felt that as a character she would be pretty good for me to latch on to.'

Guy Hamilton, who was to direct, also felt Angela was absolutely right for the part. 'She was the *only* actress we wanted,' he says. 'We should have started at the end of 1979, but we decided to wait until she had finished her year's contract in *Sweeney Todd*.

'Now, Margaret Rutherford was a divine clown, but she was *not* Agatha Christie's Miss Marple. We believed she was a more serious person, a gossip, even a bit of a snob. There was no way she was going to fall off her bicycle into the village duckpond!'

The script of *The Mirror Crack'd*, written by Jonathan Hales and Barry Sandler, remained essentially true to Agatha Christie's novel, and apart from Elizabeth Taylor, other star roles were played by Geraldine Chaplin, Kim Novak, Rock Hudson and Tony Curtis, with the cultured English actor, Edward Fox, playing Chief Inspector Craddock.

It is not generally known that a terrible tragedy before the film was made contributed very substantially to its final format. On 27 August 1979, while on holiday at Mullaghmore, County Sligo, Lord Mountbatten was murdered by a 50lb bomb planted by the IRA on his boat, the *Shadow V*. The explosion devastated the party of six on board the 30-foot boat, among whom were John Brabourne and his wife, Lady Patricia (Lord Louis' elder daughter), and their twin sons, Timothy and Nicholas.

Though John was quickly rescued from the debris of the boat, he suffered horrendous lacerations and both his legs were broken. On hearing the news, there were immediate fears that the film-maker would never work again, and *The Mirror Crack'd* seemed doomed.

However, Richard Goodwin moved quickly to maintain the American financial commitment to the picture by flying to Hollywood and recruiting the various American stars to the cast list. This saved the movie – though at the expense of considerably reducing Angela's part in order to accommodate the extra characters.

Though the film enabled Angela to fulfil her ambition to play Miss Marple, it was not a success to the same degree as EMI's two earlier Poirot pictures. The *Daily Express* called it 'Entertaining . . . though nothing caps the opening parody of an old whodunnit,' and *Variety* declared it 'a nostalgic throwback to the genteel murder mystery pix of the 1950s'. Its failure to earn a substantial profit on its $3.5 million cost ruled out the idea of a series.

Angela now looks back on what might have been and reflects:

'In a way I wish that Margaret Rutherford hadn't got there first. I would have enjoyed making Miss Marple a little bit more batty myself, but Agatha Christie didn't necessarily approve of that.'

And her enduring memory of playing the part? 'Miss Marple doesn't always say what you want her to say – she has a very prosaic way of expressing herself – but what she *thinks* is fascinating!'

Her own success in the part was not to end there, however, for the movie was seen in America by three television executives busy creating what they planned as a series about a best-selling mystery writer who finds herself being asked to help solve real-life crimes. Though the fact was never acknowledged on television, this series, *Murder She Wrote*, which was launched in the autumn in 1984, had an unmistakeable resemblance to the Miss Marple stories, and the connection was made even stronger when Angela was approached to play the writer-turned-sleuth, Jessica Fletcher.

A two-hour pilot show for the series, entitled *The Death of Sherlock Holmes*, was written by Peter Fletcher, who served as executive producer with Richard Levinson and William Link. This trio had earlier created the enormously successful TV series *Columbo*, with Peter Falk. When the pilot was announced in April 1984, Richard Levinson made no bones about the concept of the programme:

'The idea of the show,' he told the *New York Times*, 'is to imagine what might happen if Agatha Christie were alive today and people came to her to help solve mysteries.'

And when Angela took on the role, she went even further. 'The character resembles an American Miss Marple,' she said, 'and there is no doubt my preparation for the part was aided by having appeared in the two Christie films. But there are some crucial differences between the two amateur sleuths. Jessica Fletcher is a widow, not a spinster, and she is more worldly, more glamorous and less ancient than Miss Marple.

'She is an innately sophisticated person, even though she's from a small village in Maine. Jessica is also very well educated and fits in everywhere. She becomes a best-selling detective story novelist and that takes her all over the world.

'At first I was going to wear a wig with a lot of grey in it. But my family got on to me and said, "No, you go out there and play yourself." There was no reason to make her dowdy. My sense is that Jessica also embodies many of the qualities which are quintessentially American. She's very open, resilient and brave, a woman of very strong moral character.'

Though there were initial doubts whether such a sophisticated and cerebral mystery show could succeed with a television audience saturated with violent detective series, *Murder She Wrote* was screened on Sunday, 18 September 1984 and attracted a substantial audience. So substantial, in fact, that following enthusiastic newspaper reviews, CBS gave approval for a series to be made. Angela, who had been enthusiastically promoting the show as ideal viewing for 'everybody who loves a good yarn – and everyone does' was delighted, though the workload she had to undertake for a weekly, hour-long show was awesome.

'Because Jessica is on her own with no sidekick, I had to be in virtually every scene in every episode and that meant a sixteen- or seventeen-hour schedule to begin with,' she recalls today. 'After a while I was just going nuts. I didn't have time for anything but work. So I had to put my foot down and demand a twelve-hour day!'

The reward for her dedication to *Murder She Wrote* was that it caught the nation's fancy and went straight into the Top Twenty of the Nielsen Ratings. Within a matter of weeks it was a blockbuster success, topping such previously invincible series as *Dallas* and *Dynasty*.

Angela Lansbury as Jessica Fletcher, a Miss Marple in all but name, in the TV series, Murder She Wrote

Among its guest stars have been Brian Keith, Robert Culp and Lloyd Nolan.

Angela still smiles at this stunning success which has contributed to making her one of the most highly paid and powerful women in Hollywood.

'The key was that we had interesting locations and characters that gripped the audience. Another was that the audience could also play the whodunnit game and try to guess who among the other stars was the murderer. We were totally different in that we had no car chases and I didn't carry a gun. The series became a cerebral exercise.'

Murder She Wrote not only established Angela in the forefront of US television stars, but scooped several awards for her including being named 'Woman of the Year in Broadcasting'. In May 1985, the series was launched in Britain by ITV and the success story has continued.

Executive producer Robert F. O'Neill believes that it is his star who has made the show so popular. 'People tune in to watch *her*, though I believe the scripts are also very good. Angela's own character is not too far from that of Jessica, and people watch because they like both Jessica and Angela. I also think Angela has made her sleuth a role model for middle-aged women and proved that television's leading ladies do not have to be bitchy or busty to succeed.'

Underlining this fact was the announcement, as the Centenary Year dawned, that Angela had renewed her contract to appear in *Murder She Wrote*, signing a deal said to be worth $12 million a year.

'She's driven a hard bargain,' a spokesman of CBS was quoted as saying, 'but she's worth every penny.'

Angela has now come to understand her character so well that she also exercises a firm control over the making of the series from start to finish. For example, on more than one occasion she has thrown out lines from scripts that she believed were out of keeping – just as she had done as Miss Marple.

'Jessica would know all about poison,' she announced on one occasion, 'She wouldn't have to ask a doctor!'

Angela Lansbury's association with the works of Agatha Christie have undoubtedly brought about an enormous change in her fortunes, a fact she readily acknowledges.

'The success of Jessica Fletcher is that she is a healthy, energetic woman who won't be defeated by a problem and would never become involved with gratuitous violence,' she says. 'And I like to think both Agatha Christie and Miss Marple would approve of *that*!'

HELEN HAYES

'No great activist – but she gets the job done'

The veteran American actress Helen Hayes has the distinction of being the only *over*-age Miss Marple! This white-haired, gentle lady of stage and screen made her debut in the theatre at the age of five and first played Miss Marple when she was a venerable but sprightly 83 years old.

Helen also has one of the longest associations with the works of Agatha Christie: she first began to read the author's mystery books in New York in the late 1920s and made her debut in a Christie play, *Murder on the Nile*, in London in 1946.

'I've read everything by Agatha Christie,' Helen says, 'and, of course, I'm very familiar with Miss Marple. I think I see her as Agatha Christie wanted. She doesn't look like a great sleuth or a great activist of any kind – she's bland, in fact – and I think that's the way she gets the job done.'

Helen Hayes has twice played the lady detective for the American television company, CBS – in *A Caribbean Mystery* (1983), and *Murder with Mirrors* (1985) when she was 85 and co-starred with another of Hollywood's great screen veterans, the late Bette Davis. Helen brought a lifetime of experience to the role, having first appeared on stage in her native Washington in 1905: the year that Sir Henry Irving died and the first American cinemas began screening *The Great Train Robbery*.

It was Helen's mother, a former actress, who put her on the stage, and by the time she was a teenager she had become a star on Broadway in *Dear Brutus* (1918). Later, she became something of an institution and was widely known as 'The First Lady of the American Theater'. On entering films in 1931, she won an Oscar in her very first picture, *The Sin of Madelon Claudet*.

The theatre always held the greater attraction for her, Helen says, and in the Thirties and Forties she appeared in several very successful productions in New York and London. And her love of mysteries made her happy to accept the opportunity in 1946 of appearing in *Murder on the Nile*, which Agatha had adapted from her famous story.

'I read the novel when it came out,' Helen recalls, 'and even then it was easy to see that it would become a classic. But not so easy to see how it could be adapted for the stage. I was really surprised when Agatha Christie decided to cut out Hercule Poirot, but I was still happy to play the part of Miss ffolliot-ffoulkes. She and her niece, Christina Grant, were among the prime suspects.

'The play opened at the Ambassadors Theatre in London in March 1946, but it wasn't very successful. I don't know if it was because there had been too much killing in the war or the public were just a bit tired of murder mysteries then.'

Helen enjoyed much more success in 1981, however, when she was cast in a two-hour television version of *Murder Is Easy*, Agatha Christie's powerful 1939 mystery story of a lunatic killer at large in a sleepy English village. Behind the project was Stan Margulies, fresh from his triumphant series, *Roots*. The production was for CBS's *Saturday Night at the Movies* series.

Although her role in the actual story was short-lived, Helen remembers the programme for providing her with a foretaste of Miss Marple.

'I played Lavinia Fullerton, a gossipy old maid who is fascinated by murder,' she recalls. 'And though I was killed off at the beginning of the story, the character was a bit like Miss Marple. In fact, if you read the original book it's rather surprising that Miss Marple *doesn't* appear in the story!'

Interestingly, this view has been expressed by other Christie fans, and in one major study of detective fiction, *A Catalogue of Crime* by Jacques Barzun and Wendell Taylor (1971), *Murder Is Easy* is actually listed as a Miss Marple story.

The CBS adaptation of the novel was scripted by Carmen Culver and directed by Claude Whatham, with Olivia de Havilland as Honoria Waynflete, the friend of Lavinia Fullerton, who helps Bill Bixby, as amateur sleuth Luke Williams, to track down the murderer. Two other British stars, Timothy West and Lesley-Anne Down, appeared in the production which was largely shot on location in England.

The programme was well reviewed in America after its transmission on 2 January 1982, *Variety* summing up the consensus of opinion: 'A well-made English-style whodunnit that never lost its grip.'

Helen Hayes was, however, quite surprised when Stan Margulies telephoned her in New York with the news that he was going to adapt another Christie novel, *A Caribbean Mystery*, and wanted her to play Miss Marple.

'I was delighted,' she recalls, 'although I did think for a moment that I might be a bit older than Miss Marple! But *Caribbean Mystery* was one of my favourite Christie books and there were some very dear people who worked on the film with me.'

The story of an old ex-Indian Army major suddenly done to death on the holiday island of St Honore, precipitating a race against the clock to prevent a murderer carrying out his plans, was adapted by Sue Grafton and Steven Humphrey and directed by Robert Lewis. Among Helen's co-stars were Maurice Evans as the major; Barnard Hughes as the rich, irascible Mr Rafiel who helps Miss Marple unmask the killer; and suspects Lynne Moody, Beth Howland and Swoosie Kurtz.

Helen recalls the last three actors with affection. 'I was really stumbling along through television then and I didn't know my way about,' she says modestly, 'and they were really helpful to me.

Above: *Helen Hayes, the veteran actress who was actually older than Miss Marple when she played the role in 1983*

Right: *Helen Hayes as Miss ffolliot-ffoulkes in* Murder on the Nile *at the Ambassadors Theatre, London, in 1946. David Horne appeared as Father Borrowdale*

'One night, having had a very hard day, I went disconsolately home because I had had a long, long, long scene shut up in a small suite in the hotel where we worked in Santa Barbara. There was no air, and so many people in there and so many hot lights and I'm at the age when my memory isn't too sharp. And that night I was just about to fall into my bed in the little bungalow in the grounds and there was a knock on the door and there were Lynne, Beth and Swoosie and all of them with a little bouquet saying, "We love you, Helen."'

The public and press loved the new Miss Marple, too, when *A Caribbean Mystery* was first shown on CBS on 22 October 1983. 'Genteel armchair family entertainment,' the *New York Times* called the production, and voted Helen Hayes 'a delightful and resilient Miss Marple'. When the movie was screened in Britain by ITV in a prime-time Saturday evening spot on 17 September 1988, the success story was repeated.

Despite the drain on her energies making *A Caribbean Mystery*, Helen agreed to play Miss Marple again in 1985 for CBS in a new adaptation of *Murder with Mirrors*, based on the 1952 novel, *They Do It with Mirrors*, in which, disconcertingly, Miss Marple is portrayed by her creator as being only in her mid-sixties! For Helen, it marked her three-quarters of a century as an actress.

The story concerns a murder followed by the threat of poisoning at a huge country house which is being run as a home for delinquent boys. Co-starring with Helen in her search for the villain was one of her idols, Bette Davis; Sir John Mills was the man running the home; and Leo McKern was Inspector Curry. The script was by George Eckstein, and Dick Lowery directed.

Unlike its predecessor, filming *Murder with Mirrors* proved difficult – and Helen's stamina was tested to the limit. 'I am afraid dear Bette Davis seemed determined to make life difficult for us,' is her sole comment upon the production which was finally aired on US television on 20 February 1985. Its reception by the public and press was lukewarm and, at the time of writing, CBS have made no plans to continue the series.

Helen Hayes, now in her ninetieth year and living in Nyack on the Hudson River, has also indicated that she has no further intention of acting. Instead, after all her years of interest in the mystery novel, she has collaborated on one herself.

'I have always been a murder-mystery freak and never travelled anywhere without one,' she says. 'So what more natural with time on my hands than to write one myself? The book is called *Where the Truth Lies* and I have written it with Thomas Costain. The mystery takes place during the Oscar ceremonies, where everyone knows an awful lot of back-stabbing goes on! I've been able to contribute a lot of anecdotes from all my years in show business.

'I don't think I can match Agatha Christie's ingenuity,' she adds, 'but it will be a little way of saying "Thank you" to her memory for all the pleasure her books have given me.'

JOAN HICKSON

'She has integrity and strength of character'

In her picturesque sixteenth-century home in an Essex village – in some respects a little like Miss Marple's house in St Mary Mead – Joan Hickson keeps a letter she received in 1946 from Agatha Christie. It was a simple, congratulatory note on her performance in Agatha's play *Appointment with Death* in which she had appeared as Miss Pryce. But as a postscript at the bottom were two lines:

'I hope one day you will play my dear Miss Marple.'

For Joan, a life-long fan of 'The Queen of Crime', whose home is crammed with copies of

The definitive Miss Marple –
Joan Hickson with her
favourite handbag

Joan Hickson in the BBC's '4.50 from Paddington'

the authoress's books, it was a nice thought which she tucked away in a drawer and forgot all about. There it lay until fate took a hand in the veteran actress's affairs.

'The note had completely slipped my mind,' Joan admits today. 'I didn't even think about it when the BBC approached me with the idea of playing Miss Marple. It's an extraordinary coincidence, isn't it? One of those twists of the plot that Agatha would have loved.'

This 'twist of the plot' that has resulted in Joan becoming acclaimed as the definitive Miss Marple can be regarded as the crowning glory of her long career. It also played a part, she believes, in the award of an OBE, which was presented to her at Buckingham Palace in the winter of 1987.

'I was terribly thrilled to receive the letter about the gong – the morning it arrived I had to sit down and have a glass of brandy!' she smiles at the memory. 'The Queen said it was for Miss Marple. She liked the series very much.'

Joan Hickson is a remarkable, energetic 83-year-old whose career as a character actress has more often than not seen her cast as a servant or charlady – though she has actually played everything from Shakespeare to farce.

'Not being very pretty, I was never an ingenue,' she says. 'Even when I was very young I was always asked to play old ladies. But you can go on a bit longer with those sorts of parts, can't you?'

It is perhaps only fitting, therefore, that international fame should have come to this charming woman as the veteran super-sleuth in the series which the BBC says has attracted over 12 million viewers and been sold to 40 countries around the world, including Russia and China.

'What *can* they be making of Miss Marple in Chinese?' she says with a quizzical air. 'I wouldn't mind taking a slow boat to China to find out. And will they write to me? I might find that a bit foxing!'

Joan was an only child, born on 5 August 1906, in Kingsthorpe, Northamptonshire, but grew up with a large family of aunts and uncles. One of these, Aunt Lizzy, who was 'tall and tweedy' and a little eccentric might almost have been a model for Miss Marple. Joan knew she wanted to be an actress after seeing the pantomime *Cinderella* when she was five. But when she made her ambition known at the age of nineteen and said she was going to train at RADA, her family were horrified.

'Another of my aunts, Aggie, who was every inch of four feet eight inches high, drew herself to her full height and thundered, "What is Joan's destination to be?" as if I was setting off for King's Cross and the gutter.'

What it led to was a busy, if unspectacular, life in the theatre, in films, and even in television back in its pioneer days at Alexandra Palace. Her attitude to her profession has all along been very definite – to play each role as it was offered and then move on to the next.

Along the lengthy road to becoming a cult-figure Miss Marple, complete with her stylish clothes and crocodile handbag (now a prized personal souvenir), Joan has had a number of interesting associations with the work of Agatha Christie, quite apart from the role in *Appointment with Death*. Three in number, to be precise: one in films and two on television, spread over fifty years. In fact, the only entertainment medium in which she has not – so far! – played a Christie character has been on radio.

The first of these parts came in 1937 when she appeared as a maid, Emmy, in the Basil Rathbone/Ann Harding film, *Love from a Stranger*. Then, twenty-five years later, she had her first encounter with Miss Marple when she played a charlady, Mrs Kidder, in the Margaret Rutherford version of *Murder She Said*. And just prior to her own Miss Marple series, she was Mrs Rivington in the 1980 LWT adaptation of *Why Didn't They Ask Evans?*

Nor is this quite the end of Joan's association with Agatha Christie, for she knew the authoress personally, as well as being a friend of Margaret Rutherford, the actress whose achievements as Miss Marple she has now surpassed.

'Agatha Christie was charming, absolutely charming,' she recalls, 'but she was also very shy. She came on tour with us, but she didn't talk very much. I remember she was also very generous – she gave me some tea at the time when it was still rationed.

'There was certainly nothing mysterious about her, though she had an uncanny knowledge of people. I have been asked if my portrayal of Miss Marple was in any way inspired by her, and I have to say no. She was a totally different sort of person. I mean, Miss Marple's a little village spinster who knows everything that's going on. Agatha wasn't like that at all!'

And of the redoubtable Margaret Rutherford, Joan says, 'She was a very dear friend of mine, my son's godmother, in fact, and her performance is how a lot of people think of Miss

Marple. Of course, there have been several actresses who have played the role, including Americans like Helen Hayes and Angela Lansbury, but I do feel the part requires an English actress. Miss Marple is so essentially English.'

Joan admits she was very surprised when the BBC producer Guy Slater approached her to play the lady detective. He told her, 'You are the best actress to convey the character's wonderfully vague, woolly quality.'

'I roared with laughter at first,' she remembers. 'I didn't think I was right at all – not thin and small enough. She's supposed to be very old: well, I'm very old, so I decided to have a bash. I knew that if I didn't play Miss Marple there were thirty in the queue who would.

'I don't think I could be a sleuth myself, though,' she goes on. 'I'm much too vague. But after sixty-something years in the business I have become a bit of a judge of personalities. I'm very interested in people. I notice women and their mannerisms a lot. I say to myself, "She's got interesting oddities – I'd like to play her."'

Armed also with her beguiling, chintz-blue eyes, which sparkle with good humour until she narrows them into her well-known imperious look, as well as her skill at mimicry, Joan Hickson was an ideal choice. Like Miss Marple, too, she is a connoisseur of village life; is not at all sure that progress is such a good thing; and, with her faintly abstracted view, understands far more than she lets on. She also shares her alter ego's passion for gardening, and has kept her own garden immaculate since the death of her neurologist husband, Eric, some years ago.

Miss Marple at home: Joan Hickson photographed outside her picturesque Essex village house

As a life-long reader of crime fiction, the Agatha Christie stories were part of a genre in which she had a special interest.

'I think she portrayed her times very faithfully,' Joan says. 'They were lovely times – very peaceful. She was very true to life and we have been true to her stories. When I was a girl, if there was a murder case it was a sensation. We would read every paper to keep up with the latest developments. But now one hears about terrible and senseless crimes every day.'

Her interest in Christie has also grown into a genuine affection for the character she has so superbly brought to the screen.

'Oh, I adore and admire Miss Marple,' she enthuses. 'We've had wonderful times together. I think she's a wonderful woman with very high standards and a very clear outlook on life. She likes justice and likes to get things right. She must be a little unobtrusive even though she knows everything that is going on and takes everything in. I do have her natural curiosity about people – what they do, how they think, though I hope not *too* much.

'But Miss Marple is much more strong-minded than I am. I'd like to have her integrity and strength of character. That's what people like about her, because standards are not the same, are they? But she isn't prissy, she knows all about vice – nothing shocks her, while I *am* rather shockable!'

Joan admits that the lady sleuth's famous look is not all that it seems. 'When I give that thoughtful, faraway look as Miss Marple coolly solves a murder, I'm usually wondering what's for lunch!'

The actress has many fond memories of filming the Miss Marple stories, and makes light of the fact that even at her age it meant getting up at 7 a.m. and sometimes working a twelve-hour day. All the ten stories were shot on location in such places as Norfolk, Devon, Nether Wallop in Hampshire which doubled for St Mary Mead, and, in the most recent episode, the exotic Caribbean. With the series's great attention to period detail it was fun to make, Joan says, and attracted actors and actresses of the highest calibre just for the pleasure of taking part.

'I think one of the reasons for the series's success has been the fact that it has been set in such lovely parts of the English countryside, in beautiful houses and gardens,' she says. 'Viewers have been rightly nostalgic for a time when people were more gracious. Do you know I had a letter from one gentleman saying how charming it was to see the gentlemen doffing their hats to the ladies? I've also had fan letters from very young children as well as from very elderly ladies and gentlemen.'

Joan says that the film unit became rather like a family. 'I actually spent my eightieth birthday working and we had a party in the street in Woodstock, near Oxford. There was an enormous cake and flowers. It was lovely.'

She also recalls that there were tears among the unit when filming came to an end – but not from her. 'I don't go in for that sort of thing. I felt terribly sad, but I'd like to play other things as well. I do hope after what she wrote to me that dear Agatha, wherever she may happen to be, is pleased with what I've done.'

There is no doubt that the critics and the public have indeed been pleased with the series, from the very first adaptation, 'The Body in the Library', screened at Christmas 1984. George Gallaccio, who took over as producer from Guy Slater after the first three stories, says that a conscious decision was made at the BBC to set all the stories in the late Forties, 'mainly for stylistic reasons'.

'The books were written over a long period from the Twenties to the Fifties,' he says. 'We chose the Forties because it is a time that many people remember, but which isn't often portrayed on films and TV.'

'The Body in the Library', the story of Colonel Bantry's discovery of a corpse in his stately home, was adapted into a three-part story by T. R. Bowen and directed by Silvio Narizzano. The co-stars were Andrew Cruikshank, Gwen Watford and David Horovitch as Inspector Slack.

The Times greeted the first episode enthusiastically: 'once hooked, you won't be able to turn off', it said; while the *Sun* added that it was a series 'with pulling power and real class'.

An outbreak of poison-pen letters in an idyllic East Anglian village was the second case for Miss Marple in 'The Moving Finger', screened in February 1985. Scripted by Julia Jones and directed by Roy Boulting, the story featured Michael Culver, Sandra Payne, Richard Pearson and Andrew Bicknell. *The Daily Telegraph* review noted, 'Once again Guy Slater's production is built around the brilliant performance of Joan Hickson, behind whose faded blue eyes and spinsterish sibilants, the wheels of detective intelligence can be seen positively whirring around. The enterprise is impeccably cast, beautifully ordered, lovingly photographed.'

The adaptation of the famous novel, *A Murder Is Announced*, about the game that leads to death, earned even more fulsome praise when it was screened later the same month. Mary Kenny in the *Daily Mail* headlined her review, 'They've committed the perfect crime series', and added, 'My only complaint with this superbly polished Miss Marple is that every detail is so perfect that I am distracted by its perfection. Joan Hickson as Miss Marple is unsurpassable.'

With a script by Alan Plater and directed by David Giles, this third case featured Ursula Howells, Renée Asherson, John Castle, Sylvia Syms and Joan Sims. Like all the Miss Marple stories, the production was later shown in America as part of the *Mystery!* series, and found John J. O'Connor of the *New York Times* also enthusing: 'Other actresses, including Margaret Rutherford and Helen Hayes, have done well by the role, but none have captured the amateur sleuth's tiny eccentricities and enormous shrewdness as accurately as Joan Hickson.'

'A Pocketful of Rye', about murder in the Home Counties, concluded the first quartet of adaptations. Again scripted by T. R. Bowen, it was directed by Guy Slater, who handed over his producer's hat to George Gallaccio. The cast included Fabia Drake, Timothy West, Peter Davison, Tom Wilkinson, Clive Merrison and Stacy Dorning. Stanley Eveling of *The Scotsman* noted in his review that the nation was now gripped with admiration for the series: 'People sidle up with a grin on their faces to ask, "What did you think of this week's 'Miss Marple'?" and before the full critical machinery can lurch into *sprachspiel*, they mutter, "I thought it was very good. *Very* good."'

Christmas Day 1986 saw the screening of another classic, 'Murder at the Vicarage', which T. R. Bowen adapted from the novel about the murder of the unpleasant Colonel Protheroe. The cast included Paul Eddington, Robert Lang, Polly Adams and Cheryl Campbell, appearing in her second major Christie tale. Richard Last of *The Daily Telegraph* called the production his 'outstanding memory of Christmas on TV' while Wendy Cope in the *Spectator* confessed, 'The fact that I had read the book made no difference . . . everything seemed exactly right, the clothes, the setting, the casting.'

'Sleeping Murder', the bizarre story of Miss Marple's investigation into a woman's vision of a strangled body, was shown in January 1987. *The Financial Times* called it 'yet another of those beautifully produced television dramas with no sex, no swearing and no violence'. It was directed by John Davies from Ken Taylor's script and co-starred Geraldine Alexander, John Moulder-Brown, Frederick Treves and Jack Watson.

The seventh story, 'At Bertram's Hotel', dealing with an intrigue about family inheritances, was the story Agatha Christie was said to have based on the famous Brown's Hotel in London. Scripted by Jill Hyem and directed by Mary McMurray, the story featured George Baker, Caroline Blakiston, Joan Greenwood and Brian McGrath. *The Daily Telegraph* was once again full of praise: 'Seldom can dear old Agatha's computerised tales have been accorded such Rolls-Royce treatment, or so splendid a cast, even unto the peripheral characters. The period touches are laid on with such lush and loving care that you'd sign for a week at Bertram's without a second thought, except that it would be impossibly expensive!'

T. R. Bowen was again the scriptwriter of the television version of 'Nemesis', about a recently deceased millionaire who has left instructions for Miss Marple to be engaged to solve a murder while on a coach tour of some historic homes. Screened in February and directed by David Tucker, the two-part film co-starred Peter Tilbury, Margaret Tyzack, Helen Cherry, Anna Cropper and Frank Gatliff. When this story was screened on American TV at Christmas, the *New York Times* commented, 'This is the Christie detective to the very letter . . . Ms Hickson is giving a performance to be savoured by mystery buffs and just about everybody else.'

The penultimate case, the celebrated '4.50 from Paddington', about death on the railway, was also screened in Britain on Christmas Day 1987, to the delight of viewers and critics alike. Richard Last of *The Daily Telegraph* once more led the cheers: 'Drawing on the tradition so richly established by Guy Slater, producer George Gallaccio and director Martyn Friend conferred on the Christmas Miss Marple an opulence of photography and high-gloss period detail which would not disgrace *Fortunes of War* and was far more germane to the story.'

David Horovitch returned before the cameras as Inspector Slack, and there was an impressive performance from Maurice Denham, giving new life to another Christie character. Also in the story were Joanna David, David Waller and Jill Meager as Miss Marple's stalwart niece.

The most recent of the series, 'The Caribbean Mystery,' shown on Christmas Day 1989, is the last of the Miss Marple novels at present available to the BBC, and Joan Hickson has said she will not do adaptations of the short stories. The BBC, though, went out on a high note with location shooting at the Coral Reef Hotel in Barbados, at which Agatha had stayed and where the novel of multiple murders is set. This very different locale from the earlier stories provided a delightful interlude for Joan Hickson as well as her co-stars Donald Pleasence (playing Jason Rafiel), T. P. McKenna (appearing as Dr Grahame), Adrian Lukis, Sophie Ward, Sheila Ruskin, Michael Feast, Sue Lloyd, Robert Swan and Barbra Barnes.

The authenticity of the production was enhanced enormously by the fact that the twelve-acre Coral Reef complex with its holiday cottages was still owned by the same couple, Budge and Cynthia O'Hara, who 30 years earlier had inspired two of the characters (played by Adrian Lukis and Sophie Ward) and who were able to offer the cast a treasure trove of Christie memorabilia including props, costumes and photographs. On a less happy note, Hurricane Hugo appeared on the horizon while shooting was actually in progress, but thankfully just missed the island.

On returning to England after work was complete, Joan Hickson confirmed to pressmen, 'It is very likely the last – but it's good to end on a high note. Next year I think I should meet Poirot and have a long chat. I don't think they'd get on, do you?'

For the time being, Joan Hickson is busy with other projects, but does not altogether rule out a return as Miss Marple, should this prove feasible. For having earned the accolade of 'probably the oldest actress ever to take the leading role in a TV series', she has no plans to relinquish this claim to fame – or to retire, for that matter!

In a feature reviewing the series, Albert Watson of the *Western Mail* made this comment: 'Miss Marple, one of the most popular sleuths in detective fiction, is proof positive that heroes don't have to be male, young and athletic.'

They *can* be, though – and in company with brave, resourceful and pretty companions they can form appealing detective partnerships: the sort of partnership Agatha Christie brought to life in yet another creative burst, and named Tommy and Tuppence Beresford. They, too, have been widely used in the entertainment media, as the final section in this book will reveal.

The young Joan Hickson as the maid Emmy, with Ann Harding as Carol Howard, in Love from a Stranger *(1937)*

PARTNERS IN CRIME-FIGHTING

Four couples who have played the resourceful Tommy & Tuppence Beresford

CARLO ALDINI & EVE GRAY

'A young couple in search of thrills'

The fame of Hercule Poirot and Miss Marple has tended to overshadow the two young sleuths, Thomas and Prudence Beresford – better known as Tommy and Tuppence – whom Agatha Christie created in only her second book, *The Secret Adversary* (1922). She reintroduced the pair three more times during the next half century, and made them the heroes of her final mystery story, *Postern of Fate*, published in 1973. Tommy and Tuppence are of particular interest in this book as they were featured in one of the first movies based on Agatha's work as well as in the first radio serial and several television adaptations, the most recent in 1983–4.

The authoress herself enjoyed writing about this intrepid pair, a fact that was doubtless encouraged by her first review in the *Times Literary Supplement* which called them 'refreshingly original as criminal investigators'. That the public liked them, too, was evidenced when she published a later adventure, *By the Pricking of My Thumbs*, in 1968, and prefaced it with a note saying that many readers at home and abroad had written to her enquiring, 'What has happened to Tommy and Tuppence?', to which she had replied, 'I hope that you will enjoy meeting Tommy and Tuppence again, years older, but with spirit unquenched.'

The theatre critic and Christie enthusiast Charles Osborne believes there might be another reason for her affection for this couple. 'Tuppence is, perhaps, the author as Agatha Christie liked to fantasise herself,' he has written, 'and Tommy is the kind of young man who appealed to the fantasy Agatha.'

However, another fan of the adventures, the lawyer and detective novelist C. H. B. Kitchen, is convinced the explanation is simpler still. As he wrote in 1955: 'These are stories of Mrs Christie in search of thrills ... and I admit they gave me the same sensation of schoolboyish guilt as I used to have when I put down my holiday task – say *David Copperfield* or *Vanity Fair* – and took up the latest number of *The Captain!*'

Janet Morgan, too, believes that *The Secret Adversary*, in which this pair of ingenious, affectionate, and irrepressible young adventurers first appear after leaving the forces, has another significance.

'It marks the appearance of two important themes that were to figure in much of Agatha's work,' she says, 'the search for the mysterious possessor of some valuable secret or special knowledge – who may be a courier, a conspirator, the perpetrator of a crime, and who is as likely to be a woman as a man – and the identification of some powerful figure, able to buy unlimited information and arms, to travel anywhere and influence anyone, bent on domination.'

Though Tommy Beresford may seem to today's readers a rather typical cardboard, stiff-upper-lip Twenties hero, Prudence Cowley (as she is until her marriage to Tommy) is a young women well ahead of her times. She is spirited and adventurous, quite unrestrained by her age, her sex or her conventions, and limited merely by a lack of money! It is her character, I think, more than any particular contribution of her partner that has made Tuppence a TV heroine for the Eighties.

Agatha's five books of stories about this duo are unique in that they cover the couple's entire life span, and do not stand still in time like most of the stories of Poirot and Miss Marple. From unemployed young things caught up in an international Bolshevik conspiracy in *The Secret Adversary*, Tommy and Tuppence become restless newly-weds in search of excitement in *Partners in Crime* (1929); mature spycatchers in war-torn London in *N or M?* (1941); middle-aged investigators of a suspect old people's rest home in *By the Pricking of My Thumbs* (1968); and, finally, aged but still intrepid enquirers into a case of espionage and murder in *Postern of Fate* (1973), the swan song of both the author and her characters.

It was in 1929, just after the release of the first Christie film, *The Passing of Mr Quinn*, that Tommy and Tuppence were brought to the screen as a pair of 'Roaring Twenties' sleuths in an adaptation of *The Secret Adversary*. What is strange about this debut of a pair who were

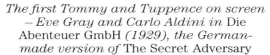

*The first Tommy and Tuppence on screen
– Eve Gray and Carlo Aldini in* Die
Abenteuer GmbH *(1929), the German-
made version of* The Secret Adversary

typical of thousands of young Britons trying to readjust to civilian life in the aftermath of the First World War (she had been a Voluntary Army Nurse and he a lieutenant in the army) was that the film should have been made by a German film company, the Fox Film Corporation. Equally strange, an Italian, Carlo Aldini, was cast as Tommy, though Tuppence was played by a vivacious English actress named Eve Gray. Among the rest of the cast directed by Fred Sauer were Hilda Bayley, Shayle Gardner and Michael Rasumny, a Russian, who later became a well-known comedy actor in Hollywood.

It has been suggested that the German passion for English crime stories about Sherlock Holmes, Jack the Ripper and Dr Crippen overruled any inhibitions the producers might have had about a tale with undertones of the war. For Aldini and Eve Gray it was an opportunity to take starring roles in the fledgling cinema where many actors' salaries still compared unfavourably with those of their contemporaries working in offices and business.

Eve Gray was an attractive, blue-eyed blonde born in Birmingham in 1904. She had been a rather sickly child, and as there were fears she might never walk properly, her father and mother emigrated to Australia in search of a healthier climate.

A bit of a daydreamer by nature, Eve found the attractions of acting more appealing than the business school her parents wanted her to attend, and, strengthened by her years in the Australian sun, she applied for a place in a dance company. Success in a number of musical comedies in Sydney and Melbourne encouraged her to return to England in 1925 where there was the promise of more work, and her undoubted beauty gained her an entrée into films with BIP at Elstree. Among the films in which she appeared were *Silver Lining* (1926), *Poppies of Flanders* (1927) and *Moulin Rouge* (1928).

'In *Moulin Rouge* I had a drunken scene which I didn't like very much, but it was apparently necessary,' Eve said in an interview in *The Picturegoer* in 1928. 'But this was seen by some Continental film-makers who thought I could play roles that demanded more than just standing around looking pretty or falling into the arms of the hero. So for almost a year I worked in France and Germany, including playing this rather dashing young lady detective in *Die Abenteuer GmbH* (Adventurers Ltd) which was made in Berlin.'

Die Abenteuer GmbH was the German title for the adaptation of the Tommy and Tuppence spy drama, and the success of this picture (it was shown in several other European countries including Britain where it was released under the title of the book) earned Eve work in a number of other crime films including *The Twickenham Mystery* (1929), *Three Witnesses* (1934) and *Murder at Monte Carlo* (1935).

The film also helped the career of Eve's co-star, Carlo Aldini, albeit somewhat briefly. Born in Bologna in 1894, Carlo developed an impressive physique as a young man and was noted in his home area as an outstanding athlete, with wrestling and high jumping his specialities. Fascinated by film-making, he decided to capitalise on his athleticism and in 1919, using the name Ajax, found work as a stunt man in the Italian action and adventure films which were then being produced in ever-increasing numbers.

In 1923, Carlo travelled to Germany and performed several dangerous stunts, including crossing the River Spree on a tightrope and jumping from a fourth-floor window, which caught the eye of film-makers on the lookout for new faces to feed the public appetite for 'sensation' movies. This led to his first major role as a warrior hero in a historical drama, *Helena*, made in 1924, and was followed by several mystery thrillers including *Der Mann Ohne Kopf*, in 1927, and, the following year, *Die Abenteuer GmbH*, in which he co-starred as the young English investigator, Tommy. Curiously, after starring in five more films, one of which he directed, Albini returned to Italy and retired from acting.

Contemporary accounts and the few remaining stills of this first Tommy and Tuppence film – now sadly lost – indicate that Eve Gray stole most of the best scenes as she outwitted the international conspiracy in which she and her partner had become enmeshed. And by so doing, she established a tradition that her successors in the role have done much to uphold . . .

LEE BOWMAN & BARBARA BEL GEDDES

'Two jazz-age crimebusters'

Although Agatha Christie published a whole collection of Tommy and Tuppence adventures entitled *Partners in Crime* in 1929 while *The Secret Adversary* was still playing in cinemas, it was not until the advent of television that the couple reappeared on the screen.

A second film did, however, nearly materialise during the Second World War when Agatha wrote her third book about Tommy and Tuppence, *N or M?*, in 1941. The authoress mentions this work in her autobiography:

> *N or M?* was in a way a continuation of *The Secret Adversary*. Now with a grown-up son and daughter, Tommy and Tuppence were bored by finding that nobody wanted them in wartime. However, they made a splendid come-back as a middle-aged pair, and tracked down spies with all their old enthusiasm.

The story told of the two investigators' dramatic search for some Nazi spies and saboteurs believed to be operating from the south-coast resort of Leahampton. *N or M?* with its espionage high jinks undoubtedly provided some light relief for readers in beleaguered Britain, and it caught the eye of the executives of Milestone Pictures in London who were searching for movie material. An option was taken out, and some pre-production work began.

There is evidence that Milestone wanted Tuppence to be played by an actress not unlike

*Lee Bowman and Barbara Bel Geddes were the first to bring
Tommy and Tuppence Beresford to American TV in 1950*

Eve Gray, and had a pretty, blonde, London film star named Sally Gray in mind. The actor pencilled in for Tommy was the darkly handsome Hugh Williams, father of the present-day actor, Simon Williams. But the uncertainty of life during the continuing blitz on London at this time appears to have put paid to the project.

It was to be almost ten years, in fact, before Tommy and Tuppence reappeared – this time on television across the Atlantic in America. And their adventure was based on one of the cases from the second book, *Partners in Crime*.

The TV programme was a 'dramatic anthology' series entitled the *Nash Airflyte Theater*, sponsored by the American automobile company of that name. The producer was attracted to the collection of Tommy and Tuppence stories, in each of which Agatha gently parodied the popular detectives of the day, and chose 'The Case of the Missing Lady'. It was aired as a 30-minute live presentation on 7 December 1950 starring Lee Bowman and Barbara Bel Geddes as the two young sleuths.

The series, which went out at 10.30 on Thursday evenings via CBS, was hosted by William Gaxton and presented an extremely varied selection of adaptations, from stories by such distinguished writers as O. Henry and John Steinbeck to Westerns and even Gilbert and Sullivan musical comedies! Among the famous actors who worked on the series were Fredric March, Otto Kruger and Grace Kelly.

'The Case of the Missing Lady' concerned a returning explorer who finds that his fiancée has gone missing and appears to be in the hands of a sinister doctor. In order to release her, he enlists the aid of Tommy and Tuppence who have set themselves up as the International Detective Agency.

The production provided interesting roles for the two American stars, Lee Bowman and Barbara Bel Geddes, as the producer retained an English feel to his sets and a jazz-age atmosphere for the story. Unfortunately, no reviews or direct comments on this *Airflyte Theater* presentation are still extant.

New York-born Barbara Bel Geddes, who is today famous as Miss Ellie Ewing in *Dallas*, did a lot of live television work in the Fifties after having appeared in a number of successful Broadway shows. She was also nominated for an Oscar as a supporting actress in the movie, *I Remember Mamma* (1948). By a twist of fate it was on the weekly TV show, *Robert Montgomery Presents*, that Barbara met her husband-to-be, Lewis, the casting director, and her co-star-to-be, Lee Bowman.

With her slight 5 foot, 3 inch figure and burnished straw-coloured hair, Barbara had made her acting mark playing well-bred young ladies who were startlingly forthright and singleminded. To this she could add a stylish way of drinking, smoking and even cursing which turned her performance as Tuppence into something of a *tour de force*.

Lee Bowman was a tall, dark and suave Cincinnati-born former stage actor and radio singer, who by the winter of 1950 had made a speciality of playing romantic leads in movies such as *Kid Glove Killer* (1942) and *Smash Up* (1947) with Susan Hayward. In the Fifties, he became one of the busiest actors in live television, appearing in series such as the *Kraft Theater*, *Studio One* and the aforementioned *Robert Montgomery Presents*. In 'The Case of the Missing Lady', he played Tommy Beresford as a wordly, wisecracking young man with an abundance of charm.

For both players, the story was just one of many performances during a busy TV era. As far as Barbara was concerned, the world-wide fame of *Dallas* lay some years ahead; while for Lee, 1951 brought the plum role of the mystery-writer/sleuth Ellery Queen in the long-running ABC TV series, *The Adventures of Ellery Queen*. Neither, though, could possibly have imagined that the story in which they had starred would be revived with considerably more impact when London Weekend Television decided to film a complete series of Tommy and Tuppence cases some 33 years later.

RICHARD ATTENBOROUGH & SHEILA SIM

'The radio detectives'

The year 1953 in Britain was dominated by the coronation of Elizabeth II. On BBC radio it also produced the first British serialisation of an Agatha Christie book, *Partners in Crime*, which attracted very substantial audiences of listeners every Monday night at 7.30 during its thirteen-week run from 13 April to 13 July.

The success of these Tommy and Tuppence episodes was undoubtedly due in no small measure to the energetic performances of the stars, Richard Attenborough and his wife, Sheila Sim, who the previous November had been acclaimed for their leading roles in Agatha's play, *The Mousetrap*.

In announcing the series in its issue of 10 April, the *Radio Times* underlined the association:

> The combination of Agatha Christie and the Attenboroughs which is responsible for the current London theatre success, *The Mousetrap*, will be continued in the new serial, *Partners in Crime*, which begins on Monday. The serial, a comedy-thriller based on Miss Christie's book of the same title, features Richard and Sheila as a young married couple, while in the play they are not related.'

The idea for this series had been put forward by the BBC producer Audrey Cameron, an admirer of Agatha Christie's work who had read most of her books and seen all her plays. It had been approved by Agatha, who was also very keen on the casting of the Attenboroughs because they had all three become friends during the staging of *The Mousetrap*.

In her autobiography, Agatha wrote: 'Richard Attenborough and his enchanting wife Sheila Sim played the two leads in the first production. What a beautiful performance they gave. They loved the play and believed in it, and Richard Attenborough gave a great deal of thought to playing his part. I enjoyed the rehearsals – I enjoyed *all* of it.'

The young couple also took on the roles of Tommy and Tuppence with similar enthusiasm, though it meant extra work recording the episodes during the day before going on stage in the evening. Both read the three existing books about the young detectives and discussed the parts thoroughly with Agatha and Audrey Cameron.

The adapting of the stories for the series had been handed to an experienced thriller writer, Rex Rienits, and extra dialogue was also provided by Colin Willock who had worked with the Attenboroughs two years earlier on a radio series, *The Braithwaites*.

The versatile Richard Attenborough was born in 1923 and made his debut on the stage in 1941, then going into films and giving a memorable performance in Graham Greene's story *Brighton Rock* in 1948. *The Mousetrap* consolidated his appeal with the public, and he later maintained his association with Agatha Christie by appearing in the 1975 film version of *And Then There Were None*, playing Judge Cannon. His work as an actor, director and producer led to a knighthood in 1976.

Sir Richard does not find it hard to remember the year 1953. 'There was all that magnificent pageantry for the coronation going on in London,' he says, 'although Sheila and I did not have much time to see things as we were so busy in *The Mousetrap* and filming.

'The radio series, *Partners in Crime*, was great fun and we had some lovely people broadcasting with us. I remember dear Agatha came to some of the rehearsals and put us all right when we made mistakes. She had a great affection for Tommy and Tuppence and I think she liked the way we played them – though you could never be quite sure, she was such a stickler for things being *just* right!'

Sheila Sim, born in Liverpool in 1922, had also begun her career on the stage in 1939, entering films in 1944, the year she married Richard. They appeared in several plays together and three films, *Dancing with Crime* (1947), *The Guinea Pig* (1948) and *The Magic Box* (1951).

'Agatha Christie was such an unlikely person to have written all those amazing murder stories,' Sheila says. 'Such a gentle, unassuming lady, like everyone's favourite aunt. She was very kind to Dickie and me, and making the radio series was a happy time for both of us.'

The series began on Monday, 13 April with 'Meet the Beresfords', based on the book's opening chapter, 'A Fairy in the Flat', which introduced the restless young couple and their detective agency which they had set up to track down spies and solve mysteries. Assisting them as the office boy was Albert, the young Cockney porter whom they had encountered in *The Secret Adversary*. He was played throughout the series by Oscar Quitak. Two other characters who were to feature regularly in the stories were Colonel Carter, also from *The Secret Adversary*, and Inspector Marriott (played by Noel Coleman and John Stevens respectively). The striking theme tune and background music for *Partners in Crime* was composed and conducted by Alan Paul.

The second episode, 'The Mysterious Stranger', was based on the story of 'The Adventure of the Sinister Stranger' in which Tommy and Tuppence come to the aid of Dr Carl Bower who fears someone is trying to steal his highly secret research papers. The story, a parody of the adventures of Desmond and Major Okewood by Douglas Valentine (1883–1946), co-starred Norman Shelley as Dr Bower, Russell Napier as Dymchurch and Philip Ray as Coggins.

The following week, in 'The House of Lurking Death', the Beresfords investigated a case of poisoned chocolates sent to a young woman, Lois Hargreaves, who has just inherited a fortune. Agatha's cunning plot was a parody of the methods of the French Inspector Hanaud, created by A. E. W. Mason (1865–1948). Two other actors who were also then appearing in London theatre presentations joined the Attenboroughs in this story: Cecile Chevreau (playing the heiress) was in *Dangerous Curves* at the Garrick, and Lockwood West (Inspector Berkshire) was in *The White Carnation* at the Globe Theatre.

'The Man in the Fog' (he had been in a mist in the original story) was a case Tommy tackled disguised as a clergyman to discover who is imperilling a glamorous actress, Gilda Glen. This imitation of the famous Father Brown created by G. K. Chesterton (1874–1936) introduced Grizelda Hervey as the actress, Bryan Coleman as Bulger and Ronan O'Casey as Benjamin Reilly. Oscar Quitak, playing Albert, also took advantage of the anonymity of radio to double as a waiter in one scene. (Coincidentally – or could this have been the work of someone with a sense of humour at the BBC? – an hour after this production, the Home Service presented a 90-minute dramatisation of Chesterton's famous novel, *The Man Who Was Thursday*!)

The fifth episode, 'The Ambassador's Boots', about the mysterious switching of an American ambassador's kitbag, saw Tommy parodying the snobbish detective Reggie Fortune, created by H. C. Bailey (1878–1961). Jimmy Dyrenforth co-starred as the ambassador, with Arthur Hill as Richards and Cecile Chevreau paying a return visit to the series, this time as Cecilia Marsh.

Episode six, 'The Thin Woman', put Tommy and Tuppence on the case of a mysterious lady threatening vengeance on a small community that she claims has wronged her. The production brought together the two stars and actor Richard Williams, who played a police inspector. (Williams had appeared as Major Metcalf in Agatha's 1947 radio play, *Three Blind Mice*, which, of course, formed the basis for *The Mousetrap*.) 'The Thin Woman' also featured Duncan McIntyre as Robert Campbell and Gwenda Wilson as Doris Evans.

'A Stab in the Back' was another murder mystery for the couple, in which Albert played a prominent part in the enquiries. The co-stars were several familiar radio names including Peter Claughton as Max Payne, Felix Felton as Morton and Marjorie Westbury as Trina.

*Richard
Attenborough
and Sheila Sim,
who played the
young sleuths on
radio in 1953*

The eighth story, 'The Man with the Gold Tooth', was based on 'The Red House', about an old and apparently haunted mansion left to Monica Deane and her mother. Tommy and Tuppence adopt the style of detection favoured by Roger Sheringham, the talkative sleuth created by Anthony Berkeley Cox (1893–1970). The parts of the two ladies were played by Betty Hardy and Mary O'Farrell, with Elsa Palmer as Mrs Crockett and Stephen Jack as the gardener.

Edgar Wallace's love of gambling plus the numerous super-villains who people his stories were the inspiration for the episode entitled 'The Crackler', which was broadcast as the ninth story in the series. This case of the couple's investigation into a flood of forged banknotes featured Philip Cunningham as Major Laidlaw, Betty Baskcomb as Marguerite

Laidlaw and Robert Ayres as Hank Ryder. Oscar Quitak went one better than in 'The Man in the Fog' by playing a barman *and* a police sergeant as well as Albert!

'In Camera', the tenth story, was based on 'The Affair of the Pink Pearl', with Tommy adopting the highly sophisticated scientific methods of Dr John Thorndyke, the creation of R. Austin Freeman (1862–1943), to recover a valuable missing pearl. Pamela Galloway played Beatrice Kingston; Laidlaw Browne was Colonel Kingston and Lewis Stringer was George Rennie.

A curious newspaper advertisement leading to murder was the theme of 'Finessing the King', in which Tommy and Tuppence solved the mystery in the manner of Timothy McCarty and his assistant Riordan, created by Isabel Ostrander (1885–1924). Deryck Guyler co-starred as Sir Arthur Merivale and Molly Rankin was Catherine Merivale.

The penultimate episode, 'The Unbreakable Alibi', in which Tommy and Tuppence tackled the seemingly impossible case of a person being in two places at once, took its inspiration from the style of Inspector French, created by Freeman Wills Crofts (1879–1957). Una Drake, the woman setting the puzzle, was played by Gwenda Wilson, with John Stevens appearing once more as Inspector Marriott.

The final episode, on 13 July 1953, was undoubtedly the *pièce de resistance* of the series. 'The Man Who Was Number Sixteen' was Agatha's joke at her *own* expense – for the detective parodied by Tommy Beresford was none other than Hercule Poirot and his 'little grey cells'! The series ended with a nail-biting finale as the young couple just managed to outwit the deadly scheme of a spy ring. Among the co-stars were Geoffrey Wincott as Wilson, Humphrey Morton as Pendlebury and John Warrington as Myers.

It is interesting to note that the role of the sinister Vladirovsky was played by that versatile actor, Maurice Denham, who was, of course, to star in other Agatha Christie mysteries, including two appearances as the series character, Parker Pyne, on television – just one more example of the coincidences that have cropped up so regularly in 'The Queen of Crime's' history in the entertainment media.

JAMES WARWICK & FRANCESCA ANNIS

'A high-living pair of super-sleuths'

The search for a new male and female detective partnership for the television audiences of the Eighties was what brought Tommy and Tuppence back to the screen. And the evident success of the London Weekend Television decision to base a series on the 'partners in crime' not only emphasised the durability of Agatha's characters after half a century, but also their appeal for modern viewers.

Despite the fact that the Beresfords had been among the pioneering duos in crime fiction, there had already been a number of such partnerships on both film and television. The Beresfords were seen as natural successors to these.

The first of these twosomes had been Nick and Nora Charles in the 'Thin Man' films of the Thirties and Forties, played by William Powell and Myrna Loy. Then John Steed and his various female partners had emerged in *The Avengers* during the Sixties, with Patrick MacNee and Honor Blackman (and her successors Diana Rigg, Linda Thorson and Joanna Lumley). And, most recently, there had been the husband-and-wife team of *Hart to Hart*, starring Robert Wagner and Stephanie Powers, which had run through the Seventies into the early Eighties.

The man charged with turning the idea into reality was the independent television producer Jack Williams, who had so successfully brought *Why Didn't They Ask Evans?* to the screen in 1980. The adventures of Tommy and Tuppence seemed to him the ideal solution – and James Warwick and Francesca Annis, who had played a pair of young sleuths in the earlier production, were clearly the ideal pairing for this series.

James Warwick has confirmed from his insider's viewpoint how the series was set up.

'What they wanted was a kind of *Hart to Hart* series,' he says. 'Now that series had been inspired by the Nick and Nora Charles stories of the Thirties. So it was decided that Tommy Beresford and his beloved Tuppence who were also from the same time period would be a good basis for a series. I suppose you could say we became a Twenties-style *Hart to Hart*!'

The tall, dark and self-contained James, the epitome of Tommy, learned his profession at the Central School of Speech and Drama in London. He followed this with five years in rep before graduating to the London stage and then television work in series such as *The Onedin Line, Edward VII* and *Lillie*. It was while filming the story of the Jersey beauty, Lillie Langtry – the actress who captured the heart of a king – that he met Francesca Annis.

'I played one of her husbands in *Lillie*,' James recalls, 'and they must have thought we worked well together because they brought us together again for *Why Didn't They Ask Evans?* Apparently this hit No 2 in the American TV ratings, so they thought of starring us together again.

'Actually, I had never read an Agatha Christie book before *Why Didn't They Ask Evans?*

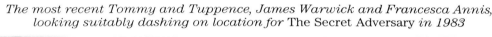

The most recent Tommy and Tuppence, James Warwick and Francesca Annis, looking suitably dashing on location for The Secret Adversary *in 1983*

A heavily disguised Tommy Beresford (James Warwick) confers with his partner, Tuppence (Francesca Annis), while on 'The Case of the Missing Lady'

So as soon as the series came along I started working my way through the whole seventy-eight of them!' he adds.

LWT decided to launch the series with a two-hour special based on *The Secret Adversary*, scripted by Pat Sandys and directed by Tony Wharmby. This story of how the couple recover a secret treaty, marry, and set themselves up as a detective agency neatly introduced viewers to the ten episodes which followed.

Francesca Annis was delighted to be working with James Warwick again and during the nine months the series took to make, their screen partnership became all that Jack Williams had envisaged.

'I really enjoyed playing Tuppence,' she said. 'I had been doing a lot of heavyweight, prestige work and it was nice to do something lighter.'

The Secret Adversary was transmitted during peak viewing hours on Sunday, 9 October 1983, and among the all-star cast were George Baker (as Whittington), Peter Barkworth (Mr Carter), Gavin O'Herlihy (Julius Hersheimmer), John Fraser (Kramenin), Donald Houston (Boris), Honor Blackman (Rita Vandemeyer) and Alec McCowen (Sir James Peel Edgerton).

The *Daily Express* was one of several newspapers that praised the programme, critic Judith Simons describing Tommy and Tuppence as 'a witty, loving, high-living pair of super-sleuths, moving in circles where people dress for dinner in country houses, play endless golf and are scared of Bolsheviks under the bed'.

A week later, *Partners in Crime* began in earnest with 'The Affair of the Pink Pearl', adapted by David Butler from the story of Tommy and Tuppence's 24-hour race against time to find a valuable missing pearl. Among the co-stars were Graham Crowden, as Colonel Kingston Bruce, and a former stage Miss Marple, Dulcie Gray, playing Lady Laura Barton. The two sleuths also acquired a day-dreaming, film-mad office boy, Albert, played then and throughout the rest of the series by a young Yorkshire actor, Reece Dinsdale.

The second case, 'The House of Lurking Death', adapted by Jonathan Hales, brought the two sleuths to a grim, isolated mansion with poisoning in the air and possible murder in the wings. The co-stars were Joan Sanderson (Miss Logan) and Liz Smith (Hannah Macpherson). Jonathan Hales also adapted the third story, 'The Sunningdale Mystery', which took Francesca back on to a golf course to solve the mystery of a murdered player. The co-stars were Denis Lill (Sessle) and Emily Moore (Doris Evans).

Episode four, 'The Clergyman's Daughter', written by Paul Annett, brought Tommy and Tuppence to another old house believed to be haunted by a poltergeist. Also appearing were Jane Booker (as Monica Deane) and Geoffrey Drew (Norman Partridge). The next week, a message in code in a newspaper led the two young sleuths into a murder case in Gerald Savory's adaptation of 'Finessing the King', with Benjamin Whitrow as Sir Arthur Merrivale and Peter Blythe playing Captain Bingo Hale.

In the sixth story, 'The Ambassador's Boot', another adaptation by Paul Annett, the US ambassador to Britain asked Tommy and Tuppence to investigate a curious incident involving his luggage while he was crossing the Atlantic in the liner *Nomadic*. The grandiloquent T. P. McKenna was cast as the ambassador, Randolph Wimot, with Jennie Linden as Cicely March. Gerald Savory's second adaptation, 'The Man in the Mist', recounted how the young sleuths, unable to solve a robbery, instead found themselves pitched into a murder mystery. The co-stars were Anne Stallybrass (Mrs Honeycott) and Constantine Gregory (as 'Bulger' Estcourt).

The eighth adventure, 'The Unbreakable Alibi', adapted by David Butler, told the curious story of a young man who enlisted Tommy and Tuppence's help to solve a seemingly impossible mystery in order to marry the girl of his dreams. Tim Meats co-starred as Montgomery Jones with Anna Nygh as Una Drake. The penultimate tale was a new version of 'The Case of the Missing Lady', about arctic explorer Gabriel Stavansson's search for his fiancée. Adapted by Jonathan Hales, the story featured Jonathan Newth as the explorer, Rowena Cooper as Irma Kleber and Ewen Hooper as Dr Horriston.

The final case for this Tommy and Tuppence was 'The Crackler', adapted again by Gerald Savory, in which Inspector Marriott enlisted the couple to track down a gang of forgers at work in high society. Arthur Cox played the police officer and Christopher Scoular was Captain Jimmy Faulkner.

For Francesca, this last story proved to be one of her favourites because of the range of glamorous clothes she was able to wear. 'The whole series was great fun, though,' she said afterwards. 'It's just a pity that Agatha Christie wrote so few stories about Tommy and Tuppence and we picked the ten best. It would have been nice to do more.'

James Warwick, on the other hand, was happy to go on to other things, even though Pamela Hodgson of the *Daily Mail* hailed him as 'a new kind of sex symbol' and added, 'He has the sculptured dark looks, firm mouth, straight nose, strong chin, but being a married man his sensuality is strictly of the "Look, don't touch" variety.'

But even with such praise ringing in his ears, James confessed as the series ended on 14 January 1984: 'Miss Christie and I have been together for some years now. I seem to have been in every one of her adaptations in the last five years. I think we may have exhausted what we have to say to one another!'

Television has not, of course, exhausted *all* the Tommy and Tuppence adventures, and though the two detectives are never likely to upstage Hercule Poirot or Miss Marple, like them they have at last been faithfully portrayed on the screen in a style which would surely have pleased their creator.

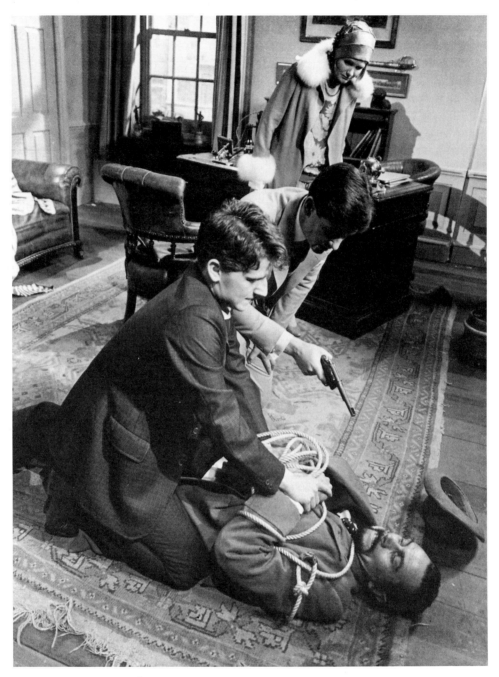

*Another Tommy and Tuppence case successfully
solved – a dramatic arrest brings the story of
'The Ambassador's Boots' to an end*

ACKNOWLEDGEMENTS

The author wishes to express his thanks to the following for their help in the writing of this book. In particular Brian Stone, Sir John Gielgud, Brian Eastman, Janet Morgan, Pamela Chamberlaine, Bill Lofts and Tise Vahimagi. Thanks also to the staffs of these organisations for their assistance with research: the Agatha Christie Centenary group; Wm. Collins & Sons; the British Film Institute; Raymond Mander & Joe Mitchenson Theatre Collection; BBC Archives; the British Museum; the British Newspaper Library; the London Library; Solo Agency; and *Illustrated London News* Archives.

Photographs in the book were kindly supplied by London Weekend Television, Thames Television, Granada Television, TVS Television, BBC TV, BFI, EMI Films, MGM Pictures, United Artists, 20th Century Fox, Seven Arts and Avco Embassy. The following newspapers and magazines have also generously given permission to quote from their pages: *The Times*, the *Daily Express*, the *Guardian*, the *Daily Mirror*, *The Financial Times*, the *Daily Mail*, *The Daily Telegraph*, *The Observer*, *Punch*, the *Times Literary Supplement*, *Radio Times*, *TV Times*, *TV Guide* (USA), *The Sunday Times*, the *Sunday Express*, *The Listener* and the *New York Times*.

P.H.